The Fruit Garden Displayed

Apple 'Sunset', a reliable cultivar of excellent flavour.

The Fruit Garden Displayed

Harry Baker, N.D.H.
Fruit Officer at the RHS Garden, Wisley

Cassell

The Royal Horticultural Society

 THE ROYAL HORTICULTURAL SOCIETY

The RHS gratefully acknowledges the unfailing help and advice of East Malling Research Station throughout the revision of this book, in particular from Brian Self.

Cassell Educational Limited
Villiers House, 41/47 Strand
London WC2N 5JE
for the Royal Horticultural Society

First published 1951
Eighth edition 1991
Reprinted 1992, 1994

British Library Cataloguing in Publication Data
  The Fruit Garden Displayed
  1. Fruit-culture
  I. Royal Horticultural Society
  634   SB356

ISBN 0-304-34016-2

Photographs by Harry Baker, Bernard Alfieri, East Malling Research Station, CRH Photographic, James Fenemore Associates, Wilf Halliday, Shell, Harry Smith Photographic Collection, Michael Warren, Joyce Maynard, Andrew Halstead, Robert Scase, Donald E. Green, Audrey V. Brooks.

Phototypesetting by RGM Associates, Lord Street, Southport, UK
Printed and bound in Singapore by Kyodu Printing Co. Ltd.

Contents

General Principles

Why grow fruit?

There is nothing better than fruit which has been allowed to ripen to its peak of perfection, eaten fresh from the plant and picked from a variety of your own choosing. This book is intended to help you achieve this delightful prospect.

Fruit has decorative, as well as utilitarian, value in the garden. There is the beauty of the blossom in the spring, the varying colours of the fruits as they ripen in the summer and autumn and the shapeliness of well trained trees to please the eye all the year round.

No matter how small the garden, there is always room for fruit, especially now that there are so many dwarfing rootstocks available. You can make use of walls and fences, pergolas and archways, and so many fruits are attractive in their own right that they can be grown in the ornamental part of the garden.

Apart from the pleasure of growing fruit, from an economic point of view it is profitable, and the larger the piece of land set aside for the purpose, the more worthwhile it becomes, particularly if there is a freezer to fill or a large family to feed. *The Fruit Garden Displayed* is written especially for the grower who produces fruit for use in the home. Numerous pictures are included to clarify the methods which must be adopted to achieve success. A wide range of fruits is described and the most up-to-date techniques explained. Efficient pest and disease control is detailed and the most suitable cultivars, both old and new, are recommended.

Geography and climate

Except in mountainous areas and the harsher coastal strips, most parts of the British Isles are relatively favourable for growing specific fruits with reasonably consistent success. The fruits described in the next pages are hardy – which means that they can be grown outdoors in this country – although there are certain limitations in connection with some of them. Exact requirements are set out in the following chapters.

The tree fruits of cool, temperate regions, such as apples, pears, plums and cherries, as well as most soft fruits grow almost anywhere; those from warm temperate regions, peaches, apricots and figs, for example, are more suited to southern parts of Britain. Further north, such fruits require the shelter of a warm wall; in the coldest areas the protection of glass may be necessary. Nevertheless, it is not possible to lay down rules on where fruit can or cannot be grown, for there is such great diversity in the British climate. Warm microclimates can occur almost anywhere: in a walled garden or a sheltered south-facing slope in the folds of a hill. On a larger scale, there is the ameliorating influence of the Gulf Stream on the climate of certain parts of the west coast. Nevertheless in both north and south there are certain basic climatic considerations to be taken into account.

Altitude. Commercially, the best tree fruits are grown at altitudes lower than 400 feet (120m), but fruits can be grown at heights of up to 600 feet (180m) or more, especially soft fruits, provided that they are adequately sheltered. The higher the altitude, the cooler and shorter the growing season.

High altitude is also associated with strong or cold winds, high humidity and low temperatures. Strong winds can damage and distort growth, inhibit the movement of pollinating insects, and blow fruits to the ground. Growing fruit on an exposed site is distinctly unrewarding, and the gardener on such land should consider planting a natural windbreak or erecting an artificial one, ideally before planting the fruit (*see* Windbreaks pp.9–12).

Rainfall. Areas of high rainfall present special problems. Tree fruits in particular may prove difficult to grow where annual rainfall totals normally exceed 40 inches (1016mm), owing to the diseases associated with wet conditions, such as scab and canker on apples and pears, and brown rot and splitting in stone fruits. Soft fruits can also suffer, especially with grey mould. There are some reasonably efficient fungicides available today which give adequate control provided a fairly regular spray programme is main-

A fan-trained cherry is more suitable for a garden than a bush or standard. This is 'Stella' on the rootstock 'Colt'.

Apple 'Sunset' in flower in May. Apple trees are very decorative at this time in spring.

tained. Gardeners reluctant to use chemicals might consider growing culinary fruit (for which skin finish is not so important) or be prepared to accept some loss of quality as far as other fruits are concerned. There are cultivars which have some resistance to certain diseases; they are listed under the individual crop.

Soils

Amateur fruit-growers usually have little choice of soil. They have to accept the soil and site on which their house is built. Most fruits are tolerant of a wide range of soils, provided that they are of good depth and well drained. (The requirements of each fruit are set out in the relevant fruit chapter.)

The ideal soil to suit nearly all fruits is a well drained medium loam at least 24 inches (60cm) deep for tree fruits or 18 inches (45cm) for bush and cane fruits. Strawberries can be grown in shallower soils, if necessary, but sweet cherries require at least 30 inches (75cm).

The soil should be slightly acid. The acidity or alkalinity of a soil is referred to in terms of a pH number. A neutral soil has a pH of 7; acid soils have pH figures below this, and alkaline soils have higher figures. Most fruits prefer a soil pH between 6.5 and 6.7. The pH for any soil can be measured by using one of the soil-testing kits on the market.

The soils that will present most difficulties are those that are extreme in one way or another. Fruits grown in very alkaline soils, for example, may suffer from lime-induced chlorosis shown by the yellowing of the leaves between the veins. It is caused by iron and/or manganese deficiency. Die-back may also occur. Affected plants require feeding with iron and manganese in a form which can be taken up by the plant (see Nutrient deficiencies, pp.24–25).

To reduce the alkalinity of the soil, the application of an acidifying agent is needed – although it should be stressed that a naturally alkaline soil (a chalky loam, for example) reverts if not regularly treated. A generous application of an acid peat (like sphagnum moss) before planting and as a mulch afterwards helps to counteract soil alkalinity.

On a long-term basis, flowers of sulphur can be used. It is quite safe to apply it where plants are growing, but its acidifying action is slow, because it depends on the activity of the sulphur-oxidizing bacteria, normally present in soils, to convert it to sulphuric acid. The process is biological (biochemical) and therefore depends on temperature, so in winter the acidifying action of sulphur is generally very slow. It is best to apply the sulphur in late winter or early spring. The quantity of sulphur required varies according to soil texture and type, and to how much the pH is intended to be reduced. For sandy loams, it may be in the region of 4 oz per sq. yd ($130g/m^2$) and for heavy loams, 8 oz per sq. yd ($260g/m^2$). It is a wise precaution to treat a small area, then test the pH after a few months, and repeat the application if necessary.

Deep soils over chalk are not necessarily very alkaline; shallow soils usually are, however, and plants not only suffer from chlorosis unless treatment is given, but are also likely to suffer stress in times of drought. Such soils are usually poor in moisture retention.

Very acid soils with a pH of 6.5 and below require liming (unless intended for blueberries), but a gardener should be careful not to over-lime. It is relatively simple to make an acid soil alkaline, but the reverse process is difficult. The usual form of lime for the treatment is the carbonate, and rates of application vary from 2 oz to 1 lb per sq. yd (65–500g/m^2), according to the acidity of the soil. Do not apply lime to ground recently fertilized because lime reacts chemically with certain fertilizers. If lime is necessary it is best applied in the autumn or early winter, well before the spring application of fertilizers. The amount needed to raise the pH to the required level depends upon the existing pH and the amount of organic matter in the soil. Soils low in organic matter need less, whereas those high in organic matter need more. In general terms, about 8 oz of ground limestone or 6 oz of burnt lime per sq. yd (250 or 180g/m^2) increases the pH by about 0.75.

As it is important not to over-lime, it is wise to apply the lime in small amounts until the required pH is reached. Thoroughly work the lime into the top 12 inches (30cm) well before planting. In established fruit plantings, apply it as a top dressing and allow the winter rains to wash the lime into the soil.

Light, sandy soils, gravels and shallow soils over chalk are liable to drought. The capacity for moisture-retention in all of them can be improved by the generous addition, thoroughly incorporated, of bulky organic materials such as farmyard or stable manure, compost or peat.

Soil drainage

Good drainage is essential although some fruits – such as plums, damsons, pears, cooking apples, blackcurrants and black-berries – tolerate slightly impeded drainage, provided that it is below 18 inches (45cm) in depth. Dessert fruits – in particular the apple 'Cox's Orange Pippin', peaches, sweet cherries, raspberries and strawberries – must have good drainage. Badly drained land can result in root death followed by die-back and wilting of the aerial parts, or the complete loss of the plant. Collar rot and canker on apples, cane death in raspberries, and red core of strawberries are related problems.

Heavy clays are more likely to be badly drained than light soils unless these happen to be over solid clay, or have a hard impermeable pan beneath. Water lying for days on the surface is an indication of bad drainage, although the reason could be that the soil has been

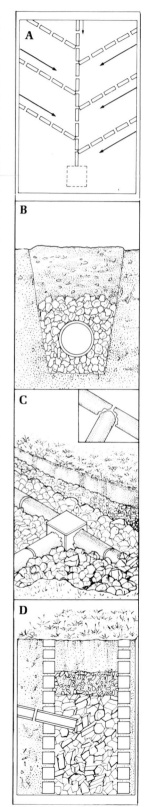

compacted and requires opening up. The presence of plants such as sedge or mare's tail indicates waterlogged conditions. Where poor drainage is suspected, dig inspection pits not less than 3 feet (90cm) deep in the area where the fruits are to be planted and examine the soil profile. If the soil is grey, greasy and "plastic" with an unpleasant smell, it is badly drained. The presence of water near the surface is another indication.

The land may be improved simply by double-digging and breaking any hard pan beneath by forking. Alternatively, more drastic measures may be required. For small areas a simple soakaway constructed of bricks loosely stacked so that water can flow through, filled with clinker or brick rubble might be the answer. For larger areas it may be necessary to lay a drain leading into the soakaway or ditch, or perhaps to construct a more sophisticated drainage system laid in herringbone fashion. Drains must run towards the ditch or soakaway at a gradient of not less than 1 in 40.

Where it is not possible to improve badly drained land, the gardener should plant trees and bush fruits on mounds and cane fruits and strawberries on ridges. It must be stressed, though, that successful growing on such ground is far from certain, and such techniques are suggested only as a last resort.

Choice of site

Where there is a choice of site in the garden, select the sunniest possible. Sunshine is needed to ripen the wood, to promote fruit bud development and to give colour, sweetness and flavour to the fruits. Ideally, most fruits should grow in the full sun – but all will tolerate a little shade, some more than others. It is important that the shade should not be dry, otherwise nearby plants will be competing for nutrients and water, nor should the plants suffer from rain dripping on to them from any overhanging branches.

Soft fruits should receive at least half the day's sun in the growing season. Cane fruits – except autumn fruiting raspberries – tolerate less than this, as do redcurrants and gooseberries. Autumn fruiting raspberries require full sun. Dessert tree fruits in which colour and flavour are important are best reserved for the sunniest site of all. Culinary fruits can take the more shady positions, if a choice has to be made.

The garden should be sheltered from strong winds which may damage growth, scorch flowers and foliage, spoil tree shape, blow fruits to the ground, remove moisture and heat from the plants and the soil, and inhibit the movement of the essential pollinating insects. If an exposed position is unavoidable for the fruit plantings, the erection of some kind of windbreak is essential.

Windbreaks

An efficient windbreak creates a favourable microclimate. The best kind of shelter surrounds the plot on all four sides, so long as it does not cast too much shade or create a frost pocket. Where a new shelter is to be provided, it should be sited on the side towards the prevailing wind – and also to the north and east in cold areas and exposed sites to give protection from cold winds, particularly at flowering time.

The windbreak may be artifical (non-living) or living. The artificial kind may be a permanent fence or wall surrounding the property or it may be a temporary one erected to shelter the fruit plants (and possibly a living windbreak) until established. The advantages of this type are that it is immediately effective, does not compete with the fruits for nutrients and water, and if permanent, can be used to support trained fruit forms.

If a temporary windbreak is erected, select a material which allows the wind to filter through but which at the same time slows it down. Solid barriers create turbulence and buffeting on the leeward side. There is a wide choice of plastic and plastic-coated materials available, as well as coir netting specially designed for windbreaks, all of which can last from 5 to 10 years. Select one which has about 50 per cent permeability; this degree of permeability reduces wind speed to an acceptable level without creating turbulence. Plastic materials should contain an ultraviolet (UV) inhibitor to prevent degradation by the sun.

The height of a fence is relative to the shelter it gives. A windbreak provides effective shelter roughly equivalent to twenty times its height on the leeward side, although the further the plants are away, the less they benefit from it.

×Cupressocyparis leylandii *makes a very solid shelter.*

A tall windbreak of poplars in late April: well in leaf before the apples flower.

Living windbreaks compete with the fruit plants for water, nutrients and light. In selecting a plant for a hedge therefore, choose a species which is not too competitive or plant it at some distance from the fruit plants. There are many hedge plants from which to choose (and a short list of suitable plants is given in table 1). Whatever the plant selected, bear in mind that the spread of the roots is roughly equivalent to the height of the hedge, and that any windbreak casts shade for at least part of the day. The taller the windbreak, the further the fruits should be away from it. Ideally, plant at a distance roughly equivalent to the height of the hedge. In a garden this is not always possible, but for fruit trees the minimum should be a distance of not less than 8 feet (2.4m), and for soft fruits 6 feet (1.8m), assuming that the hedge is clipped and well maintained.

Very large orchards, in which space is

Table 1   Living windbreaks

Species		Spacing feet (metres)	Growth period	Tolerance	Comments
a) Broad shelter belt: trees planted in staggered rows at least 40 feet (12m) away from the fruit crop					
Pinus radiata	E	6–8 (1.8–2.4)	8	1	Monterey pine. Excellent for very exposed positions as a first line of defence.
Pinus nigra	E	6 (1.8)	10	1	Austrian pine. A compact form, dense and dark green. Similar capabilities to above.
Pinus muricata	E	6 (1.8)	8	0	Bishop pine. Forms a dense head. Highly resistant to salt and wind.
b) Shelter belt: trees of narrow form planted in single or double staggered rows. Plant at least 30 feet (9m) away					
Alnus glutinosa	D	4 (1.2)	5	0	Common alder. Useful for damp situations and heavy soils. Leafs out early in the spring. Not suitable for dry soils.
Alnus incana	D	5 (1.5)	4	1	Grey alder. Can be grown on a wide range of soils. Leafs out early.
Alnus cordata	D	5 (1.5)	3	2	Italian alder. Grows strongly and fast. Suitable for dry soils. Leafs out early.
× Cupressocyparis leylandii Clone 121	E	6–8 (1.8–2.4)	5	1	Leyland cypress. Very fast-growing, but is not very well anchored except when planted as a very young tree. Also suitable as a hedge plant. Heavy pruning of branches is necessary later to maintain 50% porosity.
Populus balsamifera × P. trichocarpa 'Tacatricho 32'	D	5 (1.5)	5	3	Balsam hybrid poplar. Makes an upright tree, but more branched than Lombardy poplar. Vigorous. Resistant to leaf spot. Leafs out early to mid-April, well in advance of apple flowering.
c) Hedges: clipped and maintained at a height between 6 and 8 feet (1.8–2.4m)					
Berberis darwinii	E	1½ (0.45)	10	1	Slow-growing. Attractive leaf and flower. Forms a dense hedge.
Carpinus betulus	D	1½ (0.45)	8	1	Hornbeam. For acid soils and heavy soils. Retains its leaves throughout most of the winter. Roots are not invasive.
× Cupressocyparis leylandii Clone 121	E	3½–5 (1–1.5)	5	1	See above
Cupressus macrocarpa 'Lutea'	E	3½–5 (1–1.5)	5	2	A golden form. Fast-growing and attractive. Suitable only for mild, coastal areas.
Escallonia 'Crimson Spire' or 'C.F. Bell'	E	1½ (0.45)	6	2	Vigorous and erect with dark foliage and crimson flowers. Rapid regrowth follows wind and frost damage.
Fagus sylvatica and forma purpurea	D	1½ (0.45)	8	3	Beech and purple-leaved beech. Suitable for alkaline, but not heavy, wet soils. Leaves retained throughout the winter.
Ligustrum ovalifolium	E/D	1½ (0.45)	8	0	The common privet. Hungry and invasive. Evergreen in the milder areas. Easily clipped and makes a neat hedge.

D = Deciduous **E** = Evergreen.
Growth period is the approximate number of years needed, from planting, to reach a height of 8–10 feet (2.4–3m).
Shelter trees a) and b): very tall trees eventually reaching a height of 50 feet (15m) or more unless regularly lopped; they are intended to protect very large orchards.
Tolerance levels to wind/salt. 0 = total tolerance. 1 = high tolerance. 2 = moderate tolerance. 3 = low tolerance. 4 = damage can occur.

With acknowledgements to Rosewarne Experimental Horticulture Station, *Shelter, Hedges and Trees.*

not a problem, may be protected by fast-growing trees that reach a height of 10 to 15 feet (3–4.5m) within 4 or 5 years and which leaf out early in the spring. They may be closely planted, usually 4 to 6 feet (1.2–1.8m) apart (see table 1 under (b)).

Windbreaks sited across slopes can impede air drainage on cold nights and so create a frost pocket. In such situations, a gap of about a foot (30cm) should be left at the base of the windbreak to allow cold air to escape.

Frost

Frost in late spring is probably the greatest hazard to successful fruit-growing. Fruit plants are relatively hardy while they are dormant, but once they start to grow in spring they are extremely vulnerable to frost damage. The more forward the plants are in growth, the greater the danger.

Using the apple as an example, frost damage can occur as follows:

Stage of bud development	Temperatures at which buds are damaged	
	°F	°C
Green cluster	26	– 3.5
Pink bud	27	– 3.0
Full bloom	28	– 2.0
Petal fall	29	– 2.5
Fruitlet	30	– 1.0

Frost damage occurs in many forms, depending upon the severity of the cold, its duration and the plant's stage of fruit growth. Damage may show very soon after a frost or some time later. Typical examples are:

○ 'Scorching' and sometimes complete destruction of the young growth.

○ Blossom and fruitlet drop (not to be confused with lack of pollination and fertilization, or natural thinning); a blackened ovule within the fruitlet, apparent a day or two after the frost, is an indication.

○ Heavy russeting and cracking of the skin of apples and pears, more obvious some months later, when it may include deep circular russeted scars. Russeting and cracking on one side of the fruit is usually due to a wind frost.

○ Malformed fruits, coupled with severe russeting, typically on pears.

○ Strawberry 'black eye'; the flower centre blackened and destroyed.

○ 'Run-off', on currants, especially blackcurrants; the flowers and sometimes the young berries on the raceme dry up and drop off a number of days after the frost. Often mistakenly attributed to lack of pollination and fertilization.

Preventing frost damage. Cold air is denser than warm, and therefore gravitates to the lowest level it can. Areas in which cold air collects are called frost pockets. An obvious precaution is to avoid planting in a frost pocket, although this is not always practicable because there are very few areas of the British Isles which are frost-free every spring.

In anyone's garden a frost pocket may be natural and unavoidable – the bottom of a valley, for example. Alternatively, it may be artificial in that the escape of cold air has been impeded by a barrier of some kind, perhaps a hedge or a wall. A gardener who plants a hedge or erects a fence should take care that a frost pocket is not created. Where such a barrier already exists, the gardener should look to see whether the flow of air can be improved, possibly by making a gap in the barrier or by removing some of the lower growth from a hedge.

On the other hand, in places where a frost pocket is unavoidable, consider planting late-flowering tree and soft fruits (see Pollination tables pp.216–221 for the times of flowering of certain fruit trees.) Cane fruits such as raspberries and blackberries flower late and escape frost more often than red- and blackcurrants.

Certain cultivars are more frost-resistant than others, although none can withstand severe frost. Examples are:
Dessert apples: Beauty of Bath, Discovery, Ellison's Orange, Worcester Pearmain, Greensleeves, James Grieve, Epicure, Laxton's Superb, Laxton's Fortune, Miller's Seedling, Spartan, Sunset, Charles Ross.
Cooking apples: Emneth Early, Grenadier, Lane's Prince Albert, Lord Derby, Newton Wonder, Royal Jubilee, Wellington, Keswick Codlin, Gascoygne's Scarlet.
Pears: Dr Jules Guyot, Williams' Bon Chrétien, Louise Bonne of Jersey, Conference, Fertility, Fertility Improved, Beurré d'Amanlis, Durondeau, Hessle, Jargonelle, Onward, Beurré Dumont.
Plums: Purple Pershore, Yellow Pershore, Czar, Early Rivers, Laxton's Cropper, Marjorie's Seedling, Blue Tit.

Damsons: Prune (Shropshire), Bradley's King, Farleigh.
Acid cherries: Morello.
Blackcurrants: (late-flowering): Ben Lomond, Ben Sarek, Ben More, Malling Jet.
Redcurrants: Most are reasonably hardy, in particular Rondom.
Raspberries: Most are late-flowering, Leo even later than most. Autumn Bliss, autumn-fruiting.
Strawberries: Perpetuals which flower in flushes throughout the summer, eg. Aromel, Gento, Rapella.

Physical protection. The degree and success of frost protection depends to a large extent upon the ingenuity and fortitude of the grower. Cover the plants during the duration of the frost, but remove the covers when the danger is over. Glass and plastic which let in the light can, of course, be left on so long as provision is made for pollination.

Rows of cordons or other low-trained forms can be draped with hessian, bonded polypropylene or two or three layers of bird netting. The material should be supported by canes so that it is held away from the blossom. Fan-trained forms and bush fruits, especially blackcurrants, can be protected in a similar manner.

Cane fruits can be bundled loosely together (*see* photo p.173) and left in this way as long as possible. They should be untied once the buds break to prevent yellowing of the foliage through lack of light.

Glass cloches over strawberries give 3 or 4 degrees of frost protection. Thin polythene gives no protection however. Even under glass, with strawberries it is best when severe frosts are forecast to give them extra protection by covering the glass with newspaper.

One commercial method of protection is to sprinkle the blossom with water, a method that may be adopted in the garden (provided that permission is obtained from the local water authority, if necessary). The blossom must be kept sprinkled more or less continuously with droplets about the size of raindrops while the frost lasts. It should be noted that in long periods of sprinkling the trees may become heavily covered with ice: it may be necessary to prop up the branches to prevent breakages. Soil drainage also must be efficient so there is no danger of the soil becoming waterlogged.

Planning the fruit garden

Most fruit plants represent a long-term investment; once planted they should be there for a very long time. It is important, therefore, that they are properly sited and correctly spaced right from the start. It is wise to make a plan, ideally on graph paper and drawn to scale. A well executed plan, completed in good time, enables the gardener to make out a plant list and to assess the fertilizers and materials required, so that ordering and ground preparation can all be done well in advance. (*See also* plans, p.207.)

In planning a fruit garden, remember there will be a need to net the fruits against birds on occasions. It is simpler, and probably cheaper, to cover a plot that is square or rectangular than one which is an irregular shape. Bush and cane fruits are best planted in a block separate from tree fruits: their requirements for sprays against pests and diseases are different, and they also ripen at a different time.

Plant the smallest fruit plants at the south end of the plot and the tallest at the north so that each receives a fair share of sun. In practical terms this means planting gooseberries on the south side, currants and cane fruits in the middle, and the tallest tree fruits on the north.

Strawberries are a short-term crop and require soil rotation. They should not be planted in a permanent fruit cage and are best planted with vegetables.

The size of a fruit garden depends upon the family's requirements in relation to the ground available and the anticipated yield from each kind of fruit planted. The yield depends upon many factors, including the environment, the cultivar and the grower's skill. Good average yields from well-grown established plants are given in table 2 (p.14) under each crop but in any case vary according to cultivar and rootstock, climate, season and general growing conditions. For more details see relevant chapters.

Walls and fences
Take full advantage of walls and fences by growing against them restricted tree forms such as espaliers, fans and cordons, especially where space is limited. Arches and pergolas for climbing fruits should also be considered. The wall or fence provides support for the plant and for a fruit net, should one prove necessary.

Table 2   Good average yield from well-grown established plants

	Bush	Dwarf Bush	Dwarf Pyramid	Espalier (2-tier)	Fan	Single Cordon	Standard	
Apple	60–120	30–50	10–15	20–25	12–30	5–8	100–400	lb
	27–54	14–23	4–7	9–11	5–14	2–4	45–180	kg
Pear	40–100	20–40	8–12	15–20	12–30	4–6	80–240	lb
	18–45	9–18	3–5	7–9	5–14	2–3	36–109	kg
			Pyramid					
Plum	30–60		30–50				30–120	lb
	14–27		14–23				14–54	kg
Cherry (sweet)	30–120				12–30		30–120	lb
	14–54				5–14		14–54	kg
Cherry (acid)	30–40				12–30		30–120	lb
	14–18				5–14		14–54	kg
Peach/Nectarine	30–60				12–30		30–120	lb
	14–27				5–14		14–54	kg
Apricot					12–30		30–120	lb
					5–14		14–54	kg
Fig					12–30			lb
					5–14			kg
Blackcurrant	10–13							lb
	4–6							kg
Redcurrant	6–12							lb
	3–5							kg
Gooseberry	8–10					1–3		lb
	4–5					0.5–1.5		kg

Raspberries	2lb per foot (3kg per m) of row
Blackberries	10–20lb (4–5kg) per plant
Strawberries	8–16oz (225–450g) per plant

The aspect of the wall governs the kinds of fruit which can be grown against it, and its height dictates the tree shape or form. If necessary, the height can be increased with trellising.

Aspect. South, south-east and south-west are the warmest aspects, and all fruits can be grown against them. Such favourable sites are best reserved for those fruits which need plenty of sun, for example, figs, apricots, peaches, nectarines, dessert pears, plums and gages. Remember that the soil at the base of such a wall can become very dry in the summer, and mulching in addition to watering may be necessary.

A west wall receives the afternoon sun and is the next warmest aspect, for it has time to warm up during the day. It is suitable for apricots, peaches, nectarines, figs, gages, plums, pears, apples, sweet and sour cherries, raspberries, hybrid and blackberries, gooseberries, red- and whitecurrants. Generally this aspect receives more rain than the others, but mulching and watering in spring and summer are usually required.

An east wall receives the morning sun and is cooler than the south and west walls. It is a rather dry situation and open to cold easterly winds. It is suitable for early and mid-season pears, apples, plums, sweet and sour cherries, currants, gooseberries, blackberries, hybrid berries and raspberries.

North is the coldest aspect of all and only suitable for fruits which tolerate a lack of sun and cool conditions, such as acid cherries, early cooking apples, cordon red- and whitecurrants, gooseberries, raspberries and blackberries.

Height of wall or fence. Fences for cordon apples and pears planted obliquely need to be between 6 and 7 feet (1.8–2.1m) tall. Vertical cordons need more than this – indeed, up to the roof of the house, if so desired (see photo, p.73).

Cordon gooseberries, red- and white-

Various methods of wiring a wall: wooden battens on the perimeter to which the wires are fixed.

Wiring a wooden fence. A screwed vine eye is driven into the post and a straining bolt then slotted through the eye.

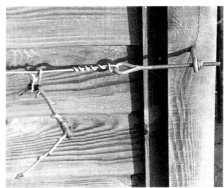

and vigour (depending on the rootstock and soil fertility). Fan-shaped apples and pears on dwarfing or semi-dwarfing root-stocks are suitable for walls 6 to 8 feet (1.8–2.4m) high; on vigorous stocks they need 8 to 12 feet (2.4–3.6m). Apricots, peaches, nectarines, plums and gages, and acid cherries require at least 7 feet (2.1m), although it is possible to grow a peach or nectarine fan on a lower structure provided that the gardener is prepared to do a lot of tying down.

Figs are very vigorous, unless the roots are restricted, and the height to which they can grow depends upon the amount of rooting area they are allowed (see p.124).

Sweet cherries are also very vigorous, even on the rootstock 'Colt', and require a wall at least 8 feet (2.4m) high.

Wiring walls and wooden fences. Fans, espaliers and cordons grown against walls and fences need some kind of support. The usual method is to fix gal-vanised wires running horizontally to the structure with the wires attached no more closely than 1½ inches (4cm), but preferably 4 inches (10cm), away so that there is air movement at the back of the plants. This is desirable to reduce the incidence of fungus diseases and the build-up of red spider mite.

For fans, the wires should be spaced about 6 inches (15cm) or two brick courses apart starting 15 inches (38cm) from the ground. The wires need to be relatively close so that the young shoots can be tied in as they grow. Because the weight of the branch framework and the crop is evenly distributed over a rela-tively wide area, it is not necessary to use heavy-gauge wire; 14-gauge (1.2mm) gal-vanised fencing wire will do. Straining bolts are not usually required except for a long run.

With cordons and espaliers, the wires can be further apart, but a heavier gauge of wire is needed. Gauge 12 (2.5mm) is recommended. Straining bolts at one end to keep the wires taut are also necessary. The spacing between the wires depends upon the ultimate height of the cordon, or the number of tiers in the espalier. Ob-lique cordons grown to a height of about 7 feet (2.1m) need horizontal wires at 2, 4 and 6 feet (60cm, 1.2m and 1.8m). With espaliers, the horizontal wires must coincide with the arms, which are usually spaced 15 to 18 inches (38–45cm) apart.

currants usually need about 4½ to 6 feet (1.3–1.8m).

Espalier apples and pears are suitable for low or high walls and fences, depend-ing on the number of tiers (arms). Generally the tiers of an espalier are spaced 15 to 18 inches (38–45cm) apart, so a two-tier espalier can be grown against a 3½- to 4-foot (1.2m) wall, a three-tier against a 5- to 5½-foot (1.6m), and a four-tier against a 6½- to 7-foot (2m) wall or fence.

Fan-trained trees require more height than other forms because of their shape

Fixing wires to masonry
The simplest method is to drive 4- or 5-inch (10–12cm) lead vine eyes into the mortar between the brickwork at 5 foot (1.5m) intervals. A hole for each vine eye is first made in the perpendicular jointing between the bricks with a masonry drill, the hole is then plugged, and the vine eye driven in not less than half-way. An alternative is to use 4- to 6-inch (10–15cm) galvanised screwed vine eyes: these are more secure in that they have a better grip. They are meant to be screwed into wood or brickwork.

A neater and a more secure way with less damage to the brickwork, especially for a long run of trained trees, is to fix 2 × 2 inches (5 × 5cm) wooden battens or a 1½ × 1½-inch (4 × 4cm) angle-iron to the wall. At the ends these can hold the straining bolts, and at the intermediate positions there can either be vine eyes at 5-foot (1.5m) intervals, or wooden battens or angle irons at 7-foot (2.1m) intervals. The wires are held with screwed vine eyes or wire staples on the intermediate battens (*see* top photo p.15).

Fences: post and wire. Cordon, espalier and fan-trained trees are long-lived and present a fair degree of wind resistance. A strong fence is therefore needed.

There are a number of materials that can be used to hold the wires. The simplest and the cheapest are wooden posts. They may be of softwood or hardwood, round, peeled and pointed and preferably pressure-treated with preservative or steeped in creosote to at least 4½ feet (1.3m) up the butts.

The thickness of the posts depends upon the length of the fence and the exposure of the garden to strong winds. Fences 30 feet (9m) or more long should have endposts 5 to 6 inches (15cm) in diameter and the intermediates 3 to 4 inches (10cm) in diameter. For shorter fences in sheltered gardens, posts of 4-inch (10cm) diameter are adequate. The posts should be sunk 2½ feet (75cm) into the ground on a light soil and 2 feet (60cm) on a heavy clay. Alternatively, they may be set in concrete and sunk only 18 inches (45cm) into the ground.

The endposts must be strutted: each strut should start two-thirds of the way up the post and be at the same distance away at the base. Intermediate posts should be spaced 12 to 15 feet (3.6–4.5m) apart.

Oak is attractive and long-lasting, but

A 6½ foot (2m) high fruit cage constructed of galvanised iron tubing and ¾ inch (2cm) mesh plastic netting.

expensive. Posts sawn to 4 inches (10cm) square and treated with a wood preservative, or with the bases charred against rot, are suitable. (Pressure-treated and oak posts last longer than posts merely dipped in wood preservative.)

A useful device is a metal post holder 2 to 2½ feet (60–75cm) long by 3 × 3 inches (8 × 8cm) or 4 × 4 inches (10 × 10cm) which is driven into the ground first. A wooden post of the appropriate size is then merely slotted in. The posts last much longer because they are not in contact with the soil.

The post holder is designed so that the anchorage is fairly secure, but strutting is still necessary for runs longer than 15 feet (4.5m).

Angle-iron fencing posts
Angle-iron is excellent for fences for cordons, espaliers, or fans. It is not obtrusive and should last for many years if properly primed with red oxide or black bitumastic or galvanised. The dimensions range from 1½ × 1½ × 3/16 inch (38 × 38 × 4.5mm) to 2 × 2 × ¼ inches (50 × 50 × 6mm), depending on whether they are intermediate or endposts. Both struts and posts are fitted with base plates.

The posts are to be set 2 feet (60cm) deep and for long runs are best set in concrete.

Concrete
Concrete can be used for ferro-concrete post holders or spurs to which the

wooden posts are bolted. Alternatively, the whole post may be made of concrete.

Concrete lasts virtually for ever, but it is heavy and can perhaps be too dominant and obtrusive in most gardens.

Wire and galvanised straining eye bolts
Galvanised fencing wire is recommended. Long fences and exposed situations require heavier-gauge wire than do short runs or sheltered gardens. For runs longer than 30 feet (9m) use gauge 10 (3.15mm) for the top wire and gauge 12 (2.5mm) for the remainder. For short fences and in sheltered gardens gauge 12 and 14 (2.5mm, 1.2mm) are adequate.

The wires must be tight, so it is advisable to use adjustable straining bolts on the endposts, and wire staples on the intermediates.

Protection from birds

The fruit cage. In most districts, in order to obtain a crop from soft fruits and from many top fruits, it is necessary to protect the plants from birds, both during the winter (when bullfinches are the main culprits) and over the ripening period (when blackbirds and thrushes are troublesome). In some areas grey squirrels are also a pest.

Trees grafted on to dwarfing rootstocks, planted close together and contained by summer pruning, can be covered by a net, but those on vigorous stocks are more difficult in that usually they grow too tall. The restricted forms grown against walls and fences or on wires are fairly easy to protect because the structure can be used to support the netting.

In its simplest form, the fruit cage is an enclosure of netting of ½ to ¾ inch (13 to 19mm) mesh 6 to 7 feet (1.8–2.1m) high. The netting is supported by wooden battens or wires stretched between the tops of posts spaced 6 feet (1.8m) apart. There are various netting materials available, such as terylene, polyethylene and nylon, as well as galvanised wire netting.

The roof netting should be made of a heavier-duty material than that of the sides, but not of galvanised wire netting because of the risk of damage to the plants through zinc toxicity from condensation drips. The galvanised wire netting can be used on the sides, in gardens where squirrels or rabbits are a nuisance.

It is not necessary to keep the nets on all the time, only during certain critical periods. Bullfinches, for example, eat the fruit buds in the winter, but the time they attack depends upon the type of fruits and the stage of bud development. Generally, buds are at risk as follows:

Type of fruit	Time of damage	Remarks
Cherries	Nov.–Jan.	Only Morello suffers severe damage.
Gooseberries	Nov.–Feb.	All cultivars attacked, but 'Leveller' most susceptible. Cultivars having a hairy berry seem partly resistant.
Plums	Nov.–Feb.	Gages especially susceptible.
Pears	Jan.–Mar.	'Williams' Bon Chrétien' may be damaged earlier. 'Doyenné du Comice' is almost immune.
Red- and whitecurrants	Variable	Sometimes not attacked.
Blackcurrants	Mar.–Apr.	Only taken after bud burst.
Apples	Mar.–Apr.	Some dormant bud damage. Most damage from bud burst until pink bud stage (see photos pp.210–211).

The nets should thus be kept on throughout the winter – except that the roof net must be taken off if a heavy fall of snow is expected, to prevent damage to the cage.

It is important to remove the netting – preferably the side netting – during the flowering period so that pollinating insects may enter easily. They tend to avoid fruit blossom in a closed cage, even if the mesh of the net is comparatively large. From this time onwards the nets can be left off to facilitate spraying and cultivation until the fruits begin to ripen when once more they require protection.

Bird repellents. There are several proprietary bird repellents, which make sprayed plants unpleasant-tasting to birds. Their main disadvantage is that the spray deposits are washed off by rain, so

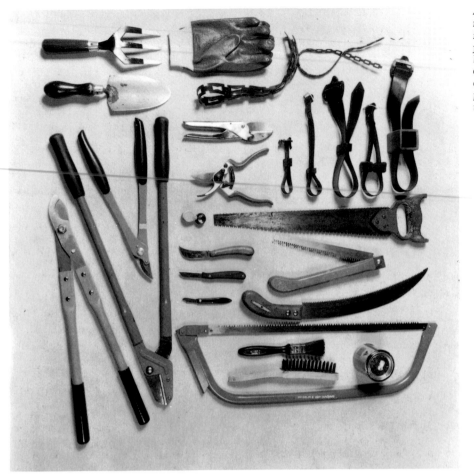

A selection of fruit grower's requirements in tools: including bow, Grecian, folding and English saws; brushes and paint for cleaning and protecting canker wounds; heavy duty pruners; knives; secateurs; tree ties; and a hand lens.

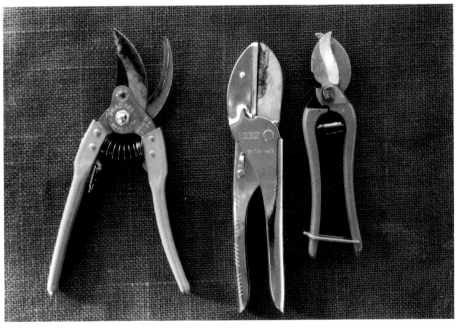

Three types of secateurs: (left) the blade cuts against but not on to a fixed bar which holds the stem; (centre) the blade cuts on to an anvil; (right) two convexly curved cutting blades cross like scissor blades.

repeated application is necessary in wet seasons. During hard winters bullfinches may become very hungry, enough to overcome their dislike of treated plants, especially if no alternative food is available.

Scaring devices. These include the traditional scarecrow, glitter strips, windmills, banging devices, 'humming' tapes, and imitations of predators such as hawks and cats. All can be quite effective initially; usually within a week, however, the birds have lost their fear and ignore the devices. To retain effectiveness, the type and position of scaring device need to be varied fairly frequently.

Tools and equipment
The basic tools include a spade, fork, rake, hoe and hand trowel; select those made of a good quality steel or stainless steel. Neither spade nor fork should be used among established fruit plants, or roots may be damaged. A dutch hoe with a 4-inch (10cm) blade is best for shallow hoeing, and an onion hoe for accurate weeding, particularly among strawberries. A trowel is useful when planting strawberries and cane fruits, and a hand fork for lifting strawberry runners. A 6-foot (1.8m) measuring-rod is an aid to marking out and spacing. It can be made from 2 × 2-inch (5 × 5cm) straight timber, scored with saw cuts every 3 inches (8cm) with extra emphasis at 6 and 12 inches (15 and 30cm).

A 2-gallon (9 litre) watering can is sufficient for a small plot, but larger areas require a garden hose and possibly sprinklers. Low-level sprinklers, lines fitted with drip nozzles or seep hoses are best in that they do not wet the foliage, so lessening the risk of infection with fungal diseases (see photo, p. 57).

A × 10 hand lens is useful for searching out small pests, such as aphid eggs in winter and red spider mite in summer.

Secateurs. A pair of strong secateurs, capable of cutting cleanly and easily wood up to ⅝ inches (16mm) in diameter with little effort is needed. This means a pair with a cutting blade about 2½ to 3 inches (7cm) long.

There are two main types. The first has a single D-shaped cutting blade which cuts against a soft brass or aluminium anvil. In the second, a convex-curved blade cuts against (but not on to) a fixed bar which holds the stem in position. The blade and bar cross in scissor fashion. The anvil type is capable of cutting heavier wood than the other, and with less effort, but the blade must be sharp, or the wood bruises badly on the anvil side. The other makes a cleaner cut and has a finer point, making it easier to manoeuvre between branches growing closely together.

There is a third type that is sometimes seen, in which two convex-curved blades cross as in a pair of scissors.

The points to note when buying a pair of secateurs are:

○ a comfortable grip: the handles should be long enough to exert good leverage;
○ a hardened steel blade, long-lasting and easily sharpened;
○ all parts replaceable: with some designs it is possible to change the blades or replace worn parts;
○ a helper-spring strong enough to return the secateurs to the open position after cutting, but not too strong to be tiring;
○ a simple and efficient safety catch.

Whichever type of secateurs is used, the stem should be positioned so that it is cut by the base of the blade, where it is firmly held. The blade must be sharp so that a clean cut is made. Good cuts cannot be made with blunt secateurs, or those incorrectly adjusted or which have been twisted or strained. Poor cuts resulting in torn edges or badly bruised wood are slow to heal and so more susceptible to infection.

Knives. A good knife is an essential part of a fruit-grower's equipment. The most useful is a 3½-inch (9cm) straight-bladed knife made from good quality steel. It has value in pruning, especially for trimming back damaged tissue or paring smooth the rough edges of a saw cut, and can also be used in grafting. For budding, a budding knife is necessary with a spatula end to the handle for lifting the rind of the bark. The pruning knife has a curved blade and handle. The blade grips the wood well and is excellent for removing snags and unwanted sideshoots flush with the stem.

Pruning saws. These are designed to cut live green wood without wet sawdust clogging the teeth. There are three basic types:

The English saw has a straight tapering blade with teeth on both sides, one set coarse and the other fine. The taper is useful when working in a confined space, but care must be taken to avoid damaging other branches with the teeth on the back of the blade.

The Grecian saw has a curved blade tapering to a fine point. The saw is set to be used with a single drawing action; provided that it is sharp, the curve of the blade enables the pruner to make a good clean cut without undue effort.

Additionally, there are folding saws both straight-bladed and curved which can be easily carried.

The bow saw is useful for heavy work, although the frame makes it difficult to use where the branches are closely spaced. The blade is easily replaced.

There is also the pole saw. Basically, this is a Grecian saw with a hollow metal handle into which a pole can be inserted. It is useful for sawing branches that cannot be reached with the ordinary pruning saw.

Long-handled pruners or limb loppers. These are heavy-duty pruners with handles 22 to 30 inches (55–75cm) long and very strong blades capable of cutting branches up to 1¼ inches (3.2cm) thick. There is also a ratchet model that can cut wood up to 2 inches (5cm) in diameter.

Limb loppers are excellent for pruning large blackcurrant bushes and for the quick removal of fairly heavy wood from a neglected tree.

Long-arm pruners. These are designed for pruning, trimming and thinning from the ground. They are particularly useful for people who cannot climb a ladder and for pruning high growth which otherwise would be difficult to reach. The best type has a blade that cuts upwards into a hook-shaped slot. The hook holds the wood securely so it cannot escape. It has a very positive rod-and-lever action for minimum effort and maximum cutting power of wood up to 1⅛-inch (3cm) diameter. The handle is made of tubular alloy and comes in various lengths, ranging from 3 to 12 feet (90cm–3.6m). With some models there is a pruning saw attachment and a fruit-picking device.

It is not easy to be as accurate in cutting to a bud with a long-arm pruner as with hand-held secateurs: where the latter can be used, it is better to do so.

Ladder. The tripod fruit-pickers' ladder is generally the most suitable. This type is easily maneouvred between branches to allow access for pruning and picking, and does not damage the tree's framework. There are two kinds; one has a folding back leg and the other is of rigid construction. The former is convenient for stacking away after use, but not as stable in operation as the rigid kind. Some also have a platform upon which tools or the picking container can be placed, as well as a leaning rail. The ladder may be made of galvanised steel, aluminium, or more rarely these days of wood, and is fitted with either rungs or steps. Steps are much easier on the feet, especially when the ladder is to be used for a long period.

Ladders are made in various sizes, ranging from about 3 to 14 treads or from about 3 feet (90cm) to 12½ feet (3.8m) high. As a general guide, a 7-step ladder should be suitable for pruning and picking from trees up to a height of about 12 to 14 feet (3.6–4.2m), and a 10-step ladder for trees up to about 17 feet (5.2m) high.

For very large trees, there are fruit-picking ladders with a tapered top and splayed bottom, ranging from 14 to 22 feet (4.2–6.7m) long, having 17 to 25 rungs. These are not self-supporting but are meant to rest against the limbs of the

Budding and grafting knives (left to right): Budding knife with spatula-ended handle; two grafting knives; a combined budding and grafting knife; a pruning and grafting knife with a slightly curved blade.

Two types of tripod ladder, a picking bucket, three pole saws, long-arm pruners and two types of sprayers.

tree, which should of course be selected to be strong enough to take the weight of the ladder and the user. In general terms, these are not for the amateur grower but are intended for the professional. Where there are only one or two trees to be dealt with, the grower might decide to make do with some kind of household ladder.

Labelling

Most fruit plants remain in the garden for a very long time and good-quality permanent labels are essential. One of the best types is the engraved label made from laminated plastic. The engraving itself requires specialised tools, but several firms will provide this service to order. Other permanent labels include the embossed lead label, embossed plastic tape which is glued to wood or plastic, and the zinc label etched with acid. Where the label is affixed to the plant, on the trunk of a tree for example, it is wise to check

the tie regularly to ensure constriction does not occur.

General principles of nutrition

The principal manures used for fruits contain nitrogen (N), phosphorus (P) and potassium (K), and should be applied on a regular basis. In certain conditions there is occasionally a need for the minor elements magnesium and calcium, and more rarely some of the trace elements, principally iron and manganese (see table 4, pp.24–25).

Nitrogen is required for growth, but the needs of fruit plants vary according to their kind. Plums, pears and black-currants, for example, benefit from heavy dressings of nitrogen, whereas if dessert apples, raspberries and strawberries are given such quantities of nitrogen, they are liable to be too vigorous, low in yield and poor in fruit quality. Excessive applications result in rank growth susceptible to disease, large dark green leaves, poor fruiting and, with apples, large fruits which do not store well.

Phosphorus, which is given in the form of phosphates, is needed for root development, growth, fruit quality and the general health of the plant. Because most soils take a long time to become depleted of phosphates, usually one application every third year is sufficient to keep the soil up to the necessary status.

Potassium, applied as potash, is a very important nutrient necessary for colour and flavour in the fruits, hardiness and fruit bud development. An annual application is usually required.

Organic matter
The importance of organic matter in fruit soils cannot be too strongly stressed. Fruit plants must have a free rooting medium for healthy growth and longevity, and this can be assured by maintaining a good content of organic matter in the soil, which improves and maintains the soil's structure and its water-holding capacity.

For tree fruits such as dessert apples and pears in an orchard, this is best achieved by growing them in grass once they are well established, usually after 3 or 4 years (see pp.56, 81). In early years they are grown in clean cultivation, but mulched with bulky organics such as well rotted manure, straw or compost. This is particularly valuable on light soils, gravel

Table 3   Commonly available fertilizers for fruit

| Fertilizer | Average nutrient content (per cent) | | | Rate of application | Notes |
	N nitrogen	P_2O_5 phosphate	K_2O potash		
Nitrogen					
Sulphate of ammonia	21	0	0	1–2 oz/sq yd 33–65 g/m^2	Makes soil acid; but useful for alkaline soils.
Nitro-chalk (ammonium nitrate/lime)	21–35	0	0	1–2 oz/sq yd 33–65 g/m^2	Useful on acid soils.
Phosphorus					
Superphosphate	0	18–19	0	1–2 oz/sq yd 33–65 g/m^2	Also contains calcium.
Triple superphosphate	0	47	0	½ oz/sq yd 15 g/m^2	Contains about three times as much phosphate as superphosphate.
Basic slag	0	18	0	4–5 oz/sq yd 125–160 g/m^2	The phosphates are released very slowly. Tends to be alkaline.
Bone meal (organic fertilizer)	3.7	21	0	3–4 oz/sq yd 100–125 g/m^2	Organic fertilizer. Both nutrients slowly available. Very useful at planting.
Potash					
Sulphate of potash	0	0	48	½–1 oz/sq yd 15–33 g/m^2	The safest form of potash to use. Slow to move into the soil, therefore best used in late winter.
Muriate of potash	0	0	60	½ oz/sq yd 15 g/m^2	A cheap form of potash, but only suitable for tree fruits and blackcurrants.
Potassium nitrate	15	0	10–15	¼–½ oz/sq yd 7–15 g/m^2	Very quickly supplies potash and nitrogen.
Magnesium					
Magnesium sulphate (Epsom salts)	0	0	0	1–2 oz/sq yd 33–65 g/m^2	For magnesium deficiency: contains 10% magnesium (see table 4, p.24).
Kieserite	0	0	0	1 oz/sq yd 33 g/m^2	Not suitable for foliar sprays, but very good for soil application, being cheaper than Epsom salts. 16% magnesium.

or shallow soils over chalk which are poor in moisture retention. Irrespective of the age of the tree, the surrounding grass and any other organic materials must be kept clear of the tree trunk to reduce the risk of collar rot.

For soft fruits the usual method is to dig in bulky manures or compost before planting, and on light soils they are also mulched afterwards.

Concentrated organic manures and in-organic fertilizers (see table 3)
Bulky organics are invaluable in maintaining structure and for improving the moisture-holding capacity of the soil, but they are low in nutrients. It is therefore usually necessary to apply concentrated organic manure or inorganic (artificial) fertilizers to the right amount. The artificial fertilizers are classified either as 'straight' or as 'compound'. The straight fertilizer supplies only one specific element, although it may sometimes contain small amounts of others. The compound fertilizer contains all three of the major elements in varying proportions to suit differing crops, and may contain other elements as well. It may be made up of

Table 3 (Continued)

Fertilizer	Average nutrient content (per cent)			Rate of application	Notes
	N nitrogen	P_2O_5 phosphate	K_2O potash		
Compound fertilizer					
Growmore	7	7	7	1–3 oz/sq yd 33–100 g/m²	A balanced fertilizer.
Bulky organic manures (Nutrient content variable: average per cent)					
Farmyard manure	0.5	0.3	0.5	10–15 lb/sq yd 5–7 kg/m²	Must be well rotted before application.
Stable manure	0.6	0.5	0.6	15 lb/sq yd 7 kg/m²	Contains straw and sometimes wood shavings: useful as a mulch.
Straw	all variable			1–2 in. (5cm) deep mulch	Best used as a mulch or composted with other bulky organics. If incorporated into the soil extra nitrogen must be added to avoid nitrogen deficiency.
Spent mushroom compost	all variable			10 lb/sq yd 5 kg/m² or as mulch	Useful for improving the soil texture and as a mulch. It usually contains chalk and care must be taken not to make the soil too alkaline. Do not use on raspberries.
Deep litter and broiler-house poultry manure	1–2	1–0	1–2	2–4 oz/sq yd 65–125 kg/m²	Extremely variable depending on the litter used and the age of the manure. Undecomposed litter can cause a shortage of nitrogen when added directly to the soil. Best mixed into the compost heap. Well made, properly dried samples are satisfactory.
Bark	—	—		Use freely	An excellent mulch and contains trace elements. Tends to be acid. Useful on alkaline soils to reduce the pH.
Garden compost	all variable			10–15 lb/sq yd 5–7 kg/m²	Generally useful and as a mulch. It must be well rotted.

purely inorganic fertilizers or may be a mixture of inorganic and organic forms.

Whichever fertilizer is used, the manufacturer is legally obliged to state the percentage contents of nitrogen, phosphate and potash. For example the widely used compound fertilizer Growmore contains 7%N, 7%P_2O_5, 7%K_2O and the straight fertilizer sulphate of ammonia contains 21%N.

Any of the usual manures and fertilizers used for other crops are suitable, although a few precautions are necessary in some cases to avoid damage. All chloride-containing fertilizers, such as muriate of potash, should be used with caution and not at all on soft fruits, because there is a danger of toxicity.

Whether to use a straight or a compound fertilizer depends on the requirements of the fruit and to a certain extent upon the personal preferences of the grower. Straight fertilizers allow the gardener to be more accurate in regard to quantities and time of application, although two or more fertilizers, and applications, may be necessary.

Compound fertilizers save time in handling, but do not always match the exact requirements of the fruit con-

Table 4 Nutrient deficiencies

Symptoms	Lack of	Occurrence	Crops most severely affected	Prevention or cure (usually no immediate treatment)
Thin, poor shoot growth; small, pale green leaves, developing early autumn tints of red and yellow and falling early; few flowers; fruits small and highly-coloured	Nitrogen	In neglected grassed orchards	Apple, plum, blackcurrant	Apply nitrogen fertilizers at recommended rates; keep the grass cut short and maintain a clear area around the plants (see table 3, p.22)
As above but dull green leaves with purplish autumn tints which fall early; small green fruits, tasting acid or unpleasant	Phosphorus	Shows in July–August on plants growing in heavy calcareous soils	Apple, black-currant, goose-berry	Apply phosphate fertilizers at recommended rates, once every three years (see table 3, p.22)
Short shoots tending to die-back; leaves bluish green with yellowing between veins, leaf margins going brown; reasonable flowering; but fruitlets mostly drop; those remaining are small, woody and taste sweet	Potassium	Can occur on plants in clay soils, but is more frequent on light sandy, peat or chalk soils	Apple, black- and red-currant, goose-berry	Apply potash fertilizer at the recommended rates (see table 3, p.22)
Brilliant orange-brown tints on leaves and/or yellowing between veins on older leaves with patches of dead tissue; then sudden severe defoliation: fruits small, immature and woody	Magnesium	From end June onwards on a light soil, in a wet season or with over-feeding with potash	Apple, black-currant, goose-berry, rasp-berry	Soil applications of Epsom salts 1 oz/sq yd (33 g/m^2) or foliar spray $\frac{1}{2}$lb in 2$\frac{1}{2}$ gal. (220g in 11 litres) plus a spreader from petal fall, and repeat 2 or 3 times
Poor shoot growth; leaves at the tips become yellow between the veins or become bleached; branches die back; fruits have pale ground colour, but are highly flushed	Iron	On alkaline soils	Apple, pear, plum, rasp-berry	Apply iron compounds (as chelates or frits) to soil or foliar sprays; try to reduce pH by digging in peat, crushed bracken, pulverized bark or by use of acidifying chemicals

cerned. This is not usually critical, provided the shortfall or excess is not large. Nevertheless, there are occasions when a compound fertilizer has to be topped up with a particular nutrient.

Nutrient deficiencies

Table 4 (above) gives brief diagnostic descriptions of the major common nutrient deficiencies in fruit. But it is often difficult even for an experienced person to be sure what the symptoms show, for they may sometimes be close to those of a disease. It is usually advisable to seek expert advice if a nutrient deficiency is suspected.

Weed control

Good control is essential, because weeds compete with the fruits for water, nutrients and light. They also create damp conditions and reduce air movement around the plants, which can encourage fungal infections such as botrytis and collar rot.

Many gardeners prefer to eliminate the weeds mechanically, by deep digging before planting, for instance, and by shallow hoeing and hand weeding afterwards, and using mulches to suppress them (see p.21). Nevertheless, there are a number of weedkillers available to the amateur which can be used in the fruit garden. The correct use of these chemicals can lessen considerably the labour of weed control, and the non-disturbance of the soil favours penetration of the roots into the warm, fertile top layer of the soil. However, great care must be taken in using these chemicals.

Table 4   (Continued)

Symptoms	Lack of	Occurrence	Crops most severely affected	Prevention or cure (usually no immediate treatment)
Leaves show yellowing between veins starting at margins and progressing inwards; terminal leaves less chlorotic or remain green	Manganese	On soils high in organic matter with pH of over 6.5	Apple, cherry raspberry	Foliar sprays of manganese sulphate 2 oz in 2½ gal. (55 g in 11 litres) plus a spreader (such as soft soap) from petal fall or as young canes develop, repeating 2 or 3 times; alternatively apply chelated or fritted manganese to soil
Die back of some shoots; leaves on some shoots small and mis-shapen; bark has roughened and pimpled appearance, fruits bumpy and malformed	Boron	On sandy or chalk soils after heavy rain; in dry periods on normally acid soils which have been over-limed	Pear	Foliar spray at petal fall with borax (sodium tetraborate) 2½ oz in 5 gal. water (70 g in 22 litres), plus a spreader
Bitter pit of apple fruits (see page 70)	Calcium	Localised deficiency within fruit, not in soil	Apple	Induced by shortage of water at critical time when wide fluctuations in rainfall and temperature (see page 70)

N.B. In gardens, deficiencies of specific major nutrients are less likely to occur than general malnutrition due to neglect. In these circumstances it is best to correct all deficiencies by applying a compound fertilizer. Applications of a foliar feed during the growing season are also beneficial to trees which have been neglected or have suffered from faulty root action as a result of drought or waterlogging. If in doubt seek expert advice before trying out any specific treatment.

Keep the chemicals in their labelled container out of reach of children; always read the label carefully before use. Use the recommended rates and observe the safety precautions stated. Apply the spray accurately; calibrate the sprayer using water only at first to find out exactly what volume is used over a specific area. Avoid spray drift and take care to prevent contamination of any water source. Wash out the sprayer and mixing containers thoroughly before and after use. Keep the sprayer specifically for weedkillers.

Simple weedkilling programmes follow (pp.26–27). The chemicals listed should be sufficient for the needs of amateur growers.

To clean up weedy ground before planting, apply glyphosate to the foliage of actively growing weeds. It destroys annual and many perennial weeds, including creeping thistle and docks, and is particularly useful against grasses, including couch. Glyphosate is inactivated on contact with the soil, and crops can be sown or planted three or four weeks after treatment, or as soon as the weeds are dead.

Weeds, or grass, should never be allowed to grow up to the trunk of a tree. As a general guide a radius of not less than 18 inches (45cm) should be maintained around dessert apples, and at least 2 feet (60cm) for cooking apples, separated either by mulches (see p.21) or by weedkillers (herbicides) (see table 5, p.26). If trees look obviously starved and fruit size is poor, the weed-free area should be made even larger.

With fruit trees grown in clean soil conditions, where herbicides are used

Table 5   **Weed control in fruits**

Time of application	Weeds controlled	Chemical name	Notes
APPLES and PEARS Before weeds appear	Nearly all weeds in germinating stage	simazine	Apply to bare, clean, moist soil, preferably in Feb. or Mar. Trees must have been established for a minimum of 12 months
After weeds appear	Annual weeds and shallow-rooted perennials	paraquat/diquat	Use as a directed spray on to weeds at any time of year. Repeated treatments kill perennials. Paraquat/diquat does not penetrate mature bark, but avoid spraying the stems of trees less than 3 years old or green bark anywhere
End winter to late bud burst	Actively growing grasses, docks and many other weeds	glyphosate	Use as a directed spray around established trees just sufficient to wet the weed foliage
alternatively: February or early March	Annuals and many perennials, including grasses	dichlobenil	Distribute granules evenly over the soil surface. Do not apply under trees within 2 years of planting
End of winter, late bud burst before white bud stage	Actively growing grasses, docks and many other weeds	glyphosate	As a carefully directed spray around established trees. Just sufficient to wet the weed foliage
alternatively: When the grass is actively growing in early spring or autumn and only when trees are dormant	Grass weeds only, will check couch, but usually some regrowth the following spring	dalapon	Use as a directed spray among trees established for at least 4 years. Spray the grass, but avoid excessive spray run-off on to soil. (May require more than one application.) Spray only between harvest and flower opening
PLUMS and CHERRIES March and repeat as frequently as necessary	Annual weeds and shallow rooted perennials	paraquat/diquat	Apply as a directed spray on to weeds, avoid wetting the bark of trees younger than 3 years old or green bark anywhere
GOOSEBERRIES and BLACK-, RED- and WHITECURRANTS Before weeds appear		simazine	*See under Apples and Pears above*
After weeds appear in late winter or in the autumn	Annual weeds and shallow rooted perennials	paraquat/diquat	Use as a directed spray on to weeds at any time of the year. Avoid wetting foliage of bushes and the buds of blackcurrants at any time, or damage results
Well before growth begins usually in February or very early March	Annuals and many perennials, including grasses	dichlobenil	Do not apply to bushes within 2 years of planting or the first year of cropping, whichever is the later. Applications should not be made to blackcurrants at any age which have been cut down to soil level until at least 1 year has elapsed after cutting back. Ensure the granules do not lodge within the buds and leaves
alternatively: Between leaf fall and end of December	Grass weeds including partial control of couch as above	dalapon	Apply as a directed spray on the grass, but avoid excessive spray run-off onto soil. Use among bushes planted out for at least 3 years

Table 5 (Continued)

Time of application	Weeds controlled	Chemical name	Notes
CANE FRUITS: RASPBERRIES, LOGANBERRIES and BLACKBERRIES			
To weed-free soil in early spring		simazine	See under Apples and Pears
After weeds appear and only when canes are fully dormant and no new suckers are present	Annual weeds and shallow-rooted perennials	paraquat/diquat	Use as a directed spray on to weeds at any time of year. Avoid wetting the foliage or canes, or damage results
November to February only	Couch and other grasses	dalapon	Protect canes from spray contact and avoid run-off into the soil
STRAWBERRIES			
Post harvest (July to November)	Nearly all weeds in germinating stage	simazine (soil acting)	Apply to clean, moist, firm soil following defoliation and general clean up of weeds, runners and older leaves after harvest. Plants must have been established for at least 12 months. Only one application should be made in a calendar year. Do not use on sandy soils or on fruiting plants

around the base of the tree year after year, the soil in this area tends to become acid rather more quickly than the grassed down part. It is important therefore to test the pH of the soil around the base of the tree and if necessary apply lime to bring the pH back to a satisfactory level (see p.8).

Pest and disease control

Proper preparation of the ground, good cultivation, careful planting and pruning are all of great importance in obtaining healthy growth and good quality fruit.

Commercial growers who have to grow fruit that is free from blemishes, use a regular programme of pesticide application to control pests and diseases. Amateurs who adopt such spray programmes can obtain dramatic improvements in their production of clean fruit but may also experience further problems, such as the development of a resistant strain of pest or disease, or the sudden increase of a previously unimportant pest when its natural predators (such as ladybirds, hoverfly larvae and lace wings) and parasites are killed. In addition, it is often difficult to apply sprays thoroughly to large trees, and inefficient applications of chemicals are wasteful and can be harmful. Chemicals should be applied only when there is a

real need, and instructions for their use must be strictly observed. In particular, a minimum interval must elapse between the last application of certain chemicals and picking and using the fruit. The length of these periods ranges from 1 day to 1 month; **always read and follow the manufacturer's instructions**.

Insecticides, fungicides and herbicides should always be handled carefully and stored safely out of reach of children and away from foods. Do not spray insecticides during blossoming when they may kill hive bees and other pollinators. The best conditions for spraying are when the weather is dry, comparatively calm, and frost-free. Spray on a dry day because the foliage or bark is then also dry and the solution sticks to them. Some arrangement should be made to screen adjacent plants, perhaps with plastic sheets, if the spray is likely to harm them. Vegetables, in particular, are vulnerable. The spray should be applied to all sides of the plant to give as good a coverage as possible, working from the top to the bottom, and from side to side.

When spraying, wear rubber gloves, goggles, adequate footwear (such as wellingtons) and, if required, other protective clothing. Ensure that the spray chemical is thoroughly mixed with the correct amount of water. First pour into the sprayer about half the required

amount of water, then the chemical and finally the remainder of the water. Wettable powders should be mixed with a little water first to make a cream and then added to the sprayer. Wash spray equipment thoroughly before and after spraying. Never use a sprayer that has been used for applying weedkiller because minute traces left in a sprayer can cause severe damage to shoots and foliage.

Thorough spraying of small bushes and trees is not at all difficult, and any one of the many hand or pressure sprayers now available should prove adequate. Some of these can be fitted with extension lances to spray larger trees, but if many such trees are to be sprayed some form of motorised sprayer is needed. As a general guide, a plastic pressurised sprayer holding 1 gallon (4.5 litres) should be adequate for a fruit garden of 30 × 30 feet (9 × 9m), 2 gallons (9 litres) for about 30 × 60 feet (9 × 18m), and a 3- to 4-gallon (14–18 litre) knapsack sprayer for 60 × 100 feet (18 × 30m) fruit plot. The sprayer should be fitted with a shoulder-strap to make it easily portable.

In addition to the use of chemicals, various non-chemical methods can reduce the incidence of pests and diseases. Good hygiene and thorough cultivation can limit the spread of some of them; barriers and traps can be used against pests such as winter moths and codling moths.

Biological control
This method of pest control is used mostly in greenhouses where specific predators and parasites can be introduced to control many of the major pests. However, one of the greenhouse biological controls can be used in gardens against glasshouse red spider mite, which damages strawberry, peach, raspberry and currants, particularly in hot summers. It is controlled by introducing a predatory mite, *Phytoseiulus persimilis*, when signs of mite damage are seen in early summer. *Phytoseiulus* can be obtained through the post from firms which breed these and other biological controls. The predator is not effective against fruit tree red spider on apple and plum and it is harmed by insecticides other than pirimicarb, which can be used if aphids are present.

Bird damage to fruit buds
Bird damage to overwintering fruit buds of apple, pear, plum, cherry and gooseberry can be devastating, and can affect cropping capacity permanently because much of the wood, devoid of buds, remains unproductive.

(Above left) *a gallon (4.5 litre) pressure sprayer which should have a shoulder strap for carrying.*

(Above right) *Two types of knapsack sprayer: (left) a 3½ gallon (16 litre) hand operated sprayer; (right) a motorised air blower type capable of carrying the spray 30 feet (9m) or more.*

(Below) *Symptoms of virus infection in strawberries, showing the harmful effect of virus in the plant on the left.*

(Above) *A motorised wheelbarrow type of sprayer for a gardener with a large area of fruit to spray.*

(Right) *Bullfinch damage to apple buds.*

The only completely effective control is to net trees and bushes between November and March (*see* pp.17–19).

Tree guards

Some kind of protection is necessary to prevent damage to the bark of fruit trees where mammals – especially rabbits and hares – are troublesome. One answer is to surround the fruit plot with a complete fence of galvanised wire netting of 1¼–1½ inch (32–38mm) mesh 18 gauge, 4½ to 5 feet (1.5m) high. Turn the bottom edge 6 inches (15cm) outwards and bury it under the soil or turf. However, if there are only a few trees to protect it is cheaper to place a guard of wire netting around each tree. The guard can be made from 3 to 3½ feet (1m) wide, 1¼-inch (32mm) mesh galvanised netting cut into strips equal in length to the required height of the guard. An alternative is a coiled ·plastic tree guard 2 to 2½ feet

(60–75cm) in length. These are quick to apply and effective against rabbits, hares and cats, but they can create damp, humid conditions around the stem of the tree, which are conducive to canker. Where plastic guards are fitted it is advisable to examine the trees fairly regularly to check that such troubles are not occurring. To protect against larger animals, such as deer, galvanised wire netting is necessary. The tree guard, to be adequate, must be of a diameter sufficient to allow the stem to grow without constriction for many years, high enough to protect against animals without itself damaging branches, and strong enough not to collapse.

Ministry of Agriculture Certification Scheme

The importance of planting healthy fruit plants cannot be too strongly emphasized. It is essential that the plants are tested. Healthy plants grow more strongly, require less feeding, crop more heavily, and give better quality fruits than infected ones.

To ensure that healthy plants are obtained, buy certified stock wherever possible. This has been grown under the Ministry of Agriculture Certification Scheme which requires the grower to grow the fruit plants concerned in isolation, to an acceptable degree of purity, health and vigour. The growing plants are inspected annually on the holding by a Ministry of Agriculture inspector, and provided that the conditions laid down have been met, the grower is given a certificate. There are two grades of certificate of interest to the gardener – S.S. (special stock) and A. The former has a higher health status than the latter. Special stock is more expensive and difficult to obtain, and for most gardens and gardeners, A certificate stock is quite acceptable.

The Ministry of Agriculture Certification Scheme does not apply to all kinds of fruit, much less every cultivar. At present it covers certain cultivars and rootstocks of apple, pear, plum and cherry, also strawberry, raspberry, blackberry, hybrid berry, blackcurrant and gooseberry.

Whether the plants are certified stock or not, however, it is in any case wise to obtain them from a reputable source.

Tree Fruits

This section of the book describes the cultivation of tree (or top) fruits. The first part covers the basic principles relevant to all these fruits, and then each fruit is discussed in detail. The order is not alphabetical but is arranged so that the most widely-grown fruits are described first, followed by the less usual kinds which are worth including in the garden for more variety.

The majority of gardens today are too small to have room for large spreading fruit trees. Most gardeners therefore want to plant trees that can be restricted in size. By planting several small trees it is possible to grow a range of fruits in a limited space. When the amount of ground available is limited, cultivars of high quality – in particular those for eating which might be difficult to obtain in the shops – are a better choice than the cooking fruits (which are often easier and cheaper to buy). With careful selection from the recommended lists (see individual fruits) it is possible to have a range of fruits over a long season. Apples and pears, for example, can be eaten in good condition from August until the following April or May.

Site and aspect

Top fruits are grown successfully in many parts of Britain, at altitudes from sea level to 400 feet (120m) or sometimes higher. South-facing slopes warm up early, giving earlier flowering. They are usually drier and get more sunlight than north-facing slopes, so the fruit is generally of good quality. Early blossom, though, runs a greater risk of damage from spring frosts. Planting on a site where cold air on a frosty night in spring can drain away to lower ground is better than planting in a hollow.

Take advantage of fences and walls with a sunny aspect by planting the restricted forms of tree against them. Their shelter and reflected warmth enables the gardener to plant those fruits that need rather higher temperatures, such as figs, apricots and peaches.

With increasing altitude, strong winds are likely to become more of a problem. A windbreak may be necessary but the siting must be carefully planned (see Windbreaks, pp.9–12). Too tall a windbreak may take away light from the trees or impede the drainage of cold air to lower levels.

Pollination

Before a tree can bear fruit, it is necessary for its blossom to be pollinated. Some cultivars of certain kinds of fruit are self-fertile and set fruits with their own pollen (like the 'Victoria' plum), but many do not, and need to be fertilized by pollen of a different cultivar, though of the same kind of fruit. Most apples, pears, cherries and many plums and gages require cross-pollination; even those which are self-fertile set a heavier crop if cross-pollinated. Often neighbours' fruit trees provide the necessary pollinators – but it is unwise to depend on this. In planning the fruit garden, therefore, cultivars should be selected that flower at the same time. Pollination tables are given on p.216 onwards.

A 'family' tree is sometimes offered by nurseries. This is a tree with a number of cultivars grafted on it. In theory this sounds ideal for the small garden where there is no room to plant another as a pollinator. In practice, however, the cultivars grafted on it are often of unequal vigour, and in later years a lot of skill may be required to maintain a well-balanced tree.

Rootstocks

Apples, pears, plums and many other cultivated tree fruits do not come true from seed. The usual means of propagating cultivars of these fruits is through uniting them by budding and grafting on to a rootstock, which is in most cases a selected type of the fruit concerned. Budding and grafting are briefly described and illustrated on pp.37–39.

There is a wide range of rootstocks used by fruit tree nurserymen which are classified according to their vigour (more details are given in the appropriate fruit chapters). The rootstock exerts a considerable influence on the ultimate size of the tree; a cultivar grafted on to a vigorous stock grows into a large tree, but the same cultivar grafted on to a dwarfing

A bush tree with a 2 to 3 foot (60–90cm) trunk. This is 'Lane's Prince Albert' apple.

Family tree with two cultivars grafted on one tree. One scion (left) is much more vigorous than the other (right) which is making an unbalanced tree.

stock remains relatively small. When ordering fruit trees some idea should be given of the amount of space available and the eventual size of the tree required; better still, the rootstocks should be stipulated. Not all fruits have a range of rootstock types from dwarfing to vigorous, but by careful selection a considerable degree of control of tree size can be obtained.

Form of tree

There are two basic types: unrestricted forms which are grown in the open and pruned in winter, and restricted forms, most of which are grown against walls and fences or on wires and pruned in summer.

Unrestricted forms

Bush. This form is a tree with a stem of 2 to 3 feet (60–90cm) and the main branches arising fairly close together to form the head. Most top fruits can be successfully grown as bush trees, and are probably the most easily managed. The

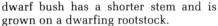

dwarf bush has a shorter stem and is grown on a dwarfing rootstock.

Standard and half standard. This a a tree with a stem 6 or 4 feet (1.8m, 1.2m) in height respectively, at which point branches arise to form a large head. These trees are grown on vigorous rootstocks and are suitable only for orchards where there is plenty of room; they are too large for a small garden.

Spindlebush. This is a cone-shaped tree with a single vertical stem. The side branches are tied down which induces the tree to form fruit buds and so the trees start to fruit earlier. It is used for apples and, less commonly, pears.

Restricted tree forms

Cordon. This is a single straight stem which has short fruit spurs along its length. Is is usually grown at an oblique angle. Side growths are restricted by summer pruning. Multiple stemmed cordons can also be developed. Cordon apples and pears are excellent for the small garden because several trees can be grown in a relatively small area.

Fan. A fan tree is trained flat against a wall or fence with branches radiating from a short trunk like the ribs of a fan. Fruits often grown in this form are plums, peaches, cherries, apricots and figs, but apples and pears also do well.

Espalier. Espaliers are made up by a central vertical main stem with pairs (tiers) of horizontal branches arising more or less opposite each other, growing out at right angles on each side. Usually it consists of 2 or 3 tiers, but there can be more. The espalier is suitable for apples and pears.

Pyramid and dwarf pyramid. This has a main stem from which, at a little higher than 1 foot (30cm) from ground level, branches begin to radiate at intervals in

(Above left) *A well-laden spindlebush; apple 'Golden Delicious'.*

(Above right) *An arch of cordons in the Bradbourne Gardens at East Malling.*

(Below) *Cordons, trained obliquely to make maximum use of the fence.*

(Above left) *An espalier pear with 4 tiers. In the border below are alpine strawberries.*

(Above right) *A dwarf pyramid apple.*

(Below) *A fan-trained plum 'Victoria', some 4 years after planting (compare with the same fan, p.93).*

gradually diminishing length. Apple and pears, and, with careful management, plums, can all make successful pyramids.

Buying the trees

The lifting season in fruit tree nurseries begins in November. To ensure a wide choice and avoid disappointment it is wise to order early. For cultivars that are rarely available, it may be necessary to order a year in advance.

A Ministry of Agriculture Certification Scheme (*see* p.29) exists for certain tree fruits and covers many of the more widely grown cultivars of apple, pear, plum and cherry. The scheme applies to the rootstocks, the source of scion material and the end product, the fruit tree. They are sometimes described as EMLA trees. Certified trees can be relied on to be free from stated viruses, substantially free from other diseases and pests and true to name. Healthy trees crop more heavily than diseased ones, so buy a certified tree whenever possible. However, not every cultivar comes within this scheme and in all cases it is wise to obtain the trees from a reputable source.

Many experienced growers like to buy their trees as 1-year-olds (maidens) and then train them in the form they want. These are cheaper, but take longer to start fruiting than older, partly trained trees. The beginner may prefer to buy the 2- or 3-year-old tree which has already been shaped in the nursery. But whatever the age of the tree bought, it is essential that the rootstock is known. When buying a maiden, choose one with side shoots (called feathers) already present on the main stem. These may be the foundation of the primary branches. Not all cultivars, however, readily produce side shoots in their first year. Some nurseries sell container-grown fruit trees in black polythene pots, which have the advantage that they can be planted at any time. But be careful to avoid trees that are not properly established in their

containers, or are so potbound that the trees are starved and the root systems congested, making the trees unlikely to become established after transplanting.

Preparing the soil for planting

Start in the late summer or early autumn, well before planting. Clear the site of perennial weeds (using a weedkiller such as glyphosate), and single or double dig, whichever may be necessary. Virgin land or grassland should be double dug, as should ground where there is a hard pan beneath the surface which should be broken up. Light and impoverished soil needs bulky organic material – well rotted manure, compost or peat – spread over the whole area about 1 or 2 inches (2.5cm) deep and then dug in.

Where closely spaced fruits are to be planted, dwarf trees perhaps, it is essential that the whole area is dug over. But if the trees are to be widely spaced – in a lawn or orchard, for example – it is not necessary to dig over all the land; it is enough to remove the turf over a radius of not less than 18 inches (45cm). With cooking fruits for which size is important (such as apples), remove the grass over a 2 foot (60cm) radius. That area should be kept clean after planting for at least four years. Bury the turf at least a foot deep (30cm) but chop it up first.

Just before planting, fork in a balanced compound fertilizer, such as Growmore, at 3 oz per sq. yd (100g/m²), plus bonemeal at 4 oz per sq. yd (130g/m²) over each planting site, or over a 2-foot (60cm) wide band down the row for a closely planted system such as cordons.

When forking in the fertilizer, ensure that any bulky organic matter still in the ground is well broken up; the roots of fruit trees should not come into contact with large lumps or organic material because there is a danger of root damage as the manure rots down.

Planting

Planting is best done between November and March, provided that weather and soil conditions are good. The earlier it can be done in the winter the better, while the soil is still relatively dry and warm, which may encourage some root growth. Do not plant when the soil is frozen or very wet because handling the soil in such conditions compacts it into lumps and air is expelled, creating bad conditions for root growth.

If planting cannot be carried out when the trees are delivered remove all the packing and heel in the trees outside. Dig a temporary hole or trench, place the roots in it, cover them with soil, and firm them in. The aerial parts of the tree are

(Left) *A tree as it will arrive from the nursery, showing thorough packing for transport.*

(Right) *Heeling-in trees that are waiting for good weather to be planted.*

Planting a maiden tree (one-year-old) to a stake. The roots are well spread out, and the tree planted to the same depth as it was in the nursery, with the union at least 4 inches (10cm) above soil level.

frost-hardy, but the roots are not. It is important, then, while the trees are out of the ground, that the roots are neither exposed to frost nor allowed to dry out. Usually the roots are packed with damp straw and then covered with hessian. This kind of packing provides adequate protection.

If the roots are dry, as may happen when the trees have been delayed on the way, soak the roots in a bucket of water for about an hour before planting, to get them thoroughly damp before planting.

If the ground is frozen keep the trees somewhere cool but frostproof, until the soil has thawed. The place of storage must not be heated, for that would induce premature growth. To ensure that the aerial parts of the plant are not forced into growth, remove the packing, but not from around the roots.

To plant balled trees with the roots wrapped, the hessian should be gently opened up so that it lies flat underneath the root system. It should be left in this way and will eventually rot away. Trees grown or packed in polythene or other types of plastic containers must have the material removed completely. If the plant is root-bound, gently comb the perimeter roots so that they spread outwards.

Container-grown trees bought during the growing season should be watered and kept in a cool, shady place if they cannot be planted immediately. Before planting, the trees should again be thoroughly watered.

All trees must be staked at planting to keep them steady until the roots anchor them. Trees on vigorous stocks are usually well anchored by the fourth or fifth year after planting, but those in dwarfing rootstocks need permanent stakes.

A single stake is usually adequate for bushes, pyramids and spindlebushes, but two vertical stakes with a crossbar give firm support to standard or half-standard trees.

Drive the stake in first to a depth of 18 inches (45cm), or 24 inches (60cm) in a light soil, and then plant the tree about 2 or 3 inches (5–8cm) from it.

Dig a hole wide and deep enough to ensure the roots are well spread out and properly covered. The union between rootstock and scion must not be buried. The position of the union on the stem may vary from 4 inches (10cm) up to 12 inches (30cm) above soil level. It is usually possible to see a mark on the stem showing where the soil came up to in the nursery, and it is correct to plant to the same depth. It is very important that the union is well above soil level so that there is no danger of the scion rooting into the soil, which would of course neutralize the influence of the rootstock.

When planting a tree against a house wall, dig a semicircular hole and spread the roots outwards, and then set the tree about 6 inches (15cm) away from the wall. This keeps the root system away from directly under the eaves so that it receives more natural rainfall and allows for the eventual expansion of the tree trunk. Incline the top of the tree slightly towards the wall. Spread the roots out so that they radiate outwards.

Replace the soil a spadeful at a time, slightly lifting and lowering the tree, so that the soil falls down well around the roots, and tread gently but firmly as the hole is filled in, so that the soil particles make good contact with the roots. A barrowload of a 50:50 mixture of sharp sand and peat is useful for mixing with the soil when planting on heavy land, to improve its structure.

Fruit trees do not thrive on poorly drained soils. Ideally, on such sites, the drainage should be improved before planting. But on very heavy land, and sites where the ground may lie wet in winter and drainage cannot be improved, the trees can be planted on a mound. Make a shallow hole for the tree and pile up the soil around the roots, sloping it away from the main stem.

Tie the tree to a stake. Use a proprietary tree tie which provides a cushion between the tree and the stake. Alternatively, use soft rope, but first wrap a piece of cloth around the trunk to prevent bark damage. Check the ties twice a year, in midsummer and in the autumn, to make sure that they are firm but not so tight as to constrict stem growth.

After planting, mulch the tree with a 2- to 3-inch (5–8cm) layer of well rotted manure, compost, old straw or peat over a radius of 18 inches (45cm). Keep the material just clear of the tree's stem to discourage fungus infection (like collar rot). The mulch helps to conserve soil moisture and to supply some nutrients throughout the growing season.

Assuming that the soil is reasonably fertile, another useful method of conserving soil moisture and suppressing weeds is to cover the soil around the base of the tree with a black polythene sheet about 2½ feet square (75 × 75cm). Bury the edges of the polythene to prevent it from blowing away, and take the sheet right up to the trunk. The sheet should last for a growing season. It is best removed in winter to allow rain to penetrate the soil, but renew it in spring after applying fertilizer.

Deblossoming newly planted trees

Remove the blossom from all trees in the first spring after planting, whatever their age. By doing this the tree's energies are channelled into good establishment and strong growth.

Pruning: general principles

Pruning is a very important operation in fruit growing and must be carried out as well as possible to obtain the best yields.

The reasons for pruning are:

○ to form a strong framework in the shape required;
○ to thin out overcrowded growth (crossing branches, etc);
○ to induce flower and fruit bud formation;
○ to stimulate shoot growth;
○ to restrict tree size;
○ to remove dead, diseased and broken branches.

Unpruned trees, although they may come early into cropping and for a year or two produce good quality fruit, gradually become less vigorous, and the fruits produced become smaller and of poor quality. Such trees also tend to bear crops every other year (biennial bearing).

The methods of pruning vary with crop and tree form; details are given on following pages. The background is given here.

Pruning can be done at two periods of the year, inducing a different response according to season.

Bush and standard trees are normally pruned in the winter, at any time between leaf fall and bud burst, although it is best not to do it in very low temperatures because of the increased danger of infection by disease at such a time.

In the first years after planting, the formative pruning is aimed at producing a strong framework of branches able to bear good crops in later years. Once the form is established and the tree is fruiting, pruning must aim to encourage the production of fruit buds while ensuring a succession of new growth to increase tree size if required, and to replace old, less productive wood.

Winter pruning stimulates vegetative growth – the greater the length of shoot removed, the more vigorous are the shoots produced by the remaining buds. A tree pruned hard tends to be vegetative rather than fruitful. A balance between growth and fruit bud production must be maintained.

In contrast, summer pruning restricts growth. The removal of leaves at the end of the main period of summer growth reduces the supply of carbohydrates (manufactured by the leaves) to the roots.

Summer pruning is used for cordons, fans, espaliers and for dwarf pyramids after the framework of the tree has been formed, to maintain them in a compact form. It can also be carried out on winter-pruned trees which are growing too vigorously, to restore the balance between shoot growth and fruit bud formation.

An additional benefit of summer pruning is that more light and air are allowed into the centre of the tree, resulting in well-ripened wood and buds, and well-coloured fruits.

Tying down branches

Horizontal growth is more fruitful: the more upright the growth is, the more vigorous and unfruitful. Tying down is a useful technique in slowing down growth, inducing fruit bud formation. It is also useful for setting upright branches at an acceptable angle, and so achieving the desired shape and filling in the allotted gap. It is widely practised on spindlebush trees (see p.32), but can be usefully adopted on any tree that tends to produce strong, vigorous, unproductive shoots. Remember also that there are other ways of slowing down vigour, such as summer pruning (p.36), bark ringing (p.137) and root pruning (p.138).

Fruit thinning

Thinning of the crop becomes necessary when there has been a heavy fruit set. Without such thinning the fruit harvested is small and of poor quality. By reducing the number of fruitlets the remaining fruits are larger and of better quality, and may still be quite plentiful.

A tree or bush that has borne a very heavy crop in one year is likely to have an "off" year the next, because the balance between shoot growth and fruiting has been upset. By reducing the crop in a fruitful year, a reasonable crop is still likely to be produced in the following year.

The definition of a heavy crop is related to the age and vigour of the cultivar and the particular plant. A vigorous healthy tree is capable of carrying a heavier crop than a weaker tree, and fruits can therefore be left closer.

Details of when and how to thin are given under each fruit.

Propagation

Most fruit trees are propagated by budding or by grafting (whip and tongue method) the selected cultivar on to the chosen rootstock.

Budding is usually carried out in July and August, and grafting in March and April. The techniques used are shown in the pictures overleaf.

Two methods of budding are shown, T-budding and chip budding. The latter has been demonstrated to give a higher proportion of successful unions.

GLOSSARY

Basal cluster The closely spaced leaves at the base of an apple or pear shoot made in the current growing season.

Diploid and triploid see p.216.

Field capacity The maximum content of water held by a soil, after excess water has drained away.

Fruit (or blossom) bud A bud which produces flowers and then fruits. It is much fatter than the slim, pointed bud which produces shoots.

Incompatible A term used to describe a rootstock and scion that will not unite. It occurs most commonly with pears. See also Pollination, p.216.

Lateral A side shoot arising from a branch or leader.

Leader The leading shoot of a branch, selected to extend the framework.

Maiden A 1-year-old tree. Those with a single straight stem are called whips; those that have side shoots are called feathered maidens.

Nicking and Notching see p.52.

Ringing see p.138.

Rootstock The plant on which fruits are grafted or budded.

Scion The shoot or bud of the fruit tree which is grafted or budded on to the rootstock.

Self-fertile or self-compatible A cultivar that can set fruit after fertilization with pollen from the same flower or from other flowers on that plant or on another plant of the same cultivar.

Self-sterile or self-incompatible Such a cultivar is one which needs the pollen from another cultivar of the same kind of fruit to set fruit. See Pollination, p.216.

Soil moisture deficit The amount, usually given as inches (or mm) of rainfall, by which the soil moisture content is below field capacity.

Spur A short branch system bearing fruit buds. A spur system is a short compound fruiting branch made up of several spurs (see photo, p.56).

Spur pruning A pruning technique with the object of achieving spur systems along the branches (see p.44).

(Left) Bud 'sticks' supply the scions for budding. They are cut from the current season's shoots in July and August. The leaf blades are cut off to leave about ½ inch (1cm) of stalk, and the individual buds are then thinly sliced off the shoot with a knife for insertion under the bark of the stock.

(Right) T-budding. The bud is ready for insertion in the T-shaped cut on the rootstock; it is slipped under the bark and any part above the cross cut is trimmed off before tying. In spring the stock is headed back immediately above the bud, stimulating it to grow, and by the autumn should have made a maiden tree.

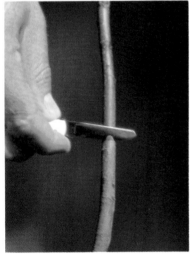

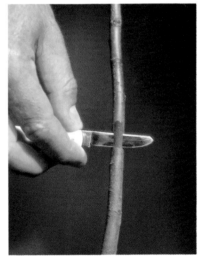

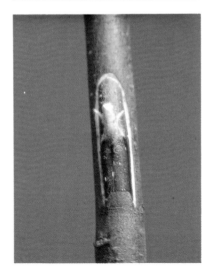

(Right) *Cleft grafting.*
A. The sawn end of the branch is pared and then cleft across with the chopping blade of the special tool (or a strong chisel). The cut end is held open (a screwdriver will do) ready to receive the scion.
B. Two scions, each 3 or 4 buds long, are prepared by 2 slanting cuts on each to form a long tapering wedge.
C. The scions are carefully inserted in the cleft so that the cambium of the scion and branch are in contact, and the tool removed leaving the scions gripped tightly in the cleft. The cut surfaces are then covered with grafting wax.

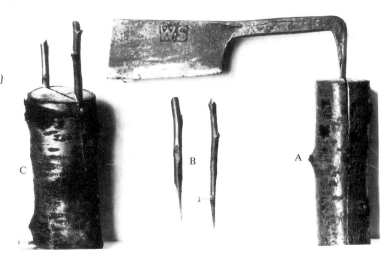

(Opposite) *Chip budding. The first cut is made at 20° to a depth of ⅛ inch (3mm). The second cut is made 1½ inches (3.5cm) above the first, cutting down to meet it, and removing the tissue. The finished cut: note the lip at the base. Exactly the same cuts are made on the bud stick and the bud removed. Stock and scion are matched together. The bud is tied in starting at the lower end using a 6- to 9-inch (15–23cm) length of 1 inch (2.5cm) wide polythene strip.*

(Right) *Whip and tongue grafting. The scion is prepared by making a flat sloping cut about 2 inches (5cm) long, and a downward pointing tongue made by an upward cut; the same cut is made in the rootstock but the tongue points upward. Both are brought together with the tongues interlocking, but the inner edge of the rind must coincide on at least one side. The union is then bound with polythene tape, and all exposed cut surfaces covered with grafting wax. A bud will start to grow out into a shoot, making a maiden tree by the end of the season.*

(Left) *A method of changing over an unsuitable cultivar to a more desirable sort. In this method the branches are sawn off and the cut ends grafted with two or three scions of the new variety.*

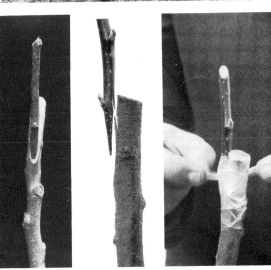

Apples

Apples are the most widely grown of all the tree fruits in this country, and the reasons for that are not hard to find. One cultivar or another will succeed in nearly all parts of Britain, and on most soils. Moreover, there is an apple – dessert or culinary – for every taste and no other fruit can provide such a range of cultivars for eating over nine months of the year.

With regular care and attention, apple trees remain healthy and fruitful for 50 years or more. For such a long-term crop it is important to start on the right lines.

Before buying trees, there are certain important points to consider:

○ the rootstock upon which the tree is grafted;
○ the tree form in which it is to be grown;
○ the pollination requirements of the chosen cultivars (see pp.216–17).

Rootstocks

The rootstock, more than any other factor, determines the eventual size of the tree. Rootstocks are classified according to their effect on the growth of the tree. By growing the cultivar on a certain rootstock, it is possible to forecast, within reasonable limits, the size the tree is likely to reach and how soon it will start to bear fruit. Many modern gardens are small, and in most situations a small- to medium-sized tree is required. For these, there is a range of dwarfing and semi-dwarfing rootstocks, upon which cultivars can be grafted to create a tree of the required size. Smaller trees have a number of advantages over larger trees. They take up less space and can be picked, pruned and sprayed from the ground, or at least from a short ladder or household steps. They also start to bear fruit sooner than larger trees on vigorous stocks, and usually produce better coloured fruits because there is less mutual shading and the framework is more open, thus letting sunlight into the tree. In general, the more dwarfing the rootstock, the younger the tree starts to bear fruit.

Before finally selecting the rootstock, however, the soil type should be considered: in a poor soil – sand or shallow soil over chalk, for example – the dwarfing effect may be too pronounced. So in a poor soil choose a more vigorous stock. The choice of stock is also dictated by the tree form selected. Apple rootstocks in order of vigour are as follows.

M.27 Extremely dwarfing. A stock which requires a very good soil and does not produce a satisfactory tree if there is competition from grass and weeds. Trees on this stock are usually very precocious, bearing within 2 or 3 years. It is excellent for the very vigorous cultivars, especially the triploids, because it substantially reduces their vigour; it is not suitable for weak cultivars. It needs support throughout its life.

M.9 Very dwarfing. A widely used stock for dwarf bushes, spindlebushes, dwarf pyramids and cordons. Trees on this stock are soon into bearing, usually within 3 years. It requires a good soil and does not tolerate neglect or competition from grass or weeds. The root system is brittle and the trees require permanent support.

M.26 Dwarfing. A good rootstock for average soil conditions. Trees on this stock are soon into bearing usually within 3 or 4 years. The stock is suitable for bush trees, dwarf pyramids and cordons.

MM.106 Semi-dwarfing. A stock widely used in nurseries, suitable for most soils

The effect of rootstock on tree size. Twelve-year-old trees of 'Cox's Orange Pippin' on 5 different rootstocks.

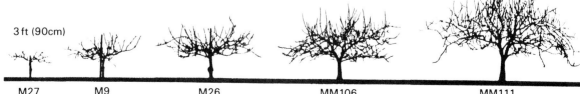

3 ft (90cm)

M27   M9   M26   MM106   MM111

An open-centred bush tree, just after planting with a "cushion" tie, stake and mulch. The plastic tree guard is for protection against rabbits.

cultivar. The sizes given in the following pages are merely guidelines to help the gardener in the overall planting plan.

Bush tree

A dwarf bush on M.27 makes a tree about 4 to 6 feet (1.2–1.8m) in height and spread which needs a 6-foot (1.8m) permanent stake. Plant at 4 to 6 feet (1.2–1.8m) apart. Such trees are not suitable for light or shallow soils and need a lot of attention, particularly in feeding and watering to keep them growing. The crop from a mature tree averages 10 to 15 pounds (4.5–7kg) per year.

A tree on M.9 makes a dwarf bush about 6 to 10 feet (1.8–3m) in height and spread. Generally this is the best choice for a small garden, but it is not suitable for light or shallow soils because the dwarfing effect is liable to be too pronounced unless the tree is fed generously and watered in dry conditions. It requires permanent staking. Plant at 8 to 10 feet (2.4–3m) apart.

Trees on M.26 grow to about 8 to 12 feet (2.4–3.6m) in height and spread. They require staking for the first four or five years. Plant at 10 to 15 feet (3–4.5m) apart.

Trees on MM.106 and M.7 (semi-dwarfing) grow to about 12 to 18 feet (3.6–5.5m) in height and spread. Plant at 12 to 18 feet (3.6–5.5m) apart. Staking is necessary for the first four or five years.

On relatively poor soils, M.26 or MM.106 can be used for obtaining small trees instead of M.9.

Pruning

Formative pruning of young bush. The object is to achieve an open-centred goblet-shaped tree with a clean stem, ranging from 18 to 24 inches (45–60cm) for a dwarf bush to about 30 inches (75cm) for a bush.

Maiden tree
There are two types of maiden tree. One is the maiden whip without laterals (side shoots) and the other is the feathered maiden with laterals. Where there is a choice, buy a well feathered maiden because well placed laterals are potential first branches.

Maiden tree without laterals. Cut back the stem to a bud at about 24 inches (60cm) for a dwarf bush or 30 inches (75cm) for a

including the lighter ones. Used for bush trees, spindlebushes, cordons, espaliers and fans. Trees on this stock bear within 3 or 4 years.

MM.111 and M.2 Vigorous. Trees on these rootstocks make large trees on good soils, but medium-sized trees on poor soils.

Tree form, spacing and yield

There are two categories of tree form to be considered: those grown in the open, such as the bush, spindlebush and dwarf pyramid, and those against walls or on fences, such as the cordon, espalier, and fan. Where there is plenty of space and a fairly large yield of apples is required, an orchard of bush trees or spindlebushes is probably to be preferred. Where space is limited, however, the restricted forms, such as the cordon, espalier and dwarf pyramid, or alternatively the dwarf bush, are more suitable.

The eventual size of any tree depends upon many factors, including soil and

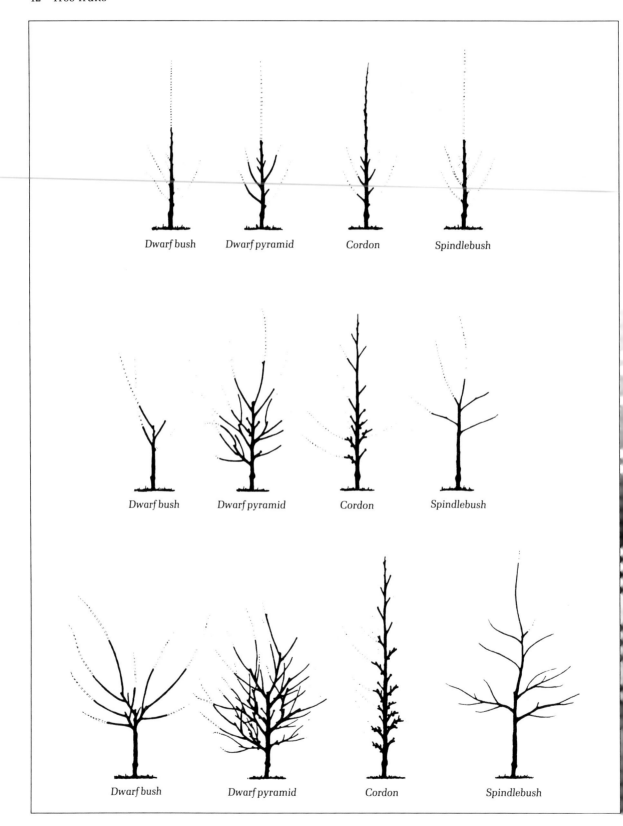

Dwarf bush   Dwarf pyramid   Cordon   Spindlebush

Dwarf bush   Dwarf pyramid   Cordon   Spindlebush

Dwarf bush   Dwarf pyramid   Cordon   Spindlebush

'Sunset' on M.26, at 12 years old.

bush, ensuring that there are at least 3 good buds beneath it. Make a sloping cut away from the bud. This pruning should stimulate the top 3 to 5 buds to produce shoots in the following spring and summer, which will be the first branches. Protect the cut with a wound paint.

Maiden tree with laterals. Cut back the central stem at about 24 to 30 inches (60–75cm) to a strong young lateral ensuring there are at least 2, preferably 3, more well-placed laterals immediately beneath it, which will be the first branches. Remove all others flush with the main stem. Cut each of the selected branches by two-thirds to an upward facing bud. Paint the wounds.

Second winter (or 2-year-old tree)
Select between 3 and 5 well-placed branches and prune the leader of each by half to two-thirds of its length, cutting to a bud facing in the required direction of growth. Usually this means cutting to an outward-facing bud, in that the aim is to encourage the branches to grow upwards and outwards. Remove any growth on the main stem lower than the selected branches, flush with the stem. Paint the wounds.

(Opposite) Methods of pruning for a dwarf bush, a dwarf pyramid, a cordon and a spindlebush, starting at the top with a 1-year-old tree, through to a 3-year-old tree at the bottom.

(Right) The tree planted, tied to the stake and mulched with black pastic. An organic mulch is preferable on a poor soil.

Pruning a feathered maiden. The central stem is cut to about 30 inches (75cm), ensuring 3 or 4 well placed laterals are beneath it. The laterals are then pruned by a third to a half to an outward facing bud.

Third winter (or 3-year-old tree)
The primary branches will by now have extended and produced laterals, some of which can be selected as secondary branches to fill any gaps. Select about 4 well-placed laterals. Prune the leaders of the primary branches and the selected laterals by about half to buds facing in the required direction of growth. Prune the remaining laterals not required as secondary branches to 4 or 5 buds.

Fourth year
Although by now the tree should be beginning to bear fruit, some formative pruning is still necessary, but it should be lighter than in previous years. Prune the leaders of the branches by about one-third. Some of the laterals on the perimeter where there is room can be left unpruned to develop fruit buds along their length. Prune other laterals to 3 or 4 buds. Cut out any shoots crowding the crotch of the tree where they receive little light in the summer and so produce poor-quality fruit.

Winter pruning of established bushes.
The objects of pruning are:

1. To maintain the tree in the form required;
2. To maintain satisfactory vigour;
3. To encourage fruit bud formation;
4. To improve and maintain quality and quantity of the fruit;

5. To prevent overcrowding of branches and thereby allow light and air to penetrate to all parts of the framework, also assisting in the control of insect pests and fungus diseases, as well as improving fruit quality and colour;
6. To remove diseased, dead and broken wood.

Before starting to prune it is important to know the bearing habit of the cultivar. Most cultivars are spur bearing, that is they produce their fruit buds on 2-year-old wood and on spurs on the older wood. These are called spur bearers. A few cultivars, however, produce most of their fruit buds at the tips of the shoots made in the previous summer, and relatively few as spurs on the older wood. These are called tip bearers. There are also the partial tip bearers which have the characteristic of producing fruit buds on the tips of 1-year-old shoots, but *also* on the older wood in the same way as a typical spur bearer. Examples are:

Spur bearers. Allington Pippin, Annie Elizabeth, Arthur Turner, Ashmead's Kernel, Beauty of Bath, Blenheim Orange, Charles Ross, Cox's Orange Pippin, Early Victoria, Edward VII, Ellison's Orange, George Cave, Golden Noble, Howgate Wonder, James Grieve, Lane's Prince Albert, Laxton's Superb, Lord Derby, Mother, Newton Wonder, Orleans Reinette, Rev. W. Wilks, Ribston Pippin, Rival, Royal Jubilee, Sturmer

An open-centre apple with a slightly crowded framework before winter pruning (left) and after pruning (right).

Pippin, Sunset, Wealthy and Wellington.

Tip bearers. Irish Peach, Kerry Pippin.

Partial tip bearers. Discovery, Bramley's Seedling, Worcester Pearmain. (*See also* notes in the table of cultivars, pp.62–67.)

Pruning spur bearers
Once the head has been formed and the tree has begun to fruit, the amount and degree of pruning should be related to the vigour of the tree. Winter pruning stimulates growth, and the harder the tree is pruned, the more growth is produced, possibly at the expense of fruit bud production. So a young tree with a strong framework, growing and cropping well, is pruned lightly. A tree with weak, drooping branches is pruned hard, at least for a number of years, until the necessary strong growth has been achieved.

(Right) Winter pruning a 2-year-old open-centre bush tree. Select 3 or 4 well placed laterals as primary branches and cut these by about half to a third to outward facing buds; prune unwanted laterals to 3 buds to form spurs or if too low down remove them completely.

As a general rule, leaders should be shortened by one-quarter to one-third of the previous summer's growth, cutting to a bud facing in the required direction of growth. This usually means cutting to an outward-facing bud to encourage the branch to extend outwards and upwards, thus maintaining an open-centred tree. Where the branch is inclined too much towards the horizontal, cut to an upward-facing bud or to an upright lateral which will then become the new leader. Prune this lateral to an outward-facing bud.

Leader-tipping should result in the growth of the topmost bud to extend the length of the branch; it should also result in the production of two or three laterals just below the leader. These will eventually become spurs or be utilized as secondary branches. The important exceptions to leader-pruning are the leaders on a very vigorous tree which are best left unpruned or lightly tipped, so as not to induce further vigorous unwanted growth.

Pruning a spur bearer ('Cox's Orange Pippin'). (Left) Note the development of fruit buds on the 2-year-old and older wood, and the effect of the previous year's pruning. (Right) The same branch: cutting the laterals back to about 5 buds, thereby extending the induced spur system provided that there is room to extend.

Next, deal with the laterals made in the previous summer, which should be spur pruned; they are cut back to a certain number of buds according to the fruit-bearing habit of the tree. Laterals on cultivars which bear fruit on short spurs (Type A) are cut back to 3 or 4 buds each winter. Laterals on cultivars which bear fruit on spurs of medium length (Type B) are cut back to 5 or 6 buds each winter.

Type A. Arthur Turner, Ashmead's Kernel, Charles Ross, Cox's Orange Pippin, Duke of Devonshire, Ellison's Orange, Epicure, Edward VII, Fortune, Howgate Wonder, Golden Noble, James Grieve, King of the Pippins, Lord Derby, Orleans Reinette, Queen, Rev. W. Wilks, Ribston Pippin, Rival, St Edmund's Pippin, Stark's Earliest, Sturmer Pippin, Sunset and Warner's King.

Type B. Allington Pippin, Annie Elizabeth, Beauty of Bath, Blenheim Orange, Claygate Pearmain, Early Victoria, Egremont Russet, Gascoyne's Scarlet, George Cave, Holstein, Lane's Prince Albert, Laxton's Superb, Mother, Newton Wonder, Royal Jubilee, Wellington and Winston.

Spur pruning – pruning to induce spurs – is done every winter, extending the length of the spur system over the years. When the spur system is long enough and there is no room to extend it, the pruner must cut back to a fruit bud on the 2-year-old wood.

Pruning tip bearers – Type C

If all the laterals are severely shortened, tip bearing cultivars produce little fruit, at least in the early part of their life. Prune only the strong laterals, those longer than 9 inches (22cm), by cutting them back to 5 or 6 buds. Prune also the leaders of each branch, removing one-quarter to one-third of the previous summer's growth. Tipping the strong laterals and leaders induces more tip bearing shoots in the next summer. Later on, some regulatory pruning may be necessary to avoid overcrowding.

Pruning partial tip bearers – Type C

Prune in the same way as spur bearing cultivars. Cut back strong laterals longer than 9 inches (22cm) to 5 or 6 buds. Laterals shorter than this probably have a fruit bud at their tips and are best left unpruned.

Pruning to establish the right system

If a cultivar not mentioned above has failed to fruit satisfactorily and it is suspected that wrong pruning has been the cause, carry out the following experiment. Divide the number of branches of the tree into three sections. Prune one section on the short spur system, another on the medium spur system, and on the third thin out overcrowded laterals, tipping the extra long ones which have been retained. Observe in due course which system of pruning has produced the most fruit buds and continue to prune accordingly.

Before (left) and after (centre) pruning a tip bearer. Strong laterals longer than 9 inches (22cm) have been cut back to 5 or 6 buds, and the leader pruned by removing a quarter to a third.

(Right) A tip bearer ('Irish Peach') at bud burst. Note the absence of spurs on the older wood, and emergence of fruit buds at the tips of the previous summer's growth.

Subsequent pruning

As the tree becomes older and larger, some regulatory pruning is necessary. Crowded and crossing branches should be removed or shortened. Branches rubbing against one another must also be cut out or shortened. Dead and diseased growth must be cut out by pruning back to healthy wood. Do not leave a stub, but cut back to the point of origin or to a branch which will take up the vigour. Pare the edges of the wound with a sharp knife and paint the cut surface. Spur systems which have become over-long and complicated, and which carry many weak fruit buds, should be simplified. Cut out a proportion of the fruit buds, removing the weaker and leaving the stronger ones where possible. This thinning should result in larger and better quality fruits (*see* photo, p.56).

Keep the centre open, but remember with cultivars which have a spreading habit – 'Beauty of Bath', for example – that it will be necessary to leave in a certain number of upright laterals near the centre for eventual replacement of branches which have become too spreading or too low. Replacement branches may also be necessary nearer the outside of the tree. With very upright cultivars – like 'Egremont Russet' – the need to provide for replacements is not as great.

Summer pruning. Summer pruning checks growth and is necessary for training and maintaining trees grown in restricted form such as the cordon, dwarf pyramid and espalier (*see* pp.49–56). But it is also useful when trees of unrestricted form have become too vigorous – when grafted on to a vigorous stock, for example. It is not recommended for such trees growing and cropping satisfactorily, and should not be carried out on a tree that is growing poorly.

The benefit obtained from summer pruning is partly due to the removal of foliage during the summer which checks root action and consequently shoot growth. It also encourages the development of fruit buds near the base of the pruned shoots. By the removal of superfluous growth, light and air are admitted to a tree, resulting in well-ripened wood and buds, and well-coloured fruits.

This type of summer pruning consists of cutting back those laterals of the current season's growth which are longer than 12 inches (30cm) and have become woody at the base to about 5 leaves from their point of origin. Do not prune all at once; start with some of the longer laterals early in August and complete the operation by the end of September. Do not summer prune the branch leaders unless to restrict their length.

Half standard and standard

Both these forms are usually grafted on to vigorous rootstocks (such as MM.111 and M.2) and eventually make large to very large trees. They are not, therefore, suitable for the average-sized garden except perhaps as shade or specimen trees in a large lawn. In time both produce more fruit than do bush trees, but they take longer to start fruiting and, being larger, require more effort in pruning, spraying and picking.

Pruning is basically the same as for the bush tree, except that the main stem is grown on to 4 to 4½ feet (1.2–1.4m) for a half standard, and 6 to 6½ feet (1.8–2m) for a standard, before cutting. This means, when starting with a maiden tree, growing on the full standard and possibly the half standard for two seasons to reach the necessary height. Train them to a stout cane during this period and leave any side shoots on to help to thicken the stem – but pinch back any vigorous laterals in the summer to about 6 leaves.

In the second winter cut the leader back to a bud 4½ feet (1.4m) for a half standard or 6½ feet (2m) for a standard. Thereafter follow the same principles as for the bush tree. Remove all laterals below the head once the tree has formed a stout trunk.

Spindlebush

The spindlebush is a cone-shaped tree supported by a permanent stake. It consists of a central stem from which, starting at about 2 feet (60cm) from the ground, branches and laterals grow at intervals evenly spaced along its length. The 3 or 4 lowest branches are permanent and carry a herringbone system of cropping laterals pruned on the renewal method. The upper branches are kept shorter than the lower branches so that the cone shape is maintained. These are not permanent but are cut out whenever they become too dominant, too crowded or unproductive. Tying down the branches and laterals is practised to obtain nearly horizontal growth, which is more fruitful and less vigorous than upright growth. This shape allows plenty of sunlight to reach the lower branches and this factor together with the wide angle of the laterals is conducive to early bearing, well-coloured fruits and good cropping. Because of the tall stake and tying down involved it is perhaps not an attractive form for the garden – and it is very important for good cropping that the tree is well maintained.

Rootstocks and spacing

On M.9 (very dwarfing), or in poor soils on M.26 (dwarfing), plant at 6 to 7 feet (1.8–2.1m) between the trees and 12 feet (3.6m) between the rows.

The extremely dwarfing rootstock, M.27, should be used for triploids (see table of cultivars on pp.62–67), such as 'Bramley's Seedling', 'Blenheim Orange' and 'Crispin'. Spacing is the same as on M.9.

On M.26 and MM.106 (semi-dwarfing), on good soils, plant at 7½ to 8½ feet (2.2–2.5m) between the trees and 8 to 10 feet (2.4–3m) between the rows. Allow the wider spacings for trees on MM.106.

Type of tree and pruning

Two or three-year-old partly-formed spindlebushes are difficult to obtain, and it is usually necessary to start with a maiden tree. Choose a well-feathered maiden, because the laterals are almost always set at a wide angle to the main stem which is ideal.

Nevertheless a maiden whip can be used and in the first winter is cut back to a bud at 3 feet (90cm).

Staking

The spindlebush needs a permanent stake. Use a post 8 to 8½ feet (2.5m) long with a minimum diameter at the top of 1¾ inches (4.5cm), treated with preservative. It should be driven 1½ to 2 feet (45–60cm) into the soil. Drive the stake in first and plant the tree to the stake. Two tree ties are necessary, one on the lower part and one on the upper part of the tree (see photo opposite).

Pruning

In the first winter cut back the maiden whip to a bud at 3 feet (90cm). For a feathered maiden choose 3 or 4 laterals at not less than 2 feet (60cm) from the ground to make the first tier of branches, and cut each back by half to a downward-pointing bud. Remove remaining laterals close to the main stem. Cut back the main stem at 3 buds above the topmost lateral.

If growth is good in the first summer it may be possible to start tying down the laterals. But if growth is moderate to weak, leave this until the second summer.

The laterals are tied down in August, after growth has stopped, at 20°, or less, to the horizontal, using fairly thick string secured to pegs or skewers in the ground. An alternative to using string is a weighted peg. The laterals chosen should be those forming naturally wide angles with the main stem, which are easily bent

A young spindlebush, showing the permanent stake; and a branch leader being tied down, on the left.

laterals arising from the central leader and from existing branches, some of which may be bearing fruit.

In the third winter prune the central leader according to its vigour, to stimulate the production of more laterals which are tied down in the summer, if necessary. The more vigorous the leader is, the more lightly it is pruned. The tree should have formed by now 8 to 10 branches arising from the central stem, those at the top being shorter than those at the bottom to form a cone shaped tree.

By the fourth year from planting, the spindlebush should be near to full cropping. The higher branches must be kept shorter to allow plenty of light to reach the lower ones. In the winter shorten them back to a fruit bud, if necessary, and similarly cut back to fruit bud any of the lower branches if they are encroaching upon neighbouring spindlebushes.

In subsequent winters, the spindlebush is pruned on a renewal basis aimed at obtaining a constant supply of young wood. Branches at the top are not permanent, but some are replaced each year by cutting out a proportion, when they are 3 or 4 years old, leaving an inch (2.5cm) stub in each case. Limb loppers can be used for this. New growth is produced from this point in the following season, which should fruit in subsequent years. Fruiting laterals and spurs on the permanent lower branches should also be cut out in the same way when they become old and unproductive.

It is important that the central leader does not become too dominant or too tall. A convenient height is between 6 and 7 feet (1.8–2.1m). The replacement of a strong, vigorous leader is necessary from time to time. This is achieved by pruning back the central stem to a weaker, 1-, 2- or 3-year-old side branch in the winter. This replacement is tied upwards to the stake.

It is equally important that strong vertical growth at the top of the tree competing with the leader is cut out at an early stage either in the winter or in the summer so that the cone shape is maintained and light can reach the lower part of the tree.

Restricted forms

Cordon

Rootstocks and spacing
M.27 (extremely dwarfing). Suitable for a small garden, but requires a very fertile soil.

down. The extension growth on the laterals of feathered maidens is tied down in the same way. Any upright, narrow-angled laterals are removed. The central leader is trained upward throughout the summer and tied to the stake when necessary.

In the second winter after planting the tree should have 1 or 2 tiers of almost horizontal branches. Cut back the central leader by a third, to a bud on the side opposite to that of the previous winter. Check the strings and remove those on branches which have set at the required angle. On those that tend to spring upwards, leave the strings for a further year, but loosen the ties if necessary to avoid constriction. Do not prune the side branches or laterals.

In the second summer, about August, repeat the process of tying down new

M.9 (very dwarfing). Best choice for a small garden, but requires a fertile soil.
M.26 (dwarfing). Suits most soils, except light shallow soils.
M.106 (semi-dwarfing). Suits most, including the lighter soils.
M.2 & MM.111 (vigorous). Only suitable on very poor soils, otherwise trees may become too vigorous.

Plant at 2½ feet (75cm) apart in the row, and 6 feet (1.8m) apart between the rows. If there is more than one row, ensure that the rows run north to south in order to reduce the amount of mutual shading.

Selection of trees
A maiden tree is the cheapest to buy, but does not usually begin cropping until its third year. It is best to choose a well feathered maiden on which the laterals represent the start of fruiting spurs, although 2- or 3-year-old cordons crop earlier. Whatever the age, remove the blossom in the first spring after planting. Select those well furnished with spurs along most of the length of the stem.

Support
A permanent post and wire system is necessary for cordons grown in the open. Wires are also required for those grown against wooden fences and walls. The posts are usually of wood, although they may be of angle-iron or concrete. Suitable posts are 8½ feet (2.6m) long if set in concrete or 9 feet (2.7m) long if set straight into the ground. This allows for 1½ feet or 2 feet (45cm or 60cm) respectively below soil level. The posts should be spaced 12 feet (3.6m) apart and the endposts be adequately strutted. Stretch three horizontal wires tightly between the posts. The bottom wire of galvanised gauge 12 (2.5mm) should be fixed at 2½ feet (75cm) above soil level, the middle wire (same gauge) at 4½ feet (1.3m), and the top wire gauge 10 (3.15mm) at 6½ feet (2m). The wires must be tight, so use straining bolts on the endposts.

For cordons against solid fences and walls the wires must be 4 to 6 inches (10–15cm) away from the structure to allow for growth and air circulation around the plants. Fix wooden battens to the walls to hold the wires and straining bolts.

Cordons are best grown at an angle of 45° to soil level (oblique cordons); this gives a longer length of stem for the same height compared with vertical cordons, and achieves the right balance between growth and fruit bud production. A disadvantage of the vertical cordon is that often the top growth becomes too dominant at the expense of growth lower down the stem.

Finally bamboo canes 10 feet long (3m) should be secured to the wires with wire to correspond to the planting position of the cordons. The base of the canes must be just clear of the soil.

Planting
Plant with the scion part of the union uppermost to reduce the risk of breakage and of the scion rooting. In a north-south row, which is preferable, the trees should be inclined towards the north in order to encourage even growth. In an east-west row, incline the trees towards the east.

Pruning

The young cordon. Immediately after planting a maiden or a 2- or 3-year-old cordon, cut back any side shoots (previous summer's growth) more than 4 inches (10cm) long to 3 buds. The leader is not pruned unless the apple is a tip bearer (see p.46), in which case it is pruned back by one-quarter to an upward-facing bud. Where there is doubt as to whether it is a tip bearer, wait until spring to see if flowers are produced at the tip of the leader. Thereafter pruning is done only in summer, unless some spur thinning becomes necessary on an older tree.

If the young tree is not producing enough side shoots, shorten the leader by up to one-third of its length in winter. This delays cropping but stimulates growth of side shoots (see also Notching, p.52).

Summer pruning (Modified Lorette System). The Modified Lorette System is recommended for all cultivars including tip bearers.

Throughout each summer the leader is trained and tied to the cane using a figure-of-eight tie so that there is no danger of rubbing.

In about the first week of August in southern England, but later further north, cut back all mature laterals of the current season's growth growing directly from the main stem to 3 leaves above the basal cluster, and those from existing side shoots or spurs to 1 leaf. Mature shoots

(Above left) *Planting an oblique cordon: note the union is well above the soil (shown by the position of the cane in the centre) and the scion is uppermost.*
(Above right) *Oblique cordons against a fence showing how to fill in the gap at the start of the row.*
(Below) *After planting, the side-shoots are pruned to a bud at 4 inches (10cm).*
(Right) *Chainlock plastic tie secures the cordon to the cane and allows for adjustment.*

are those 9 inches (22cm) long or more, with a woody base and dark green leaves. The basal cluster is the rosette of about 2 to 4 leaves closely spaced at the base of the shoot. With a mature cordon most of the summer pruning will be to 1 leaf rather than 3. If there are only a few immature shoots – those with light green leaves and bark – they can also be pruned at this time; if there are many, however, leave them until the end of September before pruning.

The timing of summer pruning is important, because if it is done too early unwanted secondary growth develops. In wet summers or in areas of high rainfall, it is better to delay summer pruning until about mid-August, and even later farther north. If it is found that despite delaying the summer pruning until mid-August excessive secondary growth occurs, leave it until September. If this fails, prune in the winter. Use the same technique, but cut back to the buds instead of the leaves.

There is sometimes secondary growth in late summer following pruning. Such immature growth, if left, may be injured by frost, possibly leading later to disease. In late October cut these shoots back to a mature bud at the base.

When the cordons reach the top wire, untie the canes and lower the cordons, by about 5° a year – but not lower than 35°, otherwise there is the risk of breaking the stems. Keep the cordon parallel with its neighbours.

Modified Lorette System – summer pruning an oblique cordon: (left) a mature shoot arising from the main stem is pruned to 3 leaves beyond the basal cluster; (right) mature shoots arising from spurs are pruned to one leaf beyond the basal cluster.

Normally the leader should not be shortened until it has reached the required height 6 inches (15cm) above the top wire – where it should be stopped in May. Thereafter the leader may be pruned annually to leave ½ inch (1cm) of the previous summer's growth.

As the tree becomes older spur shortening and simplification become necessary (see p.47). Such pruning is done in the winter; any necessary thinning of spurs should also be done in the winter.

Notching to stimulate the bud below into growth.

Notching. The removal of a small portion of bark immediately above a latent bud has the effect of stimulating it into growth. With cordons and other restricted trees it is sometimes desirable to do this in May, so preventing bare lengths of stem. Notching is also of use when the shape of a young tree is being formed. It is often used in conjunction with nicking, which consists of cutting into the bark immediately *below* a bud. This results in a weaker growth from that bud than would otherwise be the case.

Espalier

Choice of tree

Most nurseries supply 2- or 3-tier espaliers and further tiers can be made if required. The grower may prefer to start with a maiden tree (because it is cheaper), and carry out the formative pruning described below. An espalier trained at the nursery is more expensive but time is saved in the formative pruning and it comes into bearing more quickly. A 2-tier espalier is usually 2½ to 3 feet (75–90cm) high and a 3-tier one 4½ to 5 feet (1.3–1.5m).

Rootstocks and spacing

If an espalier is wanted to cover a low wall, M.9 (very dwarfing) is suitable provided that the soil is fertile. However, it is not usually possible to obtain partly-formed espaliers on this rootstock, so a maiden tree may have to be planted and the formative pruning carried out as described below. Space at 10 feet (3m) apart.

For most gardens MM.106 (semi-dwarfing) is suitable, spaced 12 to 15 feet (3.6–4.5m) apart. M.26 (dwarfing) can be used, but espaliers are difficult to obtain on this stock. Space at 10 to 12 feet (3–3.6m) apart.

For a large tree or on a poor soil, MM.111 and M.2 (vigorous) are recom-

A horizontal cordon on M.27 'Kidd's Orange Red' in fruit.

mended. Plant 15 to 18 feet (4.5–5.5m) apart on fertile land.

Support

Horizontal wires, galvanised gauge 10 (3.15mm) should be stretched 15 to 18 inches (38–45cm) apart to coincide with the tiers of the espalier. The supporting posts of wood, angle-iron or concrete may be set at 12 to 18 feet (3.6m–4.5m) intervals. The posts may be driven 2 feet (60cm) into the ground or set 18 inches (45cm) into concrete. The endposts must be strutted and the wires tightened with straining bolts.

For espaliers planted against a solid fence or wall the wires (gauge 12, 2.5mm) need to be 4 to 6 inches (10–15cm) from the wall to allow room for growth. Plant the tree so that the trunk is 6 to 9 inches (15–22cm) away from the structure.

Pruning

In the first winter after planting a maiden tree, cut it back to a good bud about 2 inches (5cm) above the first wire. Make this cut as near as possible to a point where there are two more good buds fairly close below, one facing left and the other right. Shoots from these buds will form the first tier.

In the first summer, train the shoot from the top bud upwards, tying it to a cane fastened to the wires. Train the shoots from the two lower buds to canes tied to the wires at an angle of 45°. Keep all other shoots pinched back to 6 leaves.

If one tier grows faster than the other, raise the weaker to a more upright position. At the end of the season (November) lower the arms and canes, and tie them to the first wire. This is not done initially because tying down the shoots to horizontal while actively growing reduces their vigour. Prune any other shoots arising from the main stem to 3 buds.

In the second winter form the next tier in the same way – that is, cutting to a bud just above the second wire ensuring that there are 2 good buds just beneath, one facing left and the other right. Repeat this technique each winter until the tier along the top wire has been formed. The leading shoot of each tier should not be pruned unless growth has been poor. If this has been the case extension growth can be stimulated by cutting the horizontal leader by one-quarter to one-third, to an upward-facing bud some time in winter. It also helps to tie the tiers towards the vertical (about 45°) for a

Modified Lorette System – before summer pruning an established espalier: mature shoots arising directly from existing spur systems are pruned to 1 leaf beyond the basal cluster.

Modified Lorette System after pruning.

season before tying down to the horizontal again.

Once a tier has reached the required length, prune back the leader to ½ inch (1cm) each May.

Summer pruning (Modified Lorette System). After the first tier has been formed, espaliers are pruned each summer, starting in about the first week of August in southern England but later further north. In warm, wet summers and areas of high rainfall, prune later to reduce the chance of secondary growth.

Cut back all mature laterals (those which are woody at the base, with dark green leaves) longer than 9 inches (22cm)

arising directly from the tiers, to 3 leaves above the basal cluster. Those from existing side shoots or spurs should be cut back to 1 leaf above the basal cluster. Shoots on the central stem above the first tier may be treated in the same way. If there are a few immature laterals treat them similarly, but if there are many leave them until late September before pruning. Remove any shoots produced below the first tier to create a clean stem.

Dwarf pyramid

Rootstocks

M.27 (extremely dwarfing). Makes a small pyramid, but requires a fertile soil.

A dwarf pyramid 'Welspur Red Delicious'.

apart. On other stocks plant 5 to 6 feet (1.5–1.8m) apart. Allow the wider spacing for the more vigorous rootstocks. Space the rows 6 feet (1.8m) apart for M.27 and M.9, and 7 feet (2.1m) for other rootstocks.

Trees on M.27 and M.9 must have some support throughout their lives. Trees on other rootstocks need support for the first 4 or 5 years. Support may be in the form of either stakes, or two horizontal wires at 18 inches (45cm) and 3 feet (90cm) fastened to posts.

Pruning (for illustrations *see* Pears, p.76)

Winter pruning. At planting cut back the central leader of a maiden tree to a bud 20 inches (50cm) above ground. Shorten any side shoots over 6 inches (15cm) long to a bud at about 5 inches (13cm).

In the following winter, or with a 2-year-old pyramid at planting, cut back the central leader to 8 to 10 inches (20–25cm) to a bud facing the direction opposite that of the bud chosen in the first winter. This helps to keep the stem straight. Cut laterals and branch leaders to 6 to 8 inches (15–20cm) to a downward- or outward-facing bud.

In subsequent winters, shorten the central leader to leave 8 to 10 inches (20–25cm) of new growth, cutting to a bud on the side opposite that selected the previous year.

Summer pruning (Modified Lorette System). From the second summer onwards the trees should be pruned in summer. In about the first week of August, depending upon the season and locality, cut mature branch leaders to 5 or 6 leaves beyond the basal cluster of leaves. The central leader should not be pruned at this stage. The laterals are pruned on the Modified Lorette System: mature laterals longer than 9 inches (22cm) arising directly from the branches are cut back to 3 leaves, and those from existing spurs to 1 leaf beyond the basal cluster.

In wet summers and areas of high rainfall, prune from the middle to the end of August. In mid-August or early September shorten in the same manner any shoots that were not mature earlier on. In October cut back to 1 bud any secondary growth arising from the summer pruned shoots.

When the trees have reached about 7 feet (2.1m) (or for trees on M.27, 6 feet:

M.9 (very dwarfing). Suitable for good soils.
M.26 (dwarfing). Suitable for most soils.
MM.106 (semi-dwarfing). Too vigorous on good soils, but more suitable than M.26 for less favourable conditions.

Choice of tree
Pyramids 2 and 3 years old can be obtained from nurseryies, but the grower may prefer to start with a maiden tree. Ideally, choose a feathered maiden, on which the laterals represent the first branches.

Spacing and support
Plant trees on M.27 or M.9 at 4 feet (1.2m)

A spur system with numerous fruit buds giving too many small fruits. This can happen on any type of tree fruit.

After winter pruning; a proportion of the fruit buds have been removed.

1.8m), any further growth in height can be restricted by pruning the central leader in May to $\frac{1}{2}$ inch (1cm). Any other growth that needs shortening, such as branches at the top of the tree competing with the leader, or branch leaders growing into adjacent trees, can be treated in the same way and at the same time.

In later years it may be necessary to thin out or shorten some of the spur systems in the winter if they get too congested and the tree is producing too many small fruits (*see* p.47).

Growing trees in grass

This is a traditional method of soil management for commercial orchards, although it is less often used now that weeds can be effectively controlled with herbicides. Whenever grass is used in this way it must be kept short and it must be kept away from the trunk, or the damp conditions could favour the fungus disease collar rot.

Trees grown in restricted form or on dwarfing stocks are usually grassed down in the second to fourth years after planting. Bush or larger trees are grassed down in their fifth or sixth years. For closely-planted trees it is sufficient to limit the sward to the centre 3 feet (90cm) between the rows. At a wider spacing, each tree should have an area not less than $2\frac{1}{2}$ feet (75cm) radius of clear land around the stem, but if the trees are growing very vigorously then the whole orchard can be grassed down.

A mixture of fine grasses can be used at 1 oz per sq. yd (33g/m^2).

Trickle irrigation supplies water directly to the root area. This system is being used for apples, but it is adaptable for any other fruit crop.

The grass should be kept almost as short as a lawn during the growing season, the mowings being left to lie. More nitrogen has to be applied to trees growing in grass than to those in cultivated soil.

The check to vegetative growth caused by grassing down may be of value in inducing trees to crop, but an excessive check could be detrimental to both growth and fruit size. Cooking apples are usually best grown in arable conditions.

Manuring and mulching

(For general principles, see pp.21–24). Apples have an annual requirement for potassium and nitrogen. The phosphorus requirement is not as great and it is usually sufficient to apply it every third year. Sprinkle the fertilizers as a top dressing over the rooting area of the tree (roughly equivalent to its spread and slightly beyond).

In late January apply sulphate of potash at $\frac{3}{4}$ oz per sq. yd (25g/m^2); in late February Nitro-chalk at 1 oz per sq. yd (33g/m^2) unless the soil is alkaline, in which case apply sulphate of ammonia at the same rate. Dessert apples growing in grass and cookers should be given twice this rate of nitrogen. Every third year in January apply superphosphate at 2 oz per sq. yd (65g/m^2).

In areas of high rainfall and during wet summers apples often suffer from magnesium deficiency, particularly 'Cox's Orange Pippin', and as soon as symptoms appear (see p.24) spray the trees with foliar sprays of magnesium sulphate 2 or 3 times at 14-day intervals. Once the signs of deficiency have appeared in the trees it is best to apply magnesium sulphate to the soil annually as a precaution in April, at $1\frac{1}{2}$ oz per sq. yd (50g/m^2).

Newly planted trees, particularly those on light soils, should be mulched with well rotted manure, compost or old straw to a depth of about 2 inches (5cm) over a radius of 18 inches (45cm). Keep the material clear of the tree's stem. Supplement the mulch annually for three or four years after planting. Mulch in the early spring after applying the inorganic fertilizers. On a good soil a black polythene sheet covering the soil around the base of the tree is an acceptable alternative to an organic mulch.

Watering

Young trees, especially those newly planted, need water in the growing season whenever conditions are dry. Adequate moisture helps to ensure that the tree grows well and develops a strong framework able to carry heavy crops in later years. In times of drought, water at about $4\frac{1}{2}$ gallons per sq. yd (25 litres/m^2) around the base of the tree every 10 days in the spring and summer until rain restores the moisture deficit.

Fruiting trees also benefit from watering, particularly in July, August and September in southern England when the soil moisture deficit is usually high. Water applied at this period helps to offset any check to fruit swelling and to the production of fruit buds for the next year. A tree kept well watered is less likely to lapse into a biennial pattern of fruit-bearing.

In dry weather apply about 2 inches (9 gallons per sq. yd or 50 litres/m^2) of water over the rooting area about once every 14 days, starting in early July and finishing in mid-September, unless there is appreciable rainfall and the soil is obviously back to field capacity. To lessen the risk of fungal diseases, apply the water over the ground rather than over the foliage.

Fruit thinning

The main purpose of thinning is to improve fruit size. When a tree is carrying a very heavy crop, the fruits are often small and of poor quality, and there is also the risk of branch breakage, unless they are thinned in good time. Thinning lessens the strain on the tree's resources so that while it is carrying a crop, it is able to make satisfactory growth and to develop fruit buds for the following year. A young tree allowed to crop too heavily is likely to be retarded in its growth, and instead of producing a strong framework the branches may be weak and drooping. Biennial bearing may also be induced.

Most apple cultivars, including 'Cox's Orange Pippin', shed fruitlets naturally towards the end of June and early July in what is known as the June drop. Where a heavy fruit set has occurred, however, some extra thinning is required. A little can be done before the June drop takes place, by removing malformed fruits, and the balance afterwards.   The amount of thinning depends on the cultivar, age and condition of the tree. Trees growing vigorously with strong healthy foliage are capable of supporting a heavier crop than those that are weakly. Cooking apples are thinned harder than dessert apples, in order to obtain larger fruits.

As a general guide, on bush trees thin dessert apples to about 4 to 6 inches (10–15cm) apart to obtain a good proportion of apples of $2\frac{1}{2}$ to $2\frac{3}{4}$ inches (60–75mm) diameter. Thin cooking apples to 6 to 9 inches (15–22cm) apart to obtain fruits of 3 to $3\frac{1}{4}$ inches (8cm) diameter. Thin to one fruit per cluster.

With cordons and dwarf trees on M.9, the fruits are usually larger, and heavy thinning is not always necessary. Dessert cultivars can be thinned to one, or occasionally two, fruits per cluster. If the fruit is sparse, more doubles can be left. With some cultivars such as 'Ellison's Orange', 'Laxton's Superb' and 'Charles Ross', the fruit may grow too big if reduced to singles and a good proportion of doubles should therefore be left.

Thin as soon as possible after the June drop and finish by mid-July. In addition to blemished and misshapen fruits, remove the weakest in the cluster, leaving the strongest and best shaped. Often, but not always, the king or crown apple produced from the central flower is malformed and should be removed. Certain cultivars, typically long-stalked, such as 'Golden Delicious', produce normal-shaped king fruits which may be left.

Rejected fruits should be cut off with a pair of long, thin scissors, such as vine scissors, or by gripping the stalk between the first two fingers and pushing off the fruit with the thumb.

(Above) *Thinning apples using the finger and thumb technique to push off the fruitlet. Scissors are easier for the less experienced.*

(Left) *Removing the king fruit which often has an ugly swollen stalk. This fruit need not always be removed.*

(Below) *After thinning to 1 fruit per cluster, at about 4 to 6 inches (10–15cm) apart.*

Maypoling: a dwarf bush apple on 'M.27' with string tied round the heavily laden branches to a tall temporary cane.

Picking: lift the apple in the palm of the hand and twist it slightly, when it should leave the spur easily if it is ready.

Supporting heavily laden branches

The weight of fruit on heavily laden branches, even where thinned, may be enough to cause breakages. Such branches need support. Forked stakes can be used to prop up individual branches, and particularly weak branches can be tied to stronger ones with thick string, rope or webbing. If there are several overloaded branches, a tall stake tied to the trunk or driven into the ground can be used for tying up the individual branches like a maypole.

Picking

Pick and handle fruits with the greatest care. Bruised fruits will not keep well.

Ripening varies with season and locality; the rootstock also has a slight effect, so precise dates for picking cannot be given. The season the apple can be eaten does not necessarily coincide with the time it is picked. An early dessert apple, for example, can be eaten straight off the tree, but a late-season apple is not ready to eat until after a period of storage.

There are various signs that the time for picking is approaching. The first windfalls on the ground are sometimes an indication. The fruits of many dessert apples develop much brighter colours. The seeds inside the apple turn from white to straw-coloured to brown. But this is not always a reliable guide, for some very early apples are ready when the pips are still white. The best test of readiness is to lift the fruit gently in the palm of the hand and give it a very slight twist. If the apple parts easily from spur, then it is ready for picking.

It should be noted that fruits of late cultivars picked too early may not ripen properly or develop their full flavour. Fruits harvested too late may not keep as well as they should.

All the apples on a tree do not ripen at the same time and it is best to pick in stages. Well coloured fruits, typically those at the top of the tree are usually ready first, then those at the sides, and lastly the shaded fruits in the middle of the tree.

Pick the fruits with the stalks intact; many broken stalks or torn-off spurs during picking is an indication that the apples are not yet ready. Place the fruits very carefully in the picking basket or bucket, which should be lined with a soft protective material such as paper, straw,

(Left) *Slatted apple trays with wrapped apples and apples loose in a 30 lb (14 kg) apple box. Note that each method has ample ventilation.*

(Below) *Wrapping for storage. Use tissue paper to wrap each fruit carefully; start wrapping with the stalk end upwards; fold the opposite corners over the stalk; finally fold over the other 2 corners. Newspaper can be used for wrapping cooking apples.*

Polythene bags holding about 5 lb (2kg) of fruit are also suitable. Plenty of ventilation holes should be made in the polythene, with a ballpoint pen.

cloth or a piece of foam rubber. Transfer the apples with equal care into their final container. Fruits must never be thrown or dropped into a container.

Storage

Apples can be stored in relatively simple conditions for a few weeks or even for several months depending upon the season of the cultivar.

Early apples soon go mealy and are best eaten straight off the tree or within a few weeks of picking. Mid-season cultivars keep for about 4 to 8 weeks in cool conditions. Late apples, which do not develop their full flavour until some time after storage, last from 4 or 5 weeks to several months.

The store does not need to be elaborate so long as it maintains a cool, even temperature and is frost-proof. The essential conditions for successful long-term storage are coolness, darkness, and humidity with some air circulation. Too much ventilation may cause the fruits to shrivel; too little may spoil them through lack of oxygen. The ideal temperature is from 37° to 40°F (2.7° to 4.5°C), but this is seldom possible for amateurs who can more realistically aim for a store that can maintain an average temperature of about 46°F (7°C) during the winter. A cellar, a well-built garden shed situated in the shade, or possibly a garage may

provide this kind of temperature, but the building must be frost-proof and secure against mice. Lofts and attics are not suitable because they are usually too dry with greatly fluctuating temperatures.

Store only sound fruits, ideally with stalks intact. Medium-sized apples keep better than very large or very small fruits. The larger fruits tend to break down with storage troubles, and are therefore best used first. Small apples shrivel quickly.

The fruits can be kept on wooden, slatted shelving, in wooden fruit trays with corner posts, commercial apple boxes, or on specially-made polystyrene or papier-mâché trays. The container should provide for ventilation through the sides and over the top.

The apples may be wrapped or unwrapped. Wrapped apples keep marginally longer and in better condition than unwrapped fruits. The wraps help to prevent moisture loss and the spread of rots from one apple to another. For dessert apples used oiled wraps specially made or tissue paper, and for cookers oiled wraps or newspaper cut to a convenient size. Another useful method of storage, particularly in small quantities, is in polythene bags (see below).

Keep apples which ripen at different times in separate containers. If they can be removed from the store as they approach ripeness so much the better, especially if the store is an enclosed one, because ripening apples give off volatile substances that may induce other cultivars to ripen prematurely. Keep fruit away from anything that may taint it, such as creosote, fresh paint, fertilizers, strong-smelling wood, onions and damp, dirty hay or straw. Check the apples regularly and remove any rotting fruit.

The storage of apples in polythene bags
Storage of apples in clear polythene bags (150 gauge) almost entirely prevents shrivelling and keeps the fruit clean. The same conditions for succesful storage – coolness, even temperature, darkness and some ventilation – are still essential, nevertheless.

Use clear bags holding about 5 to 7 pounds (2–3kg) of fruit. The mouth of the bag should be folded over, not sealed. For each 2 lb (1kg) of fruit, a couple of holes should be made with a pencil in different parts of the bag so that there is some air circulation. Check over the fruit regularly and remove those with rots.

Pollination

No apple cultivar is completely self-fertile, and even the few which can set a fair crop with their own pollen yield much more satisfactorily if cross-pollinated. This means no apple should be planted singly, unless it is a family tree (see p.30), but must instead be planted with at least one other different cultivar that flowers at the same time. (Details of flowering groups are given on pp.216–217.)

'Discovery', an early ripening apple.

'Worcester Pearmain', September ripening, best when eaten soon after picking.

Notes to Table 6 (opposite)
Pr = Pruning category (see p.46).
Po = Pollination group (see pp.216–217).
*Very good flavour. μ Cultivar is a very vigorous and for a small garden or in restricted form should be grafted on to a dwarfing rootstock. (T) Triploid.

Table 6	**Recommended cultivars**		
Cultivar	Pr	Po	Picking time
Dessert			
Vista Bella	A	1	late July
George Cave	B	2	early/mid-Aug.
Discovery	C	3	mid-Aug.
Irish Peach*	C	2	late Aug.
Epicure*	A	3	late Aug.
Redsleeves	A	3	late Aug.
Katy	C	3	early Sept.
James Grieve	A	3	early Sept.
Fortune*	A	3	early Sept.
Worcester Pearmain	C	3	early/mid-Sept.
St Edmund's Pippin*	C	2	mid-Sept.
Ellison's Orange	A	4	mid-Sept.
Merton Knave	A	3	mid-Sept.
Greensleeves	A	3	mid/late Sept.
Merton Beauty	A	5	mid-Sept.
Lord Lambourne	C	2	late Sept.
Jester	A	4	late Sept.
Mother* (American Mother)	B	5	late Sept.
Ribston Pippin* (T)	A	2	late Sept./early Oct.
Egremont Russet*	B	2	late Sept.
Sunset*	A	3	late Sept.
Falstaff	A	3	early Oct.
Jupiter μ (T)	A	3	early Oct.
Elstar	A	3	early Oct.
Karmijn de Sonnaville μ (T)	B	3	end Sept.
Cox's Orange Pippin*	A	3	early-mid Oct.
Fiesta	A	3	late Sept./early Oct.

(The approximate time for picking is for the south of England and is later farther north. It may vary slightly from year to year according to the season)

Season of use	Quality	Cropping	Vigour	Other characteristics
late July/mid-Aug.	Fair; soon goes soft; perfumed	Moderate	Moderate, upright, spreading	Biennial tendency
early/mid-Aug.	Good; soft, acid, juicy; nice flavour	Good	Moderate, upright, spreading	Spur bearer; soon drops, hardy
mid-Aug./mid-Sept.	Good; crisp, juicy, sweet; somewhat chewy	Good	Moderate upright, spreading	Spur and tip bearer; keeps longer than other earlies; scab resistance. Slow to crop
late Aug./early Sept.	Good; fine eating; very quickly goes soft	Irregular	Moderate, spreading	Tip bearer
late Aug./mid-Sept.	Good; firm, aromatic	Heavy	Moderate, upright, spreading	Spur bearer; tends to over-crop, small fruits; hardy
late Aug./early Sept.	Fair; sweet, crisp, juicy, pleasant flavour	Good	Moderate	Compact growth, hardy some resistance to scab and mildew
Sept./Oct.	Fair; crisp, sweet	Good	Medium	Spurs freely; tends to over-crop
Sept./Oct.	Good; juicy but soft; excellent flavour	Heavy	Moderate, spreading	Spur bearer; hardy, canker-prone bruises easily
Sept./Oct.	Excellent; crisp for a short period; sweet, aromatic	Good	Moderate, upright, spreading	Biennial tendency; spurs freely, canker-prone, some resistance to scab, fairly hardy
Sept./Oct.	Good; firm, chewy, fresh, sweet, faint strawberry flavour	Heavy	Moderate	Tip bearer; produces few spurs; hardy, reliable, resistant to mildew, scab prone.
late Sept./Oct.	Excellent; sweet, juicy, firm	Uncertain	Weak, upright spreading	Partial tip bearer; small fruits. A russet apple
Sept/Oct.	Good; soft, aniseed flavour	Good	Moderate, upright spreading	Spurs moderately well; hardy, canker-prone; fairly resistant to scab, sometimes biennial
Sept.	Fair; crisp, sweet	Good	Moderate weeping	Hardy, spurs freely; good resistance to mildew
late Sept./mid-Nov.	Good; crisp at first, soft later	Very heavy	Medium, fairly upright	Spurs freely, floriferous; hardy
Sept./early Oct.	Good; aromatic, aniseed flavour	Good	Medium, upright, spreading	Spurs freely; hardy
late Sept./mid-Nov.	Good; soft, sweet pleasant	Heavy	Moderate; compact	Partial tip bearer; spurs very freely
Oct./Nov.	Fair; crisp, juicy	Good	Compact	Spurs freely; hardy
Oct./Nov.	Very good; sweet, distinctive flavour	Irregular	Medium, very upright	Spur bearer
Oct./Dec.	Excellent; firm, aromatic	Moderate to good	Vigorous, upright spreading	Spurs freely; fruits drop easily; scab-prone
Oct./Dec.	Excellent; crisp, dry, nutty, true russet flavour	Moderate	Moderate, upright	Spurs freely; scab-resistant; bitter pit prone
Oct./Dec.	Excellent; firm, aromatic, Cox-like flavour	Good	Compact, upright, spreading	Small fruits reliable; hardy
Oct./Jan.	Good; sweet, crisp, juicy, excellent flavour	Good	Moderate	Medium-sized open tree, spurs freely; fairly hardy
Oct./Dec.	Good; firm, acid Cox-like flavour, coarse-fleshed	Very heavy	Vigorous spreading	Spurs freely; some large uneven fruits; fairly hardy, worth growing where Cox is difficult
mid-Oct./Jan.	Good; melting, soft texture	Good	Vigorous	Needs careful pruning to allow light into tree; medium-sized fruits, must be thinned rigorously to prevent biennial bearing
Oct./Jan.	Good; firm, crisp, rich, dry Blenheim Orange-like flavour	Heavy	Very vigorous upright, then spreading	Spurs freely; fruits medium to large; sometimes heavily russeted
Late Oct./Jan.	First class; crisp, fine, juicy, aromatic	Moderate/good	Moderate vigorous, upright, spreading	Spurs freely. Prone to scab, canker, mildew. Expert cultivation required: not suitable for the north
late Oct./Feb.	Good; firm, crisp, juicy, Cox-like flavour	Heavy	Moderate to vigorous	Pendulous habit; prone to toxicity and canker on acid soils lower than pH 6; partly self-fertile

'James Grieve', a September apple of excellent flavour.

'Greensleeves', a heavy cropping apple.

'Gala' is in season from November to January.

Table 6   (Continued)

Cultivar	Pr	Po	Picking time
Kidd's Orange Red	A	3	early Oct.
Spartan*	A	3	early Oct.
Gala	A	4	early Oct.
Orleans Reinette*	A	4	mid-Oct.
Jonagold μ (T)	B	4	mid-Oct.
Ashmead's Kernel*	A	4	mid-Oct.
William Crump*	C	5	mid-Oct.
Suntan μ (T)	C	5	mid-Oct.
Crispin μ (T)	A	3	mid-Oct.
Tydeman's Late Orange*	B	4	mid-Oct.
Idared	C	2	end Oct./ early Nov.
Pixie*	B	4	mid-Oct.
D'Arcy Spice*	C	3	late Oct./ early Nov.
Sturmer Pippin*	A	3	mid/ end Nov.
Culinary			
Early Victoria (Emneth Early)	B	3	mid/end July
Grenadier	A	3	mid-Aug.
George Neal*	A	2	late Aug./ early Sept.
Rev. W. Wilks*	A	2	early Sept.
Peasgood Nonsuch	A	3	mid-Sept.
Warner's King (T)	A	2	mid/end Sept.
Golden Noble*	A	4	early Oct.
Bountiful*	A	3	late Sept.
Howgate Wonder μ	A	4	early Oct.
Blenheim Orange* μ (T)	B	3	early Oct.

Season of use	Quality	Cropping	Vigour	Other characteristics
Nov./Jan.	Excellent; crisp, juicy, sweet, rich flavour, aromatic	Good	Moderate, upright spreading	Spurs freely. Small fruits unless thinned, sometimes russety appearance; fairly hardy
Oct./Feb.	Excellent; crisp, juicy, vinous flavour	Good	Moderate, upright spreading	Spurs freely; fruits can be small unless thinned; canker-prone
Nov./Jan.	Good; crisp, juicy flavour, fades later	Good	Moderate, upright, spreading	Attractive but sometimes small fruits; scab prone; Tenroy (Royal Gala) is a highly coloured clone
Nov./Jan.	Excellent, firm, rich, nutty flavour	Irregular	Vigorous, upright, spreading	Spurs fairly freely; biennial tendency; fruits shrivel easily
Nov./Feb.	Excellent; juicy, crisp, rich flavour	Very heavy	Moderate spreading	Large fruits, sometimes poorly coloured; Crowngold and Jonagored are more attractively coloured clones
Dec./Feb.	First class; firm texture, rich aromatic	Erratic	Moderate, upright, spreading	Spurs freely; a russet. Flowers prone to frost damage
Dec./Feb.	Excellent; dry, sweet, aromatic	Light	Vigorous, upright	Spurs moderately
Nov./Jan.	Good; firm, juicy, very acid, Cox-like	Good	Vigorous, wide-spreading	Spurs freely, large fruits; bitter pit-prone
Dec./Feb.	Good; crisp, juicy, acid; pleasant flavour; dual purpose	Very heavy	Very vigorous, spreading	Spurs freely, large fruits; biennial tendency with over-cropping
Dec./Apr.	Good; firm, crisp, aromatic, Cox-like flavour	Good	Vigorous, upright, spreading, long, whippy laterals	Spurs freely; tendency to over-crop, yielding small fruits
Nov./Apr.	Fair; firm, crisp, juicy, pleasant; dual purpose	Good	Moderately vigorous, upright, spreading	Spurs very freely; keeps well
Dec./Mar.	First class; crisp, juicy, fine-textured, aromatic	Good	Moderately vigorous	Spurs freely; small fruits; hardy
Dec/Apr.	Excellent; rich, sweet, tough skin	Erratic	Vigorous, upright, spreading	Spurs moderately; fruits of poor appearance, shrivel easily; requires hot, dry situation; a russet
Jan./Apr.	Good; hard, juicy, rich flavour	Good	Moderate compact	Spurs very freely; requires a warm situation
Cooking qualities				
July/Aug.	Good, soft, cooks frothily	Very heavy	Moderate, compact	Biennial tendency; fruits small unless thinned severely; hardy
Aug./Oct.	Good, sharp, intact slices at first, disintegrates later	Heavy	Moderate spreading	Spurs freely; hardy, scab-resistant
late Aug./ early Oct.	Excellent; juicy, sweet, little acidity; pale yellow intact slices	Good	Medium, spreading	Spurs very freely
Sept./Oct.	Excellent; juicy, sharp, fruity; pale yellow froth	Heavy	Compact, dwarfish	Biennial; spurs freely; large fruits
Sept./Nov.	Good; sweet, juicy, light flavour; cooks frothily	Heavy	Moderately vigorous spreading	Spurs freely; large handsome fruits
late Sept./ Feb.	Good; very acid, sharp, fruity; intact white slices	Heavy	Vigorous, upright spreading	Spurs freely; large fruits canker- and scab-prone; fairly hardy
Oct./Dec.	First class; creamy white; acid sweet and fruity; breaks up completely	Moderate	Moderately, vigorous, upright; spreading	Partial tip bearer; medium-sized fruits
Sept./Jan.	Excellent; good flavour, acid sweet; breaks down	Very heavy	Compact	Spurs freely; considerable resistance to mildew
Oct./Mar.	Fair, sweet, sub-acid; breaks up almost completely	Very heavy	Vigorous, upright spreading	Spurs freely; a large exhibition apple; hardy
Nov./Jan.	First class; dry, rich characteristic flavour, firm slices	Good, irregular	Very vigorous upright then spreading	Biennial; partial tip bearer; fairly resistant to mildew, large fruits an excellent dual

(Above) 'Sunset' has a 'Cox'-like flavour.

(Below) 'Bramley's Seedling, the best known cooking apple.

Table 6   (Continued)

Cultivar	Pr	Po	Picking time
Lane's Prince Albert	B	3	early Oct.
Bramley's Seedling* μ (T)	C	3	mid-Oct.
Newton Wonder* μ	B	5	mid-Oct.
Dumelow's Seedling* (Wellington)	B	4	mid-Oct.
Woolbrook Russet*	A	4	mid-Oct.
Crawley Beauty	A	7	mid-Oct.
Edward VII	A	6	mid-Oct.
Encore*	A	4	mid-Oct.
Annie Elizabeth	B	4	mid-Oct.

The dessert apple 'Egremont Russet', excellent flavour, in season from October to December.

Season of use	Quality	Cropping	Vigour	Other characteristics
Dec./Mar.	Good; crisp, sharp, fruity, intact slices	Very heavy	Dwarfish	Spurs freely; hardy, reliable; susceptible to mildew
Nov./Mar.	First class; acid, sweet, white, juicy, pale cream purée	Heavy	Very vigorous spreading	Partial tip bearer; sometimes biennial; fairly hardy but blossom frost susceptible
Nov./Mar.	Good; juicy, sub-acid, sweet pale purée	Heavy, irregular	Very vigorous, spreading	Biennial; even fruits; Bitter pit prone; acceptable as dessert Feb; hardy
Nov./Mar.	First class; white, firm, very juicy, very acid; pale cream purée	Good	Moderately vigorous	Spurs freely; small/medium-sized fruits; fairly hardy
Nov./Apr.	Excellent, sweet, acid, rich flavour; pale yellow purée	Good	Moderate vigorous, upright, spreading	Spurs freely; not a true russet
Dec./Mar.	Fair; crisp, sub-acid	Good	Moderately vigorously spreading	Spurs freely; small/medium fruits; flowers very late; hardy; useful in frost pocket
Dec./Apr.	Good; firm, juicy, acid, dark red; translucent purée	Moderate	Moderate, upright, compact	Spurs fairly freely; flowers very late; hardy; useful in frost pocket; scab-resistant
Dec./Apr.	Good; soft, juicy, sub-acid	Moderate	Moderately vigorous, upright, spreading	Spurs very freely; some scab-resistance
Dec./Jun.	Good; cream white, acid not very juicy; breaks up almost completely	Uncertain	Moderately vigorous	Spurs freely; a fine, late keeper; fairly hardy

Promising new dessert cultivars

Alkmene. A short-season Cox-type apple of good eating quality in October.

Rubinette. A sweet, well flavoured apple, season Sept./Jan.

Pests

CODLING MOTH caterpillars are the main cause of maggoty apples. Eggs are laid on leaves in June and July, and the caterpillars tunnel into the fruits. In mid-August they finish feeding, leave the fruits, and seek the protection of loose bark, or tree-ties under which they spin cocoons and spend the winter.

Chemical control is difficult, especially on larger trees, but if adequate spraying equipment is available, infestations may be reduced by spraying fenitrothion, pirimiphos-methyl or permethrin 4 weeks after petal fall (about mid-June) and again 3 weeks later to kill the caterpillars before they enter the fruits. Overwintering caterpillars can be trapped by tying sacking or corrugated cardboard bands around the trunks and branches in July, and then removing them and destroying the caterpillars during the winter. Such measures are likely only to affect subsequent infestations if practised rigorously over a fairly large area.

Pheromone traps, which capture male codling moths, can be used to monitor the emergence of moths and time spray applications more accurately. The traps can also help to reduce infestations by reducing the number of males and hence fertilized females.

APPLE SAWFLY caterpillars tunnel in the fruitlets and they attack earlier in the season than codling moths. Infested fruits fall off the trees in June–July. The caterpillars overwinter in the soil. Permethrin, pirimiphos-methyl or fenitrothion applied thoroughly immediately after petal fall kills the caterpillars. Picking and destroying infested fruitlets in June also helps to limit later attacks.

APPLE APHIDS of at least 4 species infest buds, young shoots and leaves, sometimes causing distortion to foliage and fruits. Eggs overwinter on the trees and hatch from March onwards. A fifth species, the WOOLLY APHID, overwinters as young nymphs, not eggs, and causes swollen lumps on the woody stems and branches.

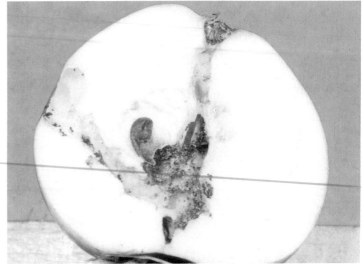

(Above) *Apple attacked by codling moth: the maggots' excrement inside the fruit.*

Canker damage which will eventually girdle and kill the branch.

Thorough spraying with tar oil in late December or early January kills overwintering eggs. Spraying with pirimicarb, dimethoate or heptenophos at the green cluster bud stage checks initial infestations. Woolly aphid colonies are spot-treated by brushing on a spray-strength solution of the above, or by applying one of them as a drenching spray when the pest is seen.

APPLE SUCKERS suck sap from blossom trusses inducing discoloration and other symptoms which resemble frost damage. The insects resemble aphids but are more

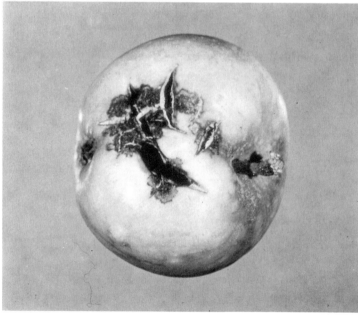

(Above) *Sawfly damage to apples; they attack the fruits earlier than codling moth caterpillars.*

(Below) *Scab infection on a 'Cox'.*

can cause a lot of damage when numerous. Thorough spraying with permethrin, fenitrothion or pirimiphosmethyl at the green cluster bud stage kills the young caterpillars. Placing greasebands around the trunks in late October may also trap wingless females as they climb up the trees from the soil to lay their eggs. Vegetable greases are used, which may be applied as prepared paper strips. Animal or mineral greases should not be used because they can cause permanent injury to the bark.

FRUIT TREE RED SPIDER MITE may build up on the leaves in early summer causing discoloration which may be followed by severe bronzing and premature leaf fall. Populations may be kept down by natural predators but the mite becomes a problem when these are destroyed by the use of tar-oil washes during the winter or by persistent insecticides after flowering. Mite eggs overwinter on the trees and hatch from May onwards. Spraying thoroughly with malathion, pirimiphosmethyl or dimethoate may check this pest when symptoms are seen. The use of mancozeb for scab also helps to suppress it. Heavy infestations are difficult to control and there is a possibility that pesticide-resistant strains of the mite may occur.

Diseases

CANKER, a serious disease of apples, shows as sunken cankers on the shoots, which can cause severe die-back if the branches are girdled. Remove badly affected smaller branches. On the larger branches cut out diseased tissues until left with a clean wound, and paint with a proprietary canker paint. The normal spraying programme designed for apple scab (*see below*) based on a systemic fungicide should keep the disease in check. In severe cases spray with Bordeaux mixture or carbendazim according to the manufacturer's instructions. Canker is often worse on trees in poorly drained soil.

SCAB shows as brown or blackish scabs on the fruit and, in severe cases, the fruit may crack. Small blisters develop on shoots and later become scab-like. Leaves are also affected and show olive-green blotches, and often fall prematurely. Remove these scabby shoots. Spray with mancozeb from the early stages of bud development according to the

flattened. Winter measures applied to control aphid eggs also control those of suckers. The active stages can be controlled at green cluster stage with dimethoate, fenitrothion or permethrin.

CAPSID BUGS feed on buds, leaves and young fruits, causing corky bumps and other malformations of the fruit, and tattered holes in the leaves. Malathion, dimethoate or fenitrothion applied immediately after flowering checks the damage.

WINTER MOTH caterpillars feed in spring on young leaves, flowers and fruitlets and manufacturer's instructions, or apply benomyl or carbendazim or thiophanate-methyl, also as instructed by the manufacturer.

POWDERY MILDEW. At bud burst diseased leaves emerge already covered with a white powdery coating of fungal spores. Affected blossoms and leaves wither and fall. The fungus overwinters in dormant buds. Remove and burn badly affected shoots. Spray with benomyl, carbendazim, thiophanate-methyl or bupirimate with triforine, starting at bud burst, and repeating according to the manufacturer's instructions.

BROWN ROT is caused by a fungus which enters through wounds. Affected fruits should be removed and burned as soon as noticed, whether on the tree, on the ground or in the store, because the disease cannot be controlled very effectively by spraying with a fungicide.

BITTER PIT affects only fruits, producing slightly sunken pits on the surface of the skin and small brown areas of tissue immediately beneath the pits and scattered throughout the flesh. The exact cause is unknown, but it appears to be connected with a shortage of water at critical times. It can be avoided to some extent by mulching well to conserve moisture and by watering in dry periods. It also apparently results from conditions within the tree that induce a deficiency of calcium (see p.25) within the fruits. The incidence of bitter pit can be greatly reduced by applying sprays of hydrated calcium nitrate at the rates and intervals suggested by the manufacturer.

HONEY FUNGUS frequently brings about the sudden death of apple trees. The fungus shows as white fan-shaped sheets of growth beneath the bark of the roots and the trunk of the tree at ground level. Affected plants should be dug out with as many of the roots as possible and the soil should be sterilized or be changed completely. A proprietary product containing a phenolic emulsion could also be used.

FIREBLIGHT see p.87.

(Top) Canker on an apple shoot, showing the damaged tissue and the red fruiting bodies of the fungus.

(Above) External signs of bitter pit.

(Left) Mildew infection on a young shoot.

'Ashmead's Kernel', a russet apple of delicious flavour, ready for eating from December to February.

'Lane's Prince Albert', a heavy cropping cooking apple, in season from December to March; susceptible to mildew.

(Right) 'St Edmund's Pippin', another russet of excellent flavour; ready from late September to October.

(Far right) 'Fiesta', an excellent eating apple, in season from October to February.

Pears

Pears need more warmth and sunshine than apples do to grow and fruit well. They flower earlier and are more at risk from late spring frosts, and young leaves are easily damaged by strong winds. Select a warm, sheltered position which is not a frost pocket. If the garden is exposed, some kind of windbreak will be needed (see pp.9–12).

Soils

Pears grow successfully in a fairly wide range of soils, from sandy loam to clay loam soils. They are less tolerant than apples of drought, but more tolerant of wetter soils.

Pears do badly on shallow soils over chalk due to lack of moisture and to lime-induced chlorosis (see p.8), which results from iron and manganese deficiences (see pp.24, 25). A satisfactory depth of soil is 18 to 24 inches (45–60cm). In a light, sandy soil, moisture retention is improved by incorporating bulky organic material.

Rootstocks

Quince selections are usually used as rootstocks for pears because they induce fruiting at an early age and, being moderately vigorous to semi-dwarfing, are ideal for most forms. 'Malling Quince A' and 'Malling Quince C' are suitable for the general range of trees in the small garden. Trees on 'Quince C' start fruiting slightly earlier and make smaller trees than those on 'Quince A', but the rootstock is not suitable for less fertile soils.

Some pear cultivars do not make a good union with quince and need to be double worked. This is a technique in which a short piece of another pear cultivar that is compatible with both is grafted between rootstock and scion. The cultivar most widely used as an intermediate is 'Beurré Hardy'. Cultivars requiring double working on quince include 'Bristol Cross', 'Dr Jules Guyot', 'Doyenné d'Eté', 'Marguerite Marillat', 'Marie Louise', 'Packham's Triumph', 'Souvenir du Congrès', 'Thompson's' and most clones of 'Williams' Bon Chrétien'.

Pollination

All pear cultivars are best regarded as self-sterile, needing pollen from another cultivar to set a good crop of fruit. If there is space for only 2 or 3 trees, choose dif-

Pear espalier ('Gorham') in blossom in spring.

Cordon pears on a building at East Malling Research Station. It is not easy to grow a cordon so tall, but has here been successfully done by experts.

ferent cultivars which can pollinate each other (*see* pp.216, 218).

Tree form and yield

Pears in the open are usually grown in bush form, as it is easily managed. When mature a bush yields an average of 40 to 50 lb (18–23 kg) of pears each year, sometimes much more, depending upon season and tree size. Standard trees are too large for most gardens.

For small gardens one of the restricted forms should be considered – a dwarf pyramid, cordon or espalier. Occasionally a pear is fan-trained. A mature dwarf pyramid bears about 8 to 12 lb (3.5–5.5 kg) of fruit, a cordon 3 to 5 lb (1.3–2.2 kg), and an espalier about 20 to 30 lb (9–13.5 kg), depending upon the number of tiers.

Bush tree

Rootstocks and spacing
'Quince A' (semi-vigorous) is the best all-round stock. Plant at 12 to 15 feet (3.6–4.5m) apart.

'Quince C' (moderately dwarfing) is suitable for fertile soils and vigorous cultivars. Plant at 10 to 14 feet (3–4.3m) apart.

Pruning

A maiden tree at planting. The aim is to produce a goblet-shaped tree with a strong framework of branches growing upwards and outwards.

In the first winter cut back the maiden whip to a good bud at about 27 to 30 inches (70–75cm) with at least 3 more good buds below it.

A feathered maiden may be cut back to a strong young lateral at about 20 to 30 inches (50–75 cm), where there are at least 2, preferably 3, more well-placed laterals immediately beneath. These represent the first branches and should then be cut back by two-thirds to an upward-facing bud. Remove all other laterals flush with the main stem.

(Above) Spur pruning in winter, showing the cut made in the previous year. The top bud has made extension growth, the lower buds have developed into fruit buds.

Opposite:
(Above left) Pruning a maiden to form an open centred bush tree: cut to a bud about 27 to 30 inches (67–75cm) above ground.
(Above right) A 2-year old tree has each leader pruned by half to two-thirds, cutting to an outward facing bud;
(Below left) Pruning completed and (below right) the wounds painted.

In the second winter, or with a 2-year-old tree at planting, select between 3 and 6 evenly spaced branches and prune the leader of each by one-half to two-thirds to an outward-facing bud (to encourage the branches to grow upwards and out-wards). Remove any shoots on the main stem below the selected branches, flush with the stem.

Pruning 3- and 4-year-old trees. In the third and fourth winters, the leading shoots of each branch should be pruned by between a half and two-thirds, to out-ward-facing buds. Laterals not wanted as part of the main framework can be spur-pruned by cutting them back to 3 or 4 buds. Strong laterals which have been selected to become branches, may be cut back by removing between one-quarter and one-third, usually to outward-facing buds (most pears are of fairly upright habit).

Remove any shoots crowding the centre unless the cultivar has a pro-nounced spreading habit, as 'Williams' Bon Chrétien' does. A few strong upright laterals may be left in the middle as even-tual replacements for branches which become too low or too far out.

Pruning established trees (winter). Nearly all pears bear fruit on short spurs on 2-year-old and older wood. Some are more vigorous than others, and the later-als of these should be pruned back to 3 or 4 buds to induce spur formation.

Spur-pruning is not suitable for tip bearers such as 'Josephine de Malines' and 'Jargonelle', and a large proportion of the laterals on these should not be pruned. The strongest ones are pruned to 3 or 4 buds. The leaders of tip bearers may be pruned by about one-third to encourage extension growth and the pro-duction of more tip-bearing laterals.

In older trees, a branch may have to be removed now and again to let in more light and air, and it can be cut back to the crotch or to a replacement branch. Spur systems which have become too long and branched may be shortened and thinned. If necessary, pears can be cut back harder than apples without producing rampant growth.

Cordon

Rootstocks and spacing
(Details of the necessary support fence are given on p.16.)

If there is a choice of rootstock, choose 'Quince C' which has a more dwarfing effect than 'Quince A'.

Plant at 2½ feet (75cm) apart, at an angle of 45°, with the scion part of the union uppermost to reduce the risk of breakage and of the scion rooting. Incline the cordons so that the tops point towards the north.

Space the rows 6 feet (1.8m) apart and, for preference, run the rows north-south to reduce the amount of mutual shading.

Pruning
If a maiden tree is planted, the only pruning needed in the first winter is to cut back any side shoots longer than 4 inches (10cm) to 3 buds. Thereafter pruning is done only in the summer except on an old neglected cordon where spur thinning might be necessary. Such pruning is done in the winter.

Two- and 3-year-old cordons at planting should not need pruning, but if there are laterals (previous summer's growth) longer than 4 inches (10cm), cut these back to 3 buds.

Summer pruning (Modified Lorette Sys-tem). Summer pruning of pears can be

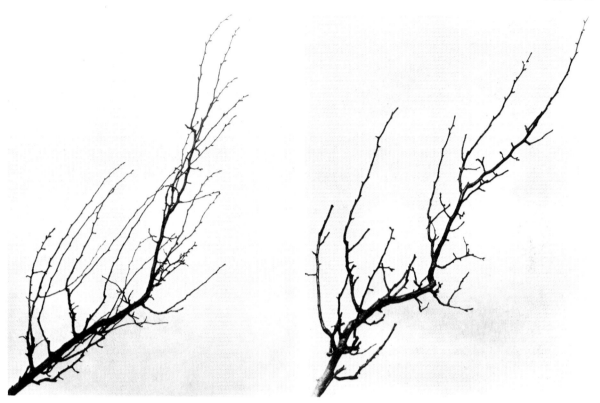

(Above) *Spur bearer before winter pruning.*

(Right) *After pruning: the laterals were spur pruned to 4 buds or to fruit buds on 2-year-old wood, where there is no room to extend the spur system. Branch leaders are cut by about a quarter.*

Opposite:
Dwarf pyramid pruning.
A. Two-year-old pear before pruning.
B. After pruning; the centre leader pruned to 10 inches (25cm), and the laterals to 8 inches (20cm).
C. Before summer pruning in July (see p.78).
D. The same tree in the following winter after the central leader has been cut back to 10 inches (25cm).
E. The same tree in the following July before summer pruning.
F. After summer pruning (see p.78).
G. A 5-year-old pyramid pear in winter.

started about a week earlier than with apples, because the shoots mature slightly earlier. At about the third week of July in southern England, later further north, cut back all mature side shoots of 9 inches (22cm) or longer arising directly from the main stem to 3 leaves above the basal cluster, and those from spur systems to 1 leaf. Mature shoots are dark brown, brittle and woody at the base. In a wet summer, or in the wetter areas of the country, it is best to delay the summer pruning until some time in August or the buds may sprout again. Leave any immature shoots until September before pruning or they too may start to grow again. Shoots shorter than 9 inches (22cm) which probably have a fruit bud at their tips should not be pruned.

The leader is not usually pruned, but trained up the cane throughout the summer. If growth has been weak, however, or if no side shoots are produced, prune the leader by about one-third in the winter. This should stimulate new growth in the following summer. (See also Notching, p.52).

To obtain an extra length of fruiting wood when the cordon has reached the top wire, it and its cane may be carefully

lowered by about 5° each year and then every time re-tied. Take it no lower than 35° to the horizontal, or the stem may break.

Once the cordon has reached the desired height, the leader (previous summer's growth) should be pruned back to ½ inch (1cm) each May.

Dwarf pyramid

Rootstocks and spacing
'Quince A' or 'Quince C' is suitable. Plant at 4 to 5 feet (1.2–1.5m) apart in the row and a minimum of 6 feet (1.8m) between the rows. The rows should run north–south if possible.

Pruning
At planting, cut back the main stem of a maiden tree to a bud about 20 inches (50cm) above the ground, and any side shoots to a bud about 5 inches (13cm) from the main stem. A well feathered maiden, however, is pruned as if it were a 2 year old. Cut central leader to 10 inches (25cm) above the topmost lateral. Shorten laterals to 8 inches (20cm).

The following winter, cut back the leader to leave about 10 inches (25cm), to a bud on the side of the shoot opposite the cut in the previous winter. This helps to keep the main stem straight. Prune laterals to 6 to 8 inches (15–20cm) to a downward- or outward-pointing bud. During the first few years remove any blossoms produced on the central leader, to encourage the growth of side branches.

In subsequent summers (late July in southern England, early August further north), cut mature branch leaders to 5 or 6 leaves beyond the basal cluster of leaves. Prune laterals arising directly from the branches to 3 leaves, and those from existing laterals or spurs to 1 leaf beyond the basal cluster. Pruning of any immature leaders or laterals should be left until late autumn, when any secondary growth from shoots pruned earlier in the summer can be cut back to 1 bud.

In subsequent winters, also continue pruning the central leader to leave 8 to 10 inches (20–25cm) of new growth. When the trees have reached about 7 feet (2.1m) they may be kept at this height by pruning the central leader in May to about $\frac{1}{2}$ inch (1cm). Any other shoots that need restriction – such as those growing into an adjacent tree, or those competing with the main leader – can be pruned in the same way at this time.

Any thinning out of the branches or spurs that is needed on older trees should be done in winter.

Espalier

Rootstocks and spacing
'Quince A' (semi-vigorous) is suitable for most conditions. Plant at 12 to 15 feet (3.6–4.5cm) apart.

'Quince C' (moderately dwarfing) is only suitable where a tree of 2 or 3 tiers is required and conditions for growth are good. Plant at 10 to 12 feet (3–3.6m) apart.

Support system
Horizontal wires (galvanised, gauge 10) should be stretched at 12 to 18 inches (30–45cm) apart to coincide with the spacing of the tiers on the espalier supplied by the nursery. If starting with a maiden tree, fix the first wire at 15 to 18 inches (38–45cm) above the ground, and those farther above at 15 inches (38cm) apart.

Pruning and training
In the first winter after planting a maiden whip, cut it back to a good bud about 2 inches (5cm) above the first wire, as near as possible to a point where there are

(Opposite) *Forming an espalier:*
(Top) *during the first summer two selected shoots to form the first tier were trained along canes set at 45°.*
(Centre) *The shoots are now tied down to the horizontal in autumn.*
(Bottom) *Pruning to form the second tier. Cut to a bud just above the wire, ensuring that there are 2 good buds just below, one pointing left and the other to the right.*

(Right) *A 4-tier espalier: just before summer pruning (above), and after pruning (below): laterals, directly from the tiers, longer than 9 inches (22cm) have been pruned to 3 leaves, and those from spurs are pruned to 1 leaf.*

2 good buds fairly close below it (not necessarily next to one another). One bud should face right and the other left. The shoots produced from these 2 buds are to form the first tier. When growth starts, rub out any bud between these three.

In the first summer, tie the shoot that grows from the top bud to an upright cane fastened to the wires. The shoots from the 2 lower buds should also be tied to canes, initially fixed at an angle of 45° from upright (because shoots grow more vigorously at a more upright angle than horizontal). If one shoot grows faster than the other, raise the slower one to a more vertical position. In October, lower both side shoots and canes to 90° with the main stem and tie them to the first wire.

To form subsequent tiers, the pruning described as for the first winter should be repeated. Cut the central leader to a bud just above the next wire, ensuring that there are 2 good buds to the left and right beneath it. Once the top wire has been reached then only 2 shoots should be allowed to grow from the vertical leader, and these are brought down to the horizontal in the same way as those of the first tier.

Each summer the shoots selected to form the new tiers should be treated in the same way as those in the first year.

(For treatment of the laterals on the tiers see below.)

The leading shoot of each existing tier should be pruned only if growth has been poor and needs to be stimulated by winter pruning. Tip the previous summer's growth by one-quarter to one-third, pruning to an upward-facing bud.

Established espalier. Each tier is pruned on the Modified Lorette System. In about the third week of July, later in the north, prune mature laterals of current season's growth that are longer than 9 inches (22cm) and arising directly from the tiers, to 3 leaves beyond the basal cluster, and those from existing spurs to 1 leaf. Spurs arising from the central stem should also be pruned in the same way.

The leading shoots from the tiers should not be pruned in the summer but tied at an angle of about 45°. In autumn, after the leaves have fallen, tie them down to the horizontal. Once a tier has reached the required length, prune back its leader to $\frac{1}{2}$ inch (1cm) every May.

On old espaliers spur systems which have become too long or complicated need to be shortened or simplified. This is done in the winter: subsequent growth is pruned in the summer (as described above).

Summer pruning: a shoot arising from an existing spur is pruned to 1 leaf beyond the basal cluster.

(Above) *Shoots that are too immature for summer pruning. These should be pruned later when they are 'ripe' and longer than 9 inches (22cm).*
(Right) *Thinning young fruits to 1 per cluster, or 2 where there is a good show of leaves.*

Grassing down

Pears grow best in clean soil conditions, because the quince rootstock on which they are grafted suffers if there is too much competition from the grass for water. But they can be grown in grass, provided that an area free of grass and weeds, and not less than 18 inches (45cm) radius, is maintained around the base. With closely-spaced trees such as cordons and dwarf pyramids, maintain a clean band 3 feet (90cm) wide down the row.

Feeding and watering

Young pear trees benefit from an annual mulch of well rotted manure, compost or straw applied in February to a depth of about 2 inches (5cm) over a radius of 18 inches (45cm), keeping it just clear of the trunk.

Round established trees apply annual top dressings of sulphate of potash at $\frac{3}{4}$ oz per sq. yd (25g/m²) in January and sulphate of ammonia at 1 to 1½ oz per sq. yd (33–50g/m²) in February. Superphosphate is needed only every third year, at 2 oz per sq. yd (65g/m²).

Pears require plenty of water in the growing season. A shortage can result in poor shoot growth, heavy fruitlet drop, small fruits, poor flavour, and cracking of the skin.

In dry weather apply about 9 gal. per sq. yd (50 litres/m²) over the rooting area every ten days, until rain restores the soil to field capacity.

Fruit thinning

Thin after the natural drop in June, when the fruitlets start to swell and turn downwards. Thin to 1 fruit or, where there is a good leaf cover, to 2 fruits per cluster.

Supporting heavily laden branches
To avoid any risk of branch breakages, support heavily laden branches by propping them up, tying them to stronger limbs or by 'maypoling' (*see photo, p.59*).

Picking

The time for picking is of great importance for pears. The fruits should not be left to ripen completely on the tree, but ought to be picked while they are still firm. Ripening varies with season and locality, but as the time of picking approaches, the ground colour of the fruits changes almost imperceptibly from dark green to a slightly lighter shade. This sign is not always reliable in our climate, however, and the best test of readiness is actually to lift the fruit slightly and then twist it gently on the stalk. If it parts easily from the spur, it is time to pick. Pick selectively, because not all pears are ready at the same time. It is particularly important with cultivars ripening in July, August and September that they are not left on the tree until they are fully ripe, because by this time they may be found to have become over-ripe and mealy in the centre. Examples are 'Jargonelle', 'Beth', 'Williams' Bon Chrétien' and 'Gorham'. Once off the tree, especially in warm conditions, they become ripe within a very short time. Store them in a cool place and check them over often to catch them at their peak of ripeness.

Late season cultivars must not be picked too early or they tend to shrivel and fail to develop their full flavour. Leave them until they part easily from the spur and then pick. They are still hard at this stage, but will soften and ripen some time afterwards.

Very late cultivars, such as 'Catillac', 'Black Worcester' and 'Olivier de Serres', should be left on the tree as long as possible. When the first fruits drop, pick the rest quickly.

Storage

The same general principles as for apples apply (see p.61), except that pears keep longer in lower temperatures, ideally between 32° and 34°F (0° and 1°C). This is seldom possible for amateurs, although pears also keep well in the bottom of a refrigerator (but not below freezing).

The fruits are best not wrapped but laid out singly on shelves or trays where they can easily be inspected frequently. This is especially important as they ripen, for most pears are at their best for only a very short period.

Pears show only a slight change in skin colour, from green to yellow-green, during normal storage, and they do not always soften as they ripen in these conditions. They can be ripened and conditioned properly if those nearing ripeness are brought into a warm room for a few days before eating. When ready, a pear should give slightly if pressed gently at the stalk end.

Pears kept in polythene bags are liable to suffer from internal rots.

(Above) 'Conference' is an old but reliable pear, and relatively hardy.

(Centre) 'Doyenné du Comice', is the best flavoured of all pears, ripening in November.

(Right) 'Merton Pride', a September pear of excellent flavour.

Table 7 **Recommended cultivars** (see ▶

Cultivar	Po	Approx. picking
Dessert		
Jargonelle + (T)	3	first week Augu
Williams' Bon Chrétien* +	3	end of August
Beth	4	late Aug./early
Onward*	4	early/mid-Sept.
Merton Pride* + (T)	3	early Sept.
Gorham	4	early Sept.
Fondante d'Automne*	3	mid-Sept.

4–5)

eason of use	Fruit size and quality	Cropping	Vigour and habit	Other characteristics
ugust	Medium; juicy, sweet, musky flavour	Heavy	Moderate, spreading straggling	Tip bearer; fruits very soon over; scab resistant
arly to mid-Sept.	Medium to large; very juicy, sweet, strong, musk flavour	Good, regular	Moderately vigorous somewhat spreading	Will not pollinate Louise Bonne of Jersey, Seckle or Fondante d'Automne; spurs freely; scab-prone; fairly hardy
eptember	Small; good, sweet, juicy flesh	Good	Moderate, upright	Spurs freely; precocious – soon into bearing like an early Williams; hardy
ate Sept./early Oct.	Medium; flesh creamy white, melting, juicy, excellent flavour	Good	Moderate, upright	Spurs freely; unsuitable as a pollinator for Doyenné du Comice and vice versa; hardy
nid- to late Sept.	Large; flesh creamy, melting, juicy, fine texture, excellent flavour	Good	Moderate to strong, spreading	Spurs freely; sometimes biennial
nid- to late Sept.	Small to medium; juicy, musky flavour	Moderate	Moderate, upright	Spurs freely; fairly hardy
ept./Oct.	Medium; flesh white, melting juicy, excellent flavour	Moderate	Dwarfish, spreading	Will not pollinate Williams', Bon Chrétien, Seckle or Louise Bonne of Jersey; fairly hardy

'Gorham', a good pollinator for 'Doyenné du Comice'.

'Louise Bonne of Jersey', for eating in October.

Table 7   (Continued)

Cultivar	Po	Approx. picking time
Bristol Cross +	4	mid-Sept.
Beurré Hardy	3	mid-Sept.
Beurré Superfin*	3	mid/late Sept.
Louise Bonne of Jersey	2	mid/late Sept.
Pitmaston Duchess (T)	4	mid/late Sept.
Durondeau	3	end Sept.
Thompson's*	3	end Sept.
Concorde*	4	end Sept.
Conference	3	end Sept.
Emile d'Heyst	2	end Sept.
Seckle*	2	end Sept.
Doyenné du Comice*	4	early/mid-Oct.
Beurré Alexandre Lucas (T)	2	early/mid-Oct.
Joséphine de Malines*	3	early/mid-Oct.
Glou Morceau	4	mid-Oct.
Olivier de Serres*	3	mid/end-Oct.
Culinary		
Catillac (T)	4	end-Oct.

Notes (see pp.216–218)
Po = Pollination group. *Very good flavour. + Incom
(T) Triploid; unsuitable as a pollinator.

on of use	Fruit size and quality	Cropping	Vigour and habit	Other characteristics
Sept./Oct.	Medium; flesh white, slightly gritty, sweet, moderate flavour	Good	Moderate, upright and then spreading	Spurs freely; does not produce much viable pollen; unsuitable as a pollinator
·ber	Medium to large; flesh white, tender, juicy, rose-water flavour	Good	Vigorous and upright	Regular, fairly hardy; slow to bear; good autumn colour
·ber	Medium; rich, sweet, perfumed flavour	Good	Moderate, spreading	Gather before fully mature; apt to rot at core during storage
·ber	Small to medium; flesh white, melting, good flavour	Good	Moderate, upright, spreading	Regular, fairly hardy; will not pollinate Williams' Bon Chrétien, Fondante d'Automne or Seckle
/Nov.	Large to very large; sweet, pleasantly flavoured; dual purpose	Heavy	Very vigorous, upright, then spreading	Unsuitable for a small garden; scab-prone; attractive autumn colour
/Nov.	Medium to large; flesh white, melting, sweet, juicy, well flavoured	Very good	Moderate, upright, compact	Regular, fairly hardy; good autumn colour; scab-prone
/Nov.	Medium to large; flesh white, melting, buttery, excellent	Irregular	Moderate, upright	Best against a warm wall; good autumn colour
Oct./Nov.	Medium; flesh yellow, buttery, juicy, with a sweet pleasant flavour	Good	Moderate, upright then spreading	Precocious, reliable cropper; fairly hardy
/Nov.	Medium; flesh yellow, slight pinkish tinge, melting, juicy, sweet	Heavy	Moderate, upright, spreading	Regular, reliable, hardy, but must be sheltered to prevent skin being marred by cold winds and frost
/Nov.	Medium; flesh yellowish melting, sub-acid, good flavour	Good	Moderate to dwarfish spreading	Hardy; attractive autumn colour
/Nov.	Small; very sweet, rich flavour	Moderate, fairly reliable	Rather weak, upright, compact	Will not pollinate Fondante d'Automne, Louise Bonne of Jersey or Williams' Bon Chrétien
Oct/Nov.	Medium large to large; flesh creamy white, melting, juicy, rich flavour	Irregular	Vigorous, upright	Requires a warm, sunny situation; susceptible to scab
/Jan.	Large; flesh white, melting, highly perfumed	Heavy	Vigorous, spreading	Fairly hardy; unsuitable as a pollinator
/Jan.	Small to medium; flesh slightly pinkish, melting, sweet, deliciously perfumed	Good	Moderate to weak; good, rather weeping	Tip bearer; requires a warm situation
/Jan.	Medium-large; flesh white, smooth, rich flavour	Good	Growth moderate; compact	Best on a sunny wall or in a sunny garden
/Mar.	Small to medium, apple-shaped; flesh white, melting, aromatic	Irregular	Growth rather weak, dwarfish, spreading	Requires a warm wall or sunny sheltered garden
/Apr.	Large; flesh hard, greenish white	Heavy	Growth stout, vigorous spreading	A stewing pear only; large flowers; fairly hardy

·rtly incompatible with quince rootstocks, therefore best double-worked.

**Promising new dessert-cultivar
Malling Concorde**. A Conference-type
pear, but promises to be of better eating
quality and with heavier cropping
capacity.

Pests

BIRDS, especially tits, peck ripening pears.
Protect them with netting or enclose
individual fruits in nylon or muslin bags.
Bullfinches destroy flower buds in the
winter, but 'Doyenné du Comice' is
relatively immune.

APHIDS infest young growth and distort
the leaves. Spray with tar oil in December
or January to kill over-wintering eggs, or
at petal fall with one of the chemicals
recommended for apple aphids (see p.68)
to kill young aphids.

PEAR LEAF BLISTER MITES produce characteristic pustules in the leaves which
first appear in May as pale green or pink
spots but later become brown or black.
Severe infestations may cause premature
leaf fall but most do little permanent
harm. If highly infested, hand-pick and
destroy affected leaves in the summer.
None of the pesticides currently available
gives good control, so extensive infestations have to be tolerated.

PEAR MIDGE is a localized pest which may
attack the same tree year after year. Small
orange-white maggots feed in the young
fruitlets, which are distorted and dis-

coloured and drop prematurely. Collection and destruction of infested fruitlets reduces the numbers of maggots
carried over from one season to the next.
Spray with HCH or fenitrothion at the
early white bud stage.

WINTER MOTH **caterpillars** see p.69.

PEAR AND CHERRY SLUGWORM caterpillars
are black, slimy, slug-like larvae that
graze away the leaf surface. Damage
occurs in May–June and July–August.

(Above) *Protecting the
fruits: a fine mesh ³⁄₁₆ inch
(4mm) nylon bag (left); a
clear polythene bag with a
hole cut in each corner to
allow moisture to drain
away (right).*

(Below) *Fruits showing
infection by pear scab.*

(Above left) *Pear leaf blister mite damages the leaves; some control can be obtained by picking off damaged leaves.*

(Above right) *Symptoms of fireblight on Pyronia (pear × quince) progressing down the twig. The brown dead leaves hanging on the shoot is a typical sign of infection although on pear the leaves usually turn a darker brown.*

(Right) *Pear midge is sometimes troublesome; the maggot-infested fruitlets will drop early.*

Control by spraying with derris, fenitrothion, permethrin or malathion.

CODLING MOTH (*see* p.68) is an occasional problem on pears but routine control measures are unnecessary in most years.

Diseases

SCAB shows on the fruit as blackish scabs and in severe cases cracking occurs. On leaves it produces olive-green blotches, and affected shoots become blistered and scabby. Diseased shoots should be cut and burned. Spray with benomyl, carbendazim or thiophanate-methyl or use mancozeb or thiram (except on fruit to be preserved) all at the rates and times suggested by the manufacturer on the label of the product.

FIREBLIGHT causes the flowers to become blackened and shrivelled. It then spreads down the shoots causing them to die back, but the leaves on affected shoots, although brown and withered, do not fall. Fireblight is no longer a notifiable disease. If it is suspected cut out and burn all infected wood to about 3 feet (90cm) past obvious damage. As this may not leave much of the plant it may be more satisfactory to cut down and burn the entire tree.

CANKER (*see* p.69) can affect pears, especially the cultivar 'Fertility'.

BROWN ROT (*see* p.70) is frequently troublesome on pears.

HONEY FUNGUS *see* p.70.

Plums

Plums form one of the main groups of the stone fruits which includes gages and the smaller fruited damsons and bullaces. The emphasis on this section is on plums and gages, because these are more widely grown in gardens. Cultivation is the same for all unless indicated otherwise.

Plums grow in a wide range of different soils, provided they are well drained. The ideal soil is a fairly heavy clay loam, at least 24 inches (60cm) deep and with a pH between 6.0 and 6.5. (Plums do not require a high lime content.)

They all flower early in spring and must be planted where there is the least likelihood of frost at flowering. Avoid a low-lying situation. Ripening gages are susceptible to splitting and rot infection in wet weather, and so are likely to do best in areas of high sunshine and low rainfall. But they like plenty of moisture at the roots throughout the growing season. Damsons do well in the wetter parts of the country.

The finest flavoured gages and dessert plums are produced on a warm south or west wall, and fans are the most suitable tree-form. An east aspect is suitable for cooking plums and early to mid-season eating plums, and early-ripening cookers can be grown in a north aspect. In the open, plums are usually grown as bushes or half standards, but pyramid trees are also suitable for gardens. Standards are too large for most gardens.

Many plums and gages, including 'Victoria', are self-fertile and fruit well when planted on their own. Others require pollen from another cultivar to fruit well. Guidance on choosing pollen associates is given in the table on p.219.

One serious problem with plums is bird damage to the flower buds in the winter, which is more likely near woodland. The only solution to this problem is to grow trees that can be netted such as fan and pyramid forms, see pp.91 and 92.

Rootstocks

Not all rootstocks used for plums are compatible with every cultivar, and some are too vigorous for the average garden. The recommended rootstocks are 'St Julien A' and 'Pixy', both of which are easily available and compatible with all plum cultivars. 'St Julian A' is semi-vigorous and suitable for all forms. As a bush it makes a tree about 12 to 15 feet (3.6–4.5m) in height and spread. 'Pixy', a relatively new rootstock, is dwarfing but requires a fertile soil and generous feeding. Trees on this stock are about half to two-thirds the size of those on 'St Julien A'. It is satisfactory for the bush and pyramid and is showing promise as being suitable for the cordon, a form not usually used for plums because of the extra vigour of other stocks. 'Mussel' (semi-dwarfing) is sometimes used by nurseries, but is inclined to sucker badly. 'Brompton' (vigorous) is compatible with all cultivars, but is rather too vigorous for the garden; it is suitable for standards. 'Myrobalan B' is another vigorous stock which produces heavy-cropping trees, but is not compatible with a few cultivars such as 'Ouillins Golden Gage' and 'Count Althann's Gage'.

The same rootstocks are suitable for damsons, but they make smaller trees.

Tree form and yield

Plums are irregular in cropping, mainly because the flowers are often damaged by spring frosts. Yields vary according to cultivar, size of tree and treatment, so the following figures should be regarded only as a rough guide. They show, nevertheless, the potential value of a few well-grown plum trees in the garden.

A well-grown bush or half standard plum on 'St Julien A' in its first 10 years of fruiting may average a harvest of 40 to 50 lb (18–23 kg) per year, and in full bearing 100 to 120 lb (42–52 kg). On 'Pixy' the yield will be about half to two-thirds of these figures. Bigger trees on 'Myrobalan' or 'Brompton' yield more. Plum pyramids yield a little less than a bush or half standard on the same rootstock.

The shy cropping cultivars, which includes most gages, may give only one-half to two-thirds of the above.

The yield from a fan-trained tree is about 15 to 25 lb (7–11 kg) of fruit.

Planting

Plant between November and March, preferably in autumn or during a mild

Feathered maiden (i.e with lateral shoots): (left) before pruning to form a bush; (right) after pruning, the central leader cut to a lateral at 3 feet (90cm), and all laterals shortened to 3 or 4 inches (8–10cm).

period in winter. Plums start to grow early in spring, and therefore late planting may check growth at the start of the season.

Plant to a stake, driving the stake in first and then taking out a hole and planting the tree (*see* pp.34–36). Large-headed half and full standards need two vertical stakes with a crossbar. Bush trees require a single vertical stake, top diameter 2½ to 3 inches (6.5–8cm), driven about 2 feet (60cm) into the ground for good anchorage. The top of the stake should be about 3 inches (8cm) below the lowest branches on that side so that there is no risk of chafing.

After planting, mulch to a depth of 2 to 3 inches (5–8cm) to help to conserve soil moisture, but keep the material just clear of the stem. An alternative, on a good soil, is to lay a piece of black polythene about 2 feet (60cm) square around the base, with the edges of the sheet buried so that it is not blown away.

Pruning

All plums fruit on 1-year-old and 2-year-old shoots, but most pruning is done in the first years to produce a tree framework. Plums are susceptible to silver leaf infection which enters through wounds, so prune in early spring when growth has started and the tree is in a better condition to repel such infection. Paint all wounds immediately after cutting.

Half standard and bush forms

The difference between a bush and a half standard is the height of the trunk. A half standard has a clean stem of about 4½ feet (1.35cm) below the head, while a bush has a stem about 2½ to 3 feet (75–90cm). Pruning of both is similar.

Maiden trees are less expensive than a 2-year-old partly-trained tree, and can be trained as desired.

Rootstocks and spacing

'Pixy' is suitable for bush trees planted 8 to 10 feet (2.4–3m) apart; 'St Julien A' for bush and half standards planted 12 to 15 feet (3.5–4.5m) apart; and 'Brompton' or 'Myrobalan B' for half standards, planted at 18 to 22 feet (5.5–6.5m) apart.

Pruning and training

First year. In the early spring an unfeathered maiden is cut back to a bud at a height of 4½ feet (1.35m) for a half standard, and about 3 feet (90cm) for a bush. Ensure that there are 3 or 4 good buds immediately below, that can grow out to form the primary branches.

In July or August check that there are 4 or 5 well-spaced shoots suitable to become primary branches growing from the main stem, and pinch out the growing point of the remainder at 4 or 5 leaves.

If the maiden tree has strong laterals (a feathered maiden) well-placed and the

head at the right height, then some of these can be used to form the primary branches. Cut back the central stem to the topmost of the selected laterals and prune each lateral by two-thirds to a bud facing outwards. Cut back lower laterals not wanted as part of the head to 3 to 4 inches (8–10cm). These may help to thicken the stem. They should not be allowed to become dominant, but kept pinched back to 4 or 5 leaves in the summer. In the second year, they should be removed completely, back to the main stem, and the wounds painted with a wound paint.

Second year or 2-year-old newly planted tree. In the early spring choose between 3 and 5 well-placed shoots as the first branches, preferably of uniform vigour and evenly spaced around the stem. Prune these by one-half to two-thirds to an outward-facing bud. Cut out any other strong growing shoots, especially those forming narrow V-angles with the main stem, which are more likely to break under the weight of a heavy crop. Paint the pruning cuts with a wound paint.

Pruning in subsequent years. Little pruning of the young tree is needed in

(Above) *Eight year old pyramid, 'Blue Tit'.*

(Right) *A fan-trained plum against a house wall, showing the maximum use of space.*

later years, although leading shoots of cultivars with a spreading growth may need to be pruned to an upward-pointing bud in order to counteract the tendency to drooping growth. Weak-growing cultivars may also need to be stimulated to produce more vigorous growth, but first make sure that the tree has adequate water and nutrients.

As the tree become older and the head more crowded, some thinning may be necessary, although a plum tolerates a more crowded head than an apple or pear. Cut out the thin, twiggy growths and remove dead wood and broken branches. This pruning is best done in the spring or early summer, or immediately after picking, and no later than the end of August.

Pyramid

(Opposite above) *'Victoria' is self-fertile, so can be grown on its own.*

(Below) *A newly planted 2-year-old bush after pruning: note alternative method of staking, using 2 stakes and a cross-piece.*

The plum pyramid is an excellent form for the garden and has a central stem grown to a height of 6 to 9 feet (1.8–2.7m). It has a clean trunk of about 18 inches (45cm) before the first branches arise. The lower branches are longer than those above, forming a pyramid-shaped tree. It is possible to net it against birds.

The pyramid is kept compact firstly by the use of a dwarfing or semi-dwarfing rootstock, and secondly by summer pruning.

Rootstocks and planting

'St Julien A' (semi-dwarfing) is the rootstock most widely used at present though the new rootstock 'Pixy' (dwarfing) is becoming more widely available and is excellent as a small pyramid.

Plant maiden trees at 10 to 12 feet (3–3.6m) apart on 'St Julien A' or 8 to 10 feet (2.5–3m) apart on 'Pixy'.

Pyramids need to be staked at planting, but the tree should be strong enough to support itself after the first 5 or 6 years. In a sheltered garden, a stout bamboo cane 6 feet (1.8m) out of the ground is effective, but in an exposed position a tree stake is necessary.

Pruning

In April, cut back the central leader to a good bud at approximately 5 feet (1.5m) for a tree on 'St Julien A', and 4 feet (1.2m) for a tree on 'Pixy'. Remove any feathers (side shoots) within 18 inches (45cm) of the ground and cut the remainder to half their length, cutting to a bud in each case.

In the first summer in late July, when the young shoots have finished growing, shorten the branch leaders to 8 inches (20cm) just above a downward-facing bud. Prune laterals growing from these branches to 6 inches (15cm). Do not prune the central leader but tie it to the cane or stake.

In subsequent years, in April cut back the central leader (previous summer's growth) by two-thirds, to a bud on the side opposite to the bud to which the previous pruning cut was made. Once a height of 8 to 9 feet (2.5m) on 'St Julien A', or 6 to 7 feet (2m) on 'Pixy', has been reached, prune the central leader in May to 1 inch (2.5cm). Repeat this annually to maintain the heights mentioned.

In late July each year, prune branch leaders (current season's growth) to about 8 inches (20cm) to a downward-facing bud, and laterals to 6 inches (15cm) preferably to downward-pointing buds.

It is important to remove any vigorous upright shoots in the summer as soon as they are noticed, particularly those competing with the centre leader and in the top half of the tree.

Fan

For the best-flavoured plums and gages, a fan-trained tree against a warm wall is the most suitable method of growing, although the training necessary is more time-consuming than with a tree grown in the open.

Rootstocks and planting
Plant in the winter. 'St Julien A' (semi-dwarfing) is the most satisfactory rootstock. The minimum wall height for a tree on this rootstock is 7 feet (2.1m). Plant at 15 to 18 feet (4.5–5.4m) apart.

For a smaller fan, the rootstock 'Pixy' is recommended. Where more than one is planted, spacing is 10 to 12 feet (3–3.6m) apart, with 6 feet (1.8m) as the minimum height of the wall or fence.

Maiden trees can be planted, or if preferred, partly-trained trees can be bought from the nursery. Plant the trees 6 to 9 inches (20–25cm) away from the wall with the stem sloping slightly towards it. This is to allow for eventual expansion of the tree trunk; the tree's root system should in any case be away from the rainshadow of the wall.

Pruning and training
Galvanised wires, gauge 16 (1.6mm)

should be fixed horizontally to the wall at 6 inches (15cm) apart or two brick courses, starting at 15 inches (38cm) from the ground. Use 2-inch square (5 × 5cm) wooden battens fixed to the masonry or lead wall eyes to hold the wires (see p.15).

In the first spring after planting, cut back the maiden tree to a lateral shoot or a good bud at about 2 feet (60cm). Ensure that there are 2 good buds below, one facing to the right and the other to the left, about 12 inches (30cm) above the ground. If there are two well-placed laterals at this point, they can be used instead to form the first 2 ribs. Cut the 2 selected laterals by two-thirds to an upward-facing bud. Remove all other laterals.

In the first summer, the 2 selected buds should develop into 2 good shoots, or the 2 selected laterals should produce extension growth. When they are about 18 inches (45cm) long, tie them to canes which are fixed to the wires at 45° to the main stem. At the same time, the main stem above the topmost shoot should be cut out and the wound painted. Pinch back all other shoots to 1 leaf.

Pyramid pruning: prune branch leaders (above) at about 8 inches (20cm) and laterals (below) to 6 leaves, about 6 inches (15cm).

(Opposite above) A young fan 'Victoria' on 'Pixy' with 6 main ribs, on a west facing fence (see also p.33).

(Below) Pruning a maiden whip to a bud at about 2 feet (60cm) to form a fan.

The following February, cut back the 2 ribs to a bud at 12 to 18 inches (30–45cm) from the main stem. In the summer, tie in the leaders of the ribs to the canes. Also select 2 more shoots spaced about 4 to 6 inches (10–15cm) apart on the upper side of each rib, and one from below, and tie these to canes as they grow. They should radiate outwards like the ribs of a fan.

In the early spring of the next year, cut back each of these 8 new ribs to 24 to 30 inches (60–75cm) of the previous summer's growth, preferably to upward-facing buds. In the summer tie in the extension growth of the ribs to the canes, and also tie new shoots to the wires to fill in available wall space. Rub out any laterals growing directly towards the wall while they are young, and pinch back laterals growing directly away to 1 leaf.

If there is plenty of room on the wall for a large tree, repeat this training over the next year. Leave filling in the centre to the last because vertical centre growth is often too vigorous at the expense of side growth.

Pruning an established fan. Remove shoots growing directly towards the wall early in the season. Thin out the remaining laterals to 4 inches (10cm) apart. These should be kept pinched back to 6 leaves unless they are required to extend the ribs of the fan.

After the crop has been picked, remove dead wood, shorten shoots that have already been pinched to 3 leaves and do any necessary tying in. This pinching and shortening induces fruit spurs, and the tree also produces natural spurs which should need no pruning. Strong vertical shoots must be cut out or tied down towards the horizontal.

Feeding and watering

Plums grow best when given plenty of nitrogen, and are therefore better grown in clean, cultivated ground, not in grass. Annual applications of farmyard manure or compost need to be supplemented with inorganic fertilizers. To trees growing in the open, apply sulphate of ammonia at $1\frac{1}{2}$ to 2 oz per sq. yd (50–65g/m^2), and sulphate of potash at $\frac{1}{2}$ oz per sq. yd (15g/m^2) each year in addition to super-phosphate at $1\frac{1}{2}$ to 2 oz per sq. yd (50–65g/m^2) every 2 or 3 years. These fertilizers can be applied during the winter, but probably early February is the most appropriate time, because nitrogen applied too early may be washed out of the soil.

Trees growing against a wall should not be given too much nitrogen, for vigorous growth is not needed. Half the amount given above is usually adequate. Potash and phosphate amounts are the same as for trees in the open. Do not dig around the trees because any damage to the roots encourages sucker production. Weed control by hoeing or by mulching is preferable. If there are any suckers, pull them up rather than cutting them off at the soil surface, because this encourages more to be produced. The soil at the base of a wall can become very dry and the trees must be watched for any signs of dryness at the roots, and watered if necessary. Mulching also helps to conserve moisture.

Frost protection

Wall trees can be protected from spring frosts during flowering by hanging a curtain of hessian, heavy-gauge polythene,

or 2 or 3 layers of bird netting over them at night. Keep these covers off the flowers with canes (see illustration p.118).

Fruit thinning

In a year of good pollination, and if too many fruits are allowed to develop, branches are liable to be broken, and the harvested fruits tend to be small and flavourless. Young fruits need to be thinned at an early age, and a good rule is

(Above) *Damson 'Bradley's King', a prolific cropper.*

(Left) *Summer pruning of a fan after harvesting. A lateral being reduced by half, having already been 'stopped' at 6 leaves earlier in the summer.*

(Opposite above) *'Kirke's', excellent flavour but shy cropping.*
(Left) *'Jefferson', good flavour, ripens in early September.*
(Right) *'Coe's Golden Drop', best grown on a warm wall.*

to leave them about 2 to 3 inches (5–8cm) apart, but at 3 to 4 inches (8–10cm) for 'Victoria'. The first thinning is done in early June and, if necessary later in the month, a second time to allow for any fruit drop during stone-hardening.

Supporting a tree

When there is a good crop, support the branches before they start to bow down, propping them up with forked poles or by maypoling (see photo, p.59).

Harvesting

The best flavour develops when fruits are allowed to ripen on the tree – but it is not always possible to allow them to remain there for so long because of wasps, birds, and also wet weather which may cause splitting of the fruits. Fruits for preserving are best picked slightly early, but all need selective picking, so pick on 2 or 3 occasions, selecting the ripest each time.

Recommended cultivars

Many plums are self-fertile (marked s.f. in the following list); others are not, and need cross-pollination. Two regularly-flowering plums that are suited to the role of pollen donor are 'Denniston's Superb' for early blossoming and 'Oullins Gage' for late ones. 'Victoria', as a mid-season flower, is a valuable pollinator for both early and late blossoming cultivars (see also pp.218–219 for other choices).

Dessert
Herman (s.f.), mid- to late July.
Early Laxton (p.s.f.), late July to early August.
Sanctus Hubertus (s.f.), late July to early August.
Opal (s.f.), early August.
Blue Tit (s.f.), mid-August.
Oullins Gage (s.f.), mid-August.
Count Althann's Gage* (s.i.), mid- to late August.
Early Transparent* (s.f.), mid- to late August.
Goldfinch (p.s.f.), mid- to late August.
Denniston's Superb (s.f.), late August.
Victoria (s.f.), dual purpose, late August to early September.
Excalibur (s.i.), late August to early September.

(Above) *Fruits before thinning.*

Reeves Seedling* (s.i.), late August to early September.
Cambridge Gage* (p.s.f.), late August to early September.
Old Green Gage* (s.i.), late August to early September.
Jefferson* (s.i), late August to early September.
Kirke's* (s.i.), late August to early September.
Golden Transparent* (s.f.), early to mid-September.
Laxton's Delight (p.s.f.), mid-September.
Severn Cross (s.f.), mid- to late September.
Ariel (p.s.f.), mid- to late September.
Coe's Golden Drop* (s.i), late September.

Cooking
Early Rivers (p.s.f.), late July to early August.
Czar (s.f.), early August.
Black Prince (s.i.), early to mid-August.
Pershore (s.f.), mid-August.
Purple Pershore (s.f.), mid- to late August.
Belle de Louvain (s.f.), late August.
Victoria see under Dessert.
Edwards (s.i.), early to mid-September.
Warwickshire Drooper (s.f.), early to mid-September.
Marjorie's Seedling (s.f.), late September to early October.

Damsons (all self-fertile)
Merryweather, early September.
Bradley's King, mid-September.
Farleigh Damson, mid-September.
Prune*, September to October.

Abbreviations:
p.s.f. = partly self-fertile
s.f. = self-fertile
s.i. = self-incompatible
* = good flavour

(Above) *Fruits after thinning.*

(Right) *Bullfinch damage to plum buds in spring, showing one bud surviving, the rest eaten.*

Pests

APHIDS infest young shoots and also colonize the undersides of older leaves later in the summer. One species causes severe leaf curling; others befoul the foliage and fruit with honeydew and sooty mould. Spray with tar oil in December to kill overwintering eggs; or as for apple aphids (p.68) at the white bud stage to kill young aphids. Further treatment may be needed in June–July against the mealy plum aphid.

BIRDS Bullfinches are responsible for considerable damage to over-wintering fruit buds, often resulting in total loss of the crop. Preventive measures should therefore be taken where possible, either by netting or cottoning.

FRUIT TREE RED SPIDER MITE (*see* p.69) sucks sap from the leaves, causing mottled discoloration and premature leaf fall.

WINTER MOTH caterpillars (*see* p.69) feed on the young foliage. Spray at the white bud stage.

PLUM SAWFLY is an occasional pest. The larvae tunnel into the fruitlets causing them to fall while immature. If this pest has been troublesome in previous years, spray at 7 to 10 days after petal-fall with dimethoate, permethrin or pirimiphos-methyl.

PLUM FRUIT MOTH caterpillars are reddish maggots that tunnel in the mature fruit; premature ripening is often associated with this pest. It is mainly a problem in southern England. Control by spraying as for codling moth (p.68) in late June, with a second spray 2 to 3 weeks later.

Diseases

SILVER LEAF can cause progressive dieback of a tree, and a purplish brown stain is produced in the inner tissues. Leaves show a silvery discoloration. All dead branches must then be cut out to 4 to 6 inches (10–15cm) behind the point where the stain ceases. Seal all wounds with a good protective paint.

FALSE SILVER LEAF is a physiological disorder which is probably more common than true silver leaf. The foliage shows a silvery discoloration but most of the leaves on a tree are affected at the same time, and there is little or no die-back. No stain is apparent in the branch bearing silvered leaves. Malnutrition and an irregular supply of moisture in the soil can cause this trouble, so affected trees should be mulched, watered and fed as necessary.

BROWN ROT (*see* p.70) can cause serious loss of fruit, if diseased plums are not removed and destroyed.

BACTERIAL CANKER shows along the branches as elongated, flattened cankers which exude copious amounts of gum. The buds of an affected branch do not burst, or if leaves do develop they are small and yellow and eventually die. On the leaves of other branches small brown spots develop and the discoloured tissues fall away, leaving holes. Remove badly cankered branches and dead wood, and paint all wounds with a good protective paint. Spray with Bordeaux Mixture according to the manufacturer's instructions.

Sweet and duke cherries

Sweet cherries are derived from the gean, mazzard or wild cherry, *Prunus avium*. Duke cherries are thought to be a hybrid between *P. avium* and *P. cerasus*, the acid cherry, and are intermediate in character between the two, but are grown in the same way as the sweet cherry. Some sweet cherry cultivars are self-fertile and can be planted singly, but most are self-sterile and with these at least two different cultivars have to be planted to obtain cross-pollination and subsequent fertilization of the flowers (*see* pp.220–21).

There is at present no dwarfing rootstock for cherries which has been thoroughly proven, though some are in the pipeline from fruit research stations. The recently introduced 'GM9' from Belgium shows promise, but has not yet been fully tested under British conditions.

The rootstock most widely used by nurserymen is 'Colt', which is described as semi-vigorous. There is also the very vigorous 'F12/1'. 'Colt' makes a tree about 18 to 25 feet (5.5–7.5m) in height and spread on a good soil, and 'F12/1' an even larger tree. Neither is suitable for the small garden.

Until a dwarfing rootstock is available to make a small bush tree, the fan is perhaps the most suitable tree form, and is therefore described here in detail. If, however, there is room to grow a sweet cherry in the open, the tree forms and pruning are the same as for plums (*see* pp.89–91). Spacing for bush, half standard and standard forms on 'Colt' are 20 to 25 feet (6–7.5m) apart.

Soils

The cherry is tolerant of a wide range of soils provided that they are well drained. The ideal is a slightly acid medium loam not less than 2 feet (60cm) deep, with a pH of 6.5 to 6.7. Shallow soil and badly drained areas are unsuitable.

Fan

Rootstocks and planting

'Colt' (semi-vigorous). Plant 15 to 18 feet (4.5–5.5m) apart, on a wall or fence at least 8 feet (2.4m) high.

'Malling F12/1' (vigorous). Plant 18 to 24 feet (5.5–7.3m) apart. The minimum height of wall or fence for this cultivar is 10 feet (3m).

A system of wires, galvanised, gauge 16, fixed horizontally and spaced at 6 inches (15cm) apart, is necessary to support the branches.

Pruning and training

There is a greater danger of infection by silver leaf disease and bacterial canker in the winter than in the growing season, and pruning is therefore carried out in the spring just as the buds break into growth.

The fan is formed in the same way as that of a peach (for details *see* pp.108–111), but because a cherry is much more vigorous, it should be possible to fill the available space in less time. Most maiden sweet cherries are strongly feathered, and it is usually possible to use 2 lower laterals for training as primary ribs from the start, and to have a total of 8 ribs (4 on each side) by the end of the first growing season. It may be possible to use 4 laterals as primary ribs provided that they are well spaced (*see* photos, p.100). The laterals should start at about 12 to 18 inches (30–45cm) from the ground. In each instance cut out the centre of the tree immediately above the topmost selected lateral. The laterals are then cut back to an upward-facing bud at about 18 to 24 inches (45–60cm) from the centre. All other laterals are removed. The ribs are tied to the wires at angles ranging between 35° and 45° so that they radiate outwards.

In the summer the pruned laterals (the primary ribs) should produce further strong shoots, some of which can be selected to form more ribs. In the case of the tree with 2 laterals initially, the topmost shoot should be trained on as the new leader. In addition, 2 more shoots – spaced about 6 inches (15cm) apart – one from the upper side of the branch and one from the lower, should then be allowed to grow on, and should be tied to the wires. The other shoots are cut out.

A similar policy is adopted in connection with the maiden tree with 4 primary ribs, except that there is only sufficient room to train in 2 extra shoots on each, one on the upper and one on the lower

(Opposite top) 'Stella', a self-fertile cultivar.
(Top right) A 2-year-old bush before pruning: note that the buds are just breaking.
(Below left) Pruning each leader on the bush by half to an outward facing bud.
(Below right) Pruning of the bush completed.

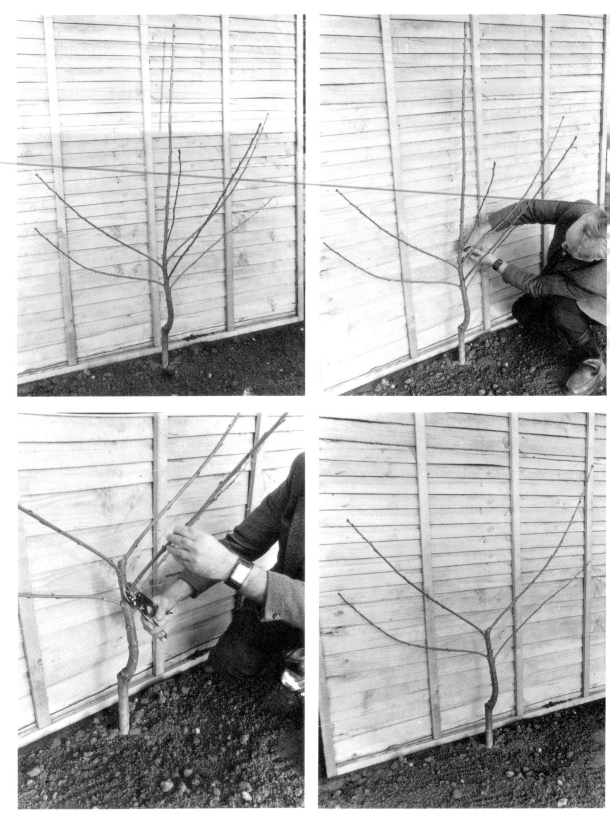

(Opposite above left) *A well-feathered maiden for training as a fan. Some of the strong well placed laterals are used for the first ribs.*

(Opposite right) *The centre leader is cut out above the topmost selected rib.*

(Opposite below left) *Remove unwanted laterals; this one is growing away from the fence.*

(Opposite below right) *Pruning nearly completed; the first four ribs are well placed.*

(Right) *Each lateral is pruned to an upward facing bud and then tied to the supporting canes.*

side. All selected shoots should be tied in as they grow.

The same pruning and training system is employed in subsequent summers until the wall space is filled. Leave the filling in of the centre of the fan to the last because vertical growth can become dominant at the expense of the growth of the side branches.

Pruning the cropping tree. Sweet cherries develop fruit buds at the base of the young laterals formed in the previous summer and on the older wood. Pruning in summer restricts vegetative growth and induces the formation of fruit buds.

Shoots growing directly towards the wall should be removed early in the spring. All others, except those that are to be trained to fill an empty space, should have their growing tips pinched out when they have made 5 or 6 leaves.

In early autumn, shorten these shoots to 3 buds, remove any dead wood, and complete the tying in of any shoots which were left to fill in wall space. Finally, check all ties and retie if there is any constriction.

Treatment of over-crowded or tall fans. After a number of years, some of the fruiting spurs become too long, project too far out from the wall, or are over-crowded. These can be shortened in the spring fairly drastically, removing one-half to two-thirds, pruning to a bud or lateral in each case. When the growth at the top of the tree has grown above the wall, either cut it back to a weaker lateral lower down or bend the shoot over and tie it down. Strong upright shoots in other parts of the fan should be cut out or tied down towards the horizontal to reduce their vigour.

All wounds larger than $\frac{1}{2}$ inch (1cm) diameter must be protected with a wound paint to guard against infection by bacterial canker or silver leaf.

Feeding

In February apply a balanced fertilizer such as Growmore at 3 oz per sq. yd (100g/m^2) over the rooting area as a top dressing. On poor soils, mulch with well rotted manure or compost to a depth of about 2 to 3 inches (5–8cm) over a radius of 18 inches (45cm), but keep the material clear of the tree trunk.

Close-up of a 2-year-old tree showing the development of fruit buds on the older wood.

A fruiting spur on a fan after pruning in summer: note the clusters of fruit buds at the base.

Cultivation

Take care that trees against walls do not become dry at the roots. A spring mulch of well rotted manure or compost helps to conserve moisture. At the start of dry weather, water around the base of the tree by applying not less than 9 gal. per sq. yd (50 litres/m²) every 10 days to keep the soil water near to field capacity. A sudden application of water to dry soil can cause ripening fruits to split.

Root pruning may be necessary if the tree becomes over-vigorous and is not fruiting (see p.137).

Netting is needed to protect the fruit from birds.

Picking

Cherries can be left on the tree until they are fully ripe, unless they start cracking because of wet weather. Pick them with the stalk intact. Once picked, eat them as soon as possible, for they quickly lose their quality. Fresh cherries freeze quite well.

Pollination

Self-fertile sweet cherries do not need cross-pollination to set a crop and therefore can be planted singly if so desired. They are also universal donors (see p.220), which means they can be used as pollinators for the self-incompatible (self-infertile) cultivars provided their times of flowering coincide. Where self-incompatible cherries are chosen, it is important to check that not only does the flowering coincide but they are compatible with each other. *See* pp.220–21 for details of flowering periods and incompatibility groups.

A sweet cherry fan, 8 years old, showing how vigorous this fruit can be and how quickly a wall or fence 15 feet × 9 feet (4.5 × 2.7m) can be filled.

Recommended cultivars

Promising new cultivar
Starkrimson, mid-July, dark red, large fruits, good quality; small tree.

Sweet cherries
Self-fertile
Stella*, late July, dark red.
Sunburst*, late July, black.
Lapins*, early August, black.

Self-incompatible
Early Rivers*, mid- to late June, dark red.
Roundel*, early July, dark red.
Merchant*, early July, black.
Merton Bigarreau*, early to mid-July, black.
Vega*, mid-July, white.
Merton Favourite, mid- to late July, dark red.
Noir de Guben*, mid- to late July, dark red.
Napoleon Bigarreau*, mid- to late July, yellow and red.
Hertford*, mid- to late July, black.
Van*, mid- to late July, dark red.

Summit*, late July, dark red.
Colney*, early August, black.

Duke cherries
May Duke (p.s.f.), early to mid-July.

Pests

BIRDS, especially starlings, eat ripe fruit; bullfinches feed on the buds during the winter. Protect with netting, if possible.
APHIDS, especially the cherry blackfly, infest young shoots causing leaf curling and checking growth. Spray tar oil in December or January to kill over-wintering eggs; or pirimicarb, dimethoate or heptenophos at the white bud stage to kill young aphids.
PEAR AND CHERRY SLUGWORM caterpillars (*see* p.86) can skeletonize the foliage.
WINTER MOTH *see* p.69.

Diseases

BACTERIAL CANKER, SILVER LEAF (*see* p.97) and BROWN ROT (*see* p.70) can affect sweet cherries.

Abbreviations:
p.s.f. = partly self-fertile
    * = good flavour

Acid cherries

Acid cherries are more suitable than sweet cherries for the garden as they form small trees. Most are self-fertile, and all tolerate some shade. As a bush in the open an acid cherry can reach a height of 10 to 12 feet (3–3.6m), and as a fan about 7 feet to 8 feet (2.1–2.4m) in height and 12 to 15 feet in spread (3.6–4.5m), depending on the rootstock. 'Morello' is the most commonly grown, and it can be grown against a north wall. The fruits are too acid for most people to eat raw, but they are excellent when cooked and make very good jam.

Trees crop regularly, provided that there is no sharp frost at flowering time; an annual yield of 12 to 20 lb (5.4–9kg) from a fan-trained tree and 30 to 40 lb (13.5–18kg) from a bush can be expected.

Tree form and rootstocks

The usual forms are bush, half standard and fan. The acid cherry can also be grown as a pyramid with the lowest branches at about 18 inches (45cm) from the ground. 'Colt', which is semi-vigorous, is the best rootstock for all forms.

Bush trees

A well feathered maiden tree is to be preferred, but a 2-year-old is also suitable. Plant at 12 to 15 feet (3.6–4.5m) apart, each tree to a stake.

Trees can be planted at any time between November and March, but autumn is preferable because cherries start to grow early in spring.

Pruning
The maiden tree. Formative pruning is done in the early spring just as the buds break into growth. At this stage growth buds can be distinguished from blossom buds, the first showing initial signs of green leaf, the second showing white. Always prune to a growth bud.

If the maiden tree has strong laterals at about the height the head is desired (see p.31), some can be used as the primary branches. Aim to start with 4 or 5 of these. Cut back the central stem to the top lateral at about about 3 to 3½ feet (1m); prune each lateral by two-thirds to a bud facing upwards. Remove lower laterals not wanted as part of the head.

A whip should be cut back to a bud at about 3½ feet (1m) with 3 or 4 good buds immediately below. These and the top bud can grow during the following summer to form the first branches. In the following 2 springs, prune the previous summer's growth of each branch by one-half to two-thirds to a bud facing in the direction of required growth – usually outwards.

The cropping tree. Acid cherries fruit almost entirely on the young shoots made the previous summer. Each year, a proportion of the older wood should be cut out to stimulate a constant supply of strong new replacement wood. Un-pruned trees usually crop only on the perimeter, the centre tending to be barren. In September, after the crop has been picked, cut back about one-quarter of the old fruiting wood to vigorous 1-year-old shoots. As the trees become older, it may be necessary to cut out a few pieces of 3- and 4-year-old wood, to strong replacement shoots. Protect the cuts with wound paint.

Fan trees

Allow 12 to 15 feet (3.6–4.5m) spacing and a height of not less than 7 feet (2.1m). Any aspects, even north, is suitable for an acid cherry. Remember to plant so that the base of the tree is 6 to 9 inches (15–22cm) away from the wall, and incline the tree towards it. A wire system, gauge 16, galvanised, tied to the wall or fence, is necessary for supports, with the wires spaced at 6 inches (15cm) apart.

Pruning

Formative pruning. A fan is formed on the same principle as that for peaches (see pp.109–110), except that if the tree is a feathered maiden and there are 2 suitable placed laterals, these can be used to form the first ribs.

The cropping tree. Once the basic framework has been formed, the fan is best pruned on a replacement system. The aim is to ensure that the fan has an adequate supply of vigorous 1-year-old shoots for fruit production.

In the spring and early summer, thin

(Opposite left) *Pruning a bush after fruiting: cut out some of the older wood, back to a strong young shoot.*

(Opposite right) *Fan training a feathered maiden:*
(Right) *the two lowest laterals make the first ribs.*

(Opposite left) *The centre leader and other unwanted laterals are cut out.*

(Opposite right) *The first ribs are cut by a third to an upward-facing bud.*

(Opposite left) *Each rib is tied to a cane and the large cut painted with protective paint.*

(Opposite right) *The older wood is pruned out immediately after harvest in late August, to a young shoot of the current season.*

out new shoots to about 2 to 3 inches (5–8cm) apart along the ribs of the fan. The retained shoots are flexible and should be tied to the wires. Allow the growing tips to extend, because the longer shoots will bear more cherries the next summer. Leave one shoot, wherever possible, at the base of each lateral bearing fruit as a replacement.

As soon as possible after the crop has been gathered, cut the fruiting laterals back to the replacement shoots; these will fruit the next summer.

As the tree ages, it becomes more likely to crop only on the perimeter. When this happens, cut a proportion of the 3- and 4-year-old wood back to young laterals to stimulate new growth, in September or March. Depending upon the vigour and condition of the tree, up to one-quarter of the older shoots in any one year may be removed.

Manuring

In late January each year apply $\frac{3}{4}$ oz per sq. yd of sulphate of potash (25g/m²) over the rooting area as a top dressing. In February apply Nitro-chalk at 2 oz per sq. yd (65g/m²), followed by a 2- to 3-inch (5–8cm) thick mulch of well rotted manure or compost. Every third year give the trees superphosphate at 3 oz per sq. yd (100g/m²).

Cultivation and watering

Acid cherries are best grown in cultivated soil so that there is no competition from grass and weeds. However, they can be grown in grass provided that an area of clean soil no less than 2 feet (60cm) in radius is maintained around the base.

Watering in times of dry weather is recommended. Keep the tree used to

A young fan-trained 'Morello' on 'Colt' in May.

(Opposite above) A 'Morello' cherry in a fruit cage, showing the heavy cropping capacity of this cherry.

(Opposite below) Picking: cut the stalks with scissors, rather than pull them, as this might damage the bark.

well-watered conditions because a sudden and heavy application of water to dry soil can cause splitting of fruits when they are near to ripening. Mulching helps to conserve soil moisture.

Netting and picking

Wall-trained trees can be fairly easily covered with netting to protect the ripening fruits from birds. But with bush or standard trees it is more difficult, and the alternative is to pick the fruits as they ripen. The cherries should be picked by cutting the stalks with scissors; pulling them off is apt to spoil the fruits or to tear the bark, thus increasing the risk of fungal infection.

Recommended cultivars

Morello (self-fertile), August/September, or later on a north wall. Dark red to black when fully ripe.
Nabella (self-fertile), August. Dark red or black.

Pests

BULLFINCHES, APHIDS (see p.103) and CHERRY SLUGWORM (see p.86).

Diseases

SILVER LEAF (see p.97), and BROWN ROT (see p.70) can be troublesome.

Peaches and nectarines

Peaches and nectarines crop quite successfully outdoors in this country, provided that they are grown in a warm, sheltered situation, that peach leaf curl fungus is controlled, and that the blossom is protected from frost. The nectarine is a smooth-skinned form of peach, and the cultural requirements for both are the same (unless otherwise stated).

They are best grown as fans planted against a sunny wall or fence. The aim is to cover the available space with branches radiating, like the ribs of a fan, from the top of the short trunk, and spaced so that each branch and shoot receives the maximum amount of light and air. A southern aspect is first choice, but one facing west is also satisfactory. North and east walls are too cold.

Peaches crop satisfactorily in the open in the south, but the site must be sunny and sheltered. The usual form for growing in the open is the bush, but trees can also be obtained as half standards and occasionally as standards.

Nectarines need more warmth than peaches and should be grown against a wall in all but mild areas. A good average yield from a mature peach fan ranges from 20 to 30 lb (9–13.5kg); from a bush the range is from 30 to 60 lb (13.5–27kg), depending on tree size.

A nectarine gives about one-half to two-thirds of these amounts. Peaches and nectarines start to bear fruit two years after planting and should be into full cropping by their fifth or sixth year.

Good yields have also been obtained from peach seedlings; the most satisfactory results are with stones from early ripening cultivars which are more likely to do well in our climate than late ripening ones. With seedling trees there is not the same control of tree size as there is with trees grafted on a rootstock. Seedling trees are usually vigorous and may take from 4 to 7 years before they start to bear.

Peaches and nectarines are self-fertile: only one tree need be planted.

Soils

Peaches and nectarines prefer a slightly acid (pH 6.5 to 7), deep, well drained, medium to heavy loam soil. They do not thrive in light, sandy soils unless their moisture retention has been improved by incorporating bulky organic material and by mulching.

Shallow soils over chalk are unsuitable because the trees are likely to suffer from lime-induced chlorosis (see p.8) and drought.

Fan trees

Rootstocks and spacing
On 'St Julien A' (semi-vigorous), plant at 12 to 15 feet (3.6–4.5m) apart.

On 'Brompton' (vigorous), plant at 15 to 20 feet (4.5–6m) apart.

The minimum recommended height of a wall or fence is 6 feet (1.8m). Fruits can be grown against structures lower than this, but much tying down and heavy pruning is then needed to limit tree growth. The height of the fence can be increased with trelliswork.

The semi-vigorous rootstock 'Mussel' is also used in nurseries. Peaches grow satisfactorily on this rootstock, but it is inclined to sucker badly. Use the same spacing as for 'St Julien A'.

Support
Wires (gauge 16) needed for support and training should be fixed horizontally at 6-inch (15cm) intervals, starting at 15 inches (40cm) from the ground.

Soil preparation
The soil at the base of a wall can be very dry, and it is important to improve its moisture retention by the generous addition of bulky organic materials, such as well rotted manure, compost or peat before planting. Good drainage is also essential. When digging in the manure, make sure any impervious subsoil is also broken up. On very heavy land, improve drainage with liberal quantities of brick rubble covered with chopped-up turf in the bottom of the planting hole.

It is not necessary to add lime unless the soil is very acid, below pH 6. Peaches and nectarines may suffer from lime-induced chlorosis if too much lime is present. Just before planting, fork in a compound fertilizer (such as Growmore at 2 oz per sq. yd/65g/m²) plus bonemeal at 4 oz per sq. yd (130g/m²).

Planting

Plant in the dormant season between November and March; autumn planting is preferable because peaches start to grow relatively early in the spring. Plant the tree 6 to 9 inches (15–22cm) away from the wall, the stem sloping slightly towards it. Plant to the same depth as it was in the nursery, ensure the roots are well spread out, and firm the soil during planting. Finally, mulch the tree with well rotted manure, peat or compost over a radius of about 18 inches (45cm) to a depth of 2 or 3 inches (5–8cm), but keep the mulch just clear of the stem.

Pruning and training

A peach bears its fruit mainly on wood of the previous year's growth. When pruning a peach it is necessary to be able to distinguish between wood buds (pointed) and fruit buds (plump and round). Fruit buds never produce shoots, but a triple bud consists of 2 blossom buds and a wood bud, and such a bud may produce a shoot after pruning.

Maiden tree. In the spring after planting, just as growth is starting, if the peach is well feathered and there are two strong laterals, one to the left and one to the right which can be used as ribs, then cut out the centre to the topmost shoot. Prune the ribs by a quarter to a third cutting to an upward facing bud in each case. With a poorly feathered tree cut back to about 24 inches (60cm) to a lateral shoot, or to a good growth bud. Select 2 well placed buds below this, one to the left and the other to the right, about 9 to 12 inches (22–30cm) above ground.

In the early summer, when shoots should have grown from the selected buds or laterals, pinch back all other shoots to one leaf, except those right at the top or the topmost lateral, as the case may be.

When the 2 side shoots are about 18 inches (45cm) long tie each to a cane fixed to the wires at an angle of 45° or a little lower. Cut out the main stem immediately above these 2 shoots and paint the wound with tree paint. If one shoot grows more strongly than the other, it should be temporarily trained at a somewhat lower angle until the growth of the two shoots is more or less equal.

By the end of the summer, with the strong tree starting with 2 ribs, there should be an 8-ribbed fan; 4 ribs on either side, with the centre fairly open (see photos p.111). This is typical of the partly-trained fan sold by the nursery, although the number of ribs may range from 5 to 12, depending on the age and vigour of the peach or nectarine.

Second year. In February, dealing with a 2-ribbed fan, cut back the 2 side branches to a growth bud 12 to 18 inches (30–45cm) from the main stem. These are the first ribs of the fan.

In the summer train in 4 shoots in the same way as described above. Allow 2 suitably spaced side shoots (about 4 inches, 10cm, apart) on the upper side of each branch and one on the lower side to grow; pinch all other shoots back to one leaf. The selected shoots must be trained along canes or tied in to the wires.

Third winter or newly planted partly-trained fan. A newly planted fan should have its branches tied to canes as detailed above. In February, cut back each shoot, to a triple or a growth bud (pointing upwards, if possible), to leave about 2 to 2½ feet (60–75cm) of ripened wood of the previous summer's growth. In the summer allow the end bud of each rib to grow on again as described above, and train in more shoots as part of the permanent framework until all the available space on the wall or fence is filled. Leave filling in the centre of the fan to the last, because vertical growth in the centre can become too dominant at the expense of the vigour of the sides of the fan.

The tree is now nearing the fruit-bearing stage. The shoots that grow in the summer will bear fruit the following year. Indeed it is possible that the tree is already carrying some fruits. These can be left on to develop and ripen, provided that the tree is making strong growth and the peaches are well spaced out, not less than 9 inches (22cm) apart. But a young tree at this formative stage should not be allowed to carry a heavy crop.

The young shoots produced along the framework branches throughout the early summer should be thinned and tied in so that they are spaced about 4 to 6 inches (10–15cm) apart on the upper and lower sides of the ribs. These are to become the fruit-carrying laterals the next summer. Those growing towards the wall can be tied in parallel if needed, but if not should be cut out completely. Any other surplus shoots are pinched back to 1 leaf.

The selected shoots may be allowed to grow to about 18 inches (45cm), when the tip should be pinched out. If they overlap the ribs, they should be pinched back shorter than this. Stop any secondary shoots on these at 1 leaf. This is the end of the formative period.

Pruning the established cropping tree. Peaches fruit almost entirely on the growth made in the previous summer. Pruning for fruiting is aimed at obtaining an adequate and constant supply of new shoots so that fruits are produced on all parts of the fan; this is the replacement system of pruning.

Start pruning in the spring soon after new growth begins. At the base of the last year's shoots, which should be carrying blossom and wood buds, there are usually 2 or more wood buds. Allow one of these to grow to form the replacement shoot. Another bud about half-way up may be also allowed to grow as a reserve in case the first should die or be damaged. Pinch back all other young shoots on the fruit-carrying lateral to 1 leaf. Do not remove them completely because this would result in bare wood. The leaves help to feed the peaches.

The terminal bud of the fruiting lateral should be allowed to grow on without stopping if there is plenty of room. If not, allow it to produce about 6 leaves and pinch it back to 4 leaves. The replacement and the reserve shoots should be stopped at about 18 inches (45cm), provided that there is room to tie them in. If not, stop them shorter than this so that they do not overlap adjoining branches. Any secondary growth produced on the stopped shoots is pinched back to 1 leaf.

The operation of deshooting and pinching back should be done in the spring and early summer while the growth is still soft. Tie in the young growth regularly so that it is exposed to the sun and the fan is neat and flat. Shoots to be used as an extension of the existing framework should also be tied in, and young laterals on this extension growth thinned to 4 to 6 inches (10–15cm) apart.

Immediately after the fruits have been picked, and no later than the end of September, cut back the shoots that have fruited to the replacement shoot, unless they are needed to extend the framework or fill in any gaps. Tie the new shoots to the wires. If necessary, thin out the current season's growth, remove dead

(Opposite) *Peach 'Peregrine' ripens in early August.*

(Opposite) *By the end of June the peach has produced enough shoots for 4 to be selected on each side: 1 shoot to extend the leader, 2 shoots on the upper side, and one on the lowest side of the rib on each side.*

(Opposite right) *A similar fan in September.*

(Opposite top left) *A blossom-carrying lateral on a fan with a replacement shoot at the base and a reserve in the middle.*

(Opposite top right) *A mature fan after the shoots have been thinned to about 4 inches apart (10cm) on the upper and lower sides of each branch.*

(Opposite below left) *De-shooting: thinning out the young shoots to 4 to 6 inches (10–15cm) apart on each side of the framework branches.*

(Opposite below right) *A shoot growing towards the fence is removed.*

(Above) *Pinch back the tip of the fruit-carrying lateral to 4 leaves, when it has made about 6 leaves.*

(Right) *Later in the summer the replacement shoot has grown out, at the base of the fruit-carrying lateral; the lateral will be cut back to this shoot after harvest.*

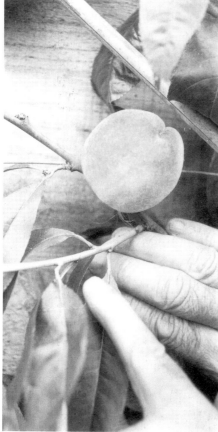

and diseased shoots, and space out the remaining shoots to encourage wood ripening.

Feeding and watering

Peaches should be well manured and watered to obtain an adequate fruit set and produce good-sized fruits and the replacement shoots.

In February each year apply a balanced compound fertilizer (such as Growmore at 3 oz per sq. yd/100g/m²), as a top dressing over the rooting area, followed by a light mulch of well rotted stable manure or garden compost. Spread the mulch about 2 inches (5cm) thick over a radius of about 18 inches (45cm). The mulch helps to conserve soil moisture.

At intervals of 10 to 14 days from flowering onwards, give the tree a high potash liquid feed, at about 1 gal. (4.5 litres) per tree, each time. Stop as the fruits begin to ripen.

Watering is usually necessary for wall-trained trees, especially when there is a good fruit set. Water copiously in dry weather. Apply about 1 inch (4½ gal. per sq. yd/25 litres/m²) every 10 days until rain restores the soil to field capacity.

Hand pollination and frost protection

Peaches flower early in the spring usually when there are few pollinating insects about. Hand pollination is well worth while to ensure a good set. The pollen is transferred from one flower to the next by very gently dabbing the centre of the flower using a rabbit's tail, a soft camel-hair brush or a piece of cotton wool on a match stick. This is best done in bright sunny weather, but should be done every day until the flowers are over.

Protection against frost is essential from the pink bud stage onwards. Drape the tree with hessian or a similar material, or 2 or 3 layers of bird netting whenever frost is forecast. Keep the covering just clear of the flowers and remove it during the day. A polythene lean-to as recommended for the control of peach leaf curl gives 2 or 3 degrees of frost protection (*see* pp.118, 119).

Fruit thinning
To obtain good-sized peaches, thinning is necessary. Aim to have a final spacing of one fruit every 9 inches (22cm) of wood. A first thinning should be carried out when the fruit is the size of a hazel nut, usually in June. Reduce the fruits to singles, spaced at about 4 inches (10cm) apart. Remove all those next to the wall and in places where there is no room for them to swell. The final thinning should be done about the end of June when the fruits are roughly the size of walnuts. Thin them to about 9 inches (22cm) apart. Nectarines should be thinned to about 6 inches (15cm) apart.

Bush form

Rootstocks
'St Julien A' (semi-vigorous), plant at 15 to 18 feet (4.5–5.5m) apart.
'Brompton' (vigorous), plant at 18 to 24 feet (5.5–7.5m) apart.

Planting
Prepare the site as described under Fan (*see* p.108). A maiden tree is the most suitable for planting. 'Rochester' is the best peach cultivar for growing as a bush. Nectarines are not suited for growing as a bush tree, unless in a particularly warm situation.

Pruning
Prune in the spring after planting when the buds have started to grow. The formative pruning is basically the same as for a bush plum (*see* pp.89–90).

Usually a maiden peach tree is well feathered, and some of the laterals can be

(Above) *Hand pollinating the peach flowers with a rabbit's tail.*

(Right) *Thinning the fruits to singles.*
(Far right). *The second thinning at the end of June is to 9 inches (22cm) apart*

(Opposite above) *Frost protection: hessian is unrolled each evening during flowering when frost is forecast, and rolled up the next morning.*

(Opposite below) *A young cropping fan in the summer with the shoots tied to the wires and the fruits thinned to 6 to 9 inches (15–22cm) apart.*

used to form the first branches if they are at the right height. Aim for a tree with a clean stem of about 1½ to 2 feet (45–60cm) and a head consisting of 4 to 6 primary branches.

Cut back the central stem to the topmost of the selected laterals and cut each of these by two-thirds to a bud facing outwards. Remove the unwanted lower laterals back to the main stem. Paint the cuts with a wound paint.

By the second spring the primary branches should have extended and produced side shoots, some of which can be used to form secondary branches. Select about 9 or 10 to form the framework and cut each leader by one-half to a growth bud facing in the required direction, usually outwards. Cut back the other side shoots to about 4 inches (10cm).

The objective in subsequent years is to obtain plenty of strong new growth each year to bear fruit in the next summer.

The centre should be fairly open, but not barren, because some growth in the middle of the tree is needed later on to replace perimeter branches which have become too low. Each spring cut out some of the 2- or 3-year-old wood that has become bare, back to young healthy shoots. Removed crowded and crossing branches as well as dead shoots.

When cropping has pulled down the lower branches, cut them back to a suitable vertical branch.

Thinning
Cropping should start in the third year, but thin hard in the third summer to concentrate the tree's energy into new growth. In subsequent years thin to give a final spacing of 9 inches (22cm) apart.

Manuring and watering
Generous feeding and copious watering as advocated for the fan-trained tree is necessary (see p.113).

Picking

Handle ripe fruits with great care. The test for ripeness is to cup the fruit lightly in the palm of the hand and press it gently at the base near the stalk with the finger tips. If the flesh gives, it is ready to pick and usually parts easily from the shoot without pulling. Place the fruits in shallow containers lined with a soft material such as cotton wool. Keep the

Pruning a feathered maiden for a bush tree. Cut back the central stem to a lateral at 2 to 2½ feet (60–75cm) above the ground, where there are 2 or 3 laterals below. (continued opposite)

fruits in a cool place until they are to be eaten.

Peaches from stones

Peaches do not grow true from seed, so if they are raised from stones the chances are that the progeny will be inferior to or equal to, but rarely better than, its parents. But there are many unnamed peach trees grown from stones in gardens throughout the country which yield quite a useful crop of peaches. Provided that the gardener is prepared to take this chance and wait perhaps 4 or 5 years before the tree starts to fruit, growing from seed is worth trying.

Select stones from fruits which are early-ripening – for example, imported peaches from Italy sold here in June or early July, or from named peaches grown outdoors in this country. Clean the stones and dry them outside in the sun for a day or two. Percentage germination is variable, so retain more stones than are needed.

The seed must undergo a period of cold to break dormancy. The simplest method is to bury the seed in a 50:50 mixture of

(Left) *Cut the laterals by about half to an outward facing bud.*

(Right) *Pruning completed: the badly placed lower laterals have been removed.*

damp peat and sharp sand (⅛-inch, 2mm grit) in a 10-inch (25cm) plastic plant pot. Store this in a cool cellar or a dark corner of a garden shed, or bury it in a shady part of the garden for the rest of the summer and during the winter. Protect the pots from hard frost; if plunged outside cover them with straw. Protect all pots from mice. The compost must not be allowed to dry out during this period.

In late February sow the seed. The best method is to sow it singly in 6-inch (15cm) pots filled with John Innes potting compost No. 1. Place the pots under glass on a propagating bench in which a basal heat of about 60° to 68°F (15–20°C) is maintained. Alternatively, place the pots on a sunny kitchen windowsill or sow outside in a nursery row. Plant them 2 inches (5cm) deep and 9 inches (22cm) apart in well-prepared ground into which some peat and bone meal has been incorporated. As each seedling appears, train it to a cane. A peach seedling in a pot must be carefully potted on into a 9- or 10-inch (22–25cm) pot once the roots have filled the original pot. Give the seedling a liquid feed high in potassium every 14 days throughout the growing season. The seedling can be placed outside when the danger of frost is over. At the end of the

season, when it is dormant, the peach can be planted in open ground.

In the second year give the seedlings more room. Space them 2 feet (60cm) apart. Continue training the centre leader up a cane. Gradually remove the lower laterals to create a clean stem of about 2 feet (60cm), allowing the higher laterals to form the head of the tree.

Plant out the seedling tree in its permanent position in the third winter. It should bear fruit in its fourth or fifth year.

Recommended cultivars

Peaches
Amsden June, mid-July.
Duke of York*, mid-July.
Hale's Early, mid- to end July; good for freezing.
Peregrine*, early August.
Rochester, early August.
Redhaven, mid-August.
Royal George*, late August.
Alexandra Noblesse*, early September.
Bellegarde*, early to mid-September.
Barrington*, early to mid-September.

Nectarines
Early Rivers*, mid-July.

*good flavour

Peach leaf curl, symptoms on the opening shoots.

John Rivers*, mid-July.
Lord Napier*, early August.
Humboldt*, mid-August.
Elruge*, late August.
Pine Apple*, early September.

*good flavour

Compact cultivars

These are naturally dwarf compact forms, useful for growing in containers in a sunny paved garden where they will receive plenty of reflected warmth. Most flower very early and need protection from frosts, which can easily be given because of their small size. The following are all self-fertile and yellow-fleshed.

Peaches
Bonanza, early to mid-July.
Garden Lady, mid-July.

Nectarines (all August)
Garden Delight.
Nectarina.
Nectarella.

Pests

APHIDS suck sap from the leaves during spring and early summer. Affected leaves become sticky, curled and crinkled.

Opposite:
(Top left) *A polythene lean-to for protection from leaf curl infection will also give some frost protection.*

(Top right) *Nectarine 'Elruge' ripens in late August.*

(Below left) *A polythene cover is easily moved during the day if necessary.*

(Below right) *Peach leaves showing yellowing (chlorosis) caused by iron deficiency.*

Overwintering eggs can be destroyed by thorough spraying with tar oil in December. Alternatively, the trees can be sprayed with pirimicarb, dimethoate or heptenophos shortly after flowering.
GLASSHOUSE RED SPIDER MITE are sap-feeding pests more likely to occur on a wall-trained tree than one in the open. The mites are yellowish green with darker markings, and only just visible to the naked eye. They feed on the undersides of leaves, causing the upper surface to develop a fine mottled discoloration. In heavy infestations leaves dry up and fall prematurely. Thorough spraying with dimethoate, pirimiphos-methyl or malathion when symptoms appear, with further applications at 7- to 10-day intervals, check the mites but control is not easy. Biological control with the predatory mite, *Phytoseiulus persimilis*, may be effective, although this technique is less certain on outdoor plants.
BROWN SCALE is a sap-feeding insect seen mainly on the branches. The adults are covered by dark brown, convex shells up to ¼ inch (6mm) long. Heavy infestations can develop which reduce the tree's vigour. Control by spraying with a tar oil wash in December, or use malathion or pirimiphos-methyl in early July.

Diseases

PEACH LEAF CURL shows on the leaves as large blisters which are first red but later swell up and turn white. Affected leaves fall early in the season. Spray with a copper fungicide in January or February, repeating 10 to 14 days later, and again in the autumn immediately before leaf fall. A temporary glass or polythene overhead cover to shelter wall peaches, open at both ends, should prevent infection. Cover from the end of December until late May, though the cover is usually left on later than this to take advantage of extra warmth and protection it provides.
BACTERIAL CANKER and SILVER LEAF (see p.97) and BROWN ROT and HONEY FUNGUS (see p.70) can also affect peaches.
SPLIT STONE shows as a deep crack at the stalk end of affected fruit, and within the stone, which is split into two, the kernel rots. This is often caused by several adverse cultural factors, but can be prevented by applying lime if the soil is very acid, by mulching and watering so that the soil does not dry out, and by hand pollination of the flowers.

Apricots

An apricot tree requires a warm, sunny and sheltered position. It is one of the earliest tree fruits to flower – usually in March and April, but occasionally in February – and so the blossom may be damaged by frost, and pollination or fertilization may be affected by the cold. Apricots are self-fertile, and one tree on its own will bear a crop.

In colder parts of the country, trees are best grown under glass. The most successful trees in the south and midlands are those against a warm wall with a substantial coping or a house wall with wide eaves that help to ward off the frost. The best form is as a fan on a south- or (as second choice) a west-facing wall. Apricots are fairly vigorous, so the wall must be at least 8 feet (2.4m) high. The eventual width of the tree depends upon the rootstock used (see below).

An apricot can be grown in the open in the warmer parts of the country as a bush tree. It must, however, be in a sunny, sheltered position and grown in a chalky clay loam. Do not expect a regular crop because of its early flowering; there will be frequent years when the crop is nil or very light. The bush apricot should be trained and pruned in the same way as a bush plum (see p.89). The usual rootstock upon which it is grafted is 'St Julien A' which makes a tree of about 15 to 18 feet in height and spread (4.5–5.5m).

Soil

The ideal soil is a deep, slightly alkaline medium loam over limestone, but apricots tolerate a wide range of soils (of pH between 6.5 and 7.5) provided that they are well drained. Light, sandy soils which tend to dry out quickly are unsuitable, but they can be improved by incorporating bulky organic materials before planting.

Rootstocks and spacing

Plum rootstocks are used for apricots. 'St Julien A' (semi-vigorous) is widely used because it is the least vigorous of those now available. Trees on this rootstock are spaced 14 to 15 feet (4.2–4.5m) apart. Trees on 'Common Mussel' (vigorous) are spaced 15 to 20 feet (4.5–6m) apart, and 'Brompton' (very vigorous) 20 to 25 feet (6–7.5m) apart.

Choice of tree

A partly-formed fan is quicker to fruit than a maiden tree, and is therefore preferable – although it is more expensive to buy from the nursery.

Soil preparation and planting

If the soil is very acid, the pH can be brought up to between 6.7 and 7.0 by applying lime (see p.8) 6 to 8 weeks before planting.

Just before planting dig in some well rotted manure, compost or peat – a $2\frac{1}{2}$-gal. bucketful over 1 sq. yd (13 litres /m^2) – then fork in 2 oz (65g) of a balanced compound fertilizer (such as Growmore) plus 4 oz of bone meal over a square yard (130g/m^2).

Plant at any time in the dormant season from November to March, but preferably in the autumn while the soil is still warm. Set the tree 6 to 9 inches (15–22cm) away from the wall, with the top inclined slightly towards it. After planting, mulch with organic material.

Pruning

Formative pruning and training
The system of wirework on the wall and the formative pruning is the same as for a fan-trained peach (see pp.108, 109), except that pruning is done in early February.

Pruning the cropping tree
Apricots fruit on shoots made in the previous summer and on short spurs produced on older wood. Spurs form naturally, but others can be induced by summer pruning. When the laterals are about 3 inches (8cm) long, usually in May, pinch out their tips with the fingers and thumb; pinch back any subsequent sublaterals to 1 leaf. If growth tends to be vigorous, pinch the laterals to 6 inches (15cm). Shoots needed to fill up spaces should be tied into position while still pliable.

A maiden apricot: (left) the centre leader cut back to two well placed laterals in February to form the first ribs of a fan; (right) the laterals cut back by two-thirds of their length and any other laterals removed.

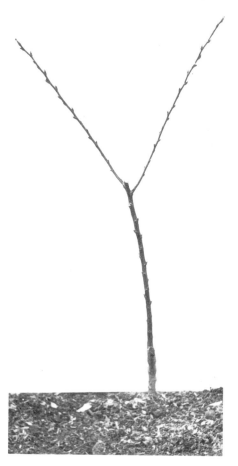

Frost protection and hand pollination

For a good crop of fruit, apricots need special attention during flowering. A few degrees of frost protection at the pink or white bud stage is given by draping the tree with two or three layers of bird netting or heavy-gauge (500g) clear poly-thene sheet (*see* Peaches, p.114). The covering must not come in contact with the blossom but be held away from the tree with canes. If the covering is opaque, remove it during the day so that light reaches the flowers.

Hand pollination is carried out using a soft camel-hair brush or, ideally, a rab-bit's tail, by lightly touching the flowers at midday. Do it every day until flowering is over.

At this time of the year the atmosphere is often very dry, which means that the pollen dries quickly and can be easily distributed. But if the stigma of the flower becomes too dry the pollen may not stick, so on a fine, dry day mist over the tree immediately after pollination in time for the blooms to dry before dark.

Thinning

Thinning is necessary only when many fruits have been set; it is done in stages. The first stage is when the fruits are about ½ inch (1cm) long. Remove the very small and badly placed fruits, and thin to about 1 inch (2.5cm) apart. The final thinning is done after the 'stoning' period is over, when the fruits are a little larger than hazel nuts. Thin to singles, aiming for an average spacing of 2 to 3 inches (5–8cm) apart.

There may be some natural fruit drop when the fruits are about the size of garden peas.

Feeding and watering

Apricots need potash and nitrogen. In late January apply a top dressing of sulphate of potash at 1oz per sq. yd (33g/m²) over the rooting area. In April apply Nitro-chalk at ¾oz per sq. yd (25g/m²) followed by a mulch of well rotted manure, compost or peat. Every third year, in January, apply superphosphates at 3oz per sq. yd (100g/m²).

The soil at the base of a wall can become extremely dry, so it is important to keep the tree well watered, particularly following a heavy fruit set. In dry weather apply at least 1 inch (2.5cm) at a time, 4½ gal. over 1 sq. yd (25 litres/m²) every 7 days, until rain restores the field capacity.

Harvesting

Fruits usually ripen from late July until the end of August, according to cultivar, and for fruits in the best of condition, they should be allowed to ripen fully on the tree.

Netting against bird damage is sometimes necessary.

When picking, be careful not to tear the fruits away from the stalk because this spoils its keeping qualities. Store in a cool place.

Recommended cultivars

New Large Early, July.
Early Moorpark, July/August.
Hemskerk, July/August.
Farmingdale, July/August; less prone to die-back.
Alfred, July/August; less prone to die-back.
Moorpark, August/September; the most widely planted and reliable cultivar.

Pests

Apricots can be affected by the same pests as peach (see p.119), but are generally less susceptible.

Diseases

DIE-BACK of apricots often results in the death of a large branch that shows a copious exudation of gum near its base, caused by a weak parasitic fungus which enters through wounds and can be prevented by avoiding winter pruning and by coating larger pruning cuts immediately with a wound paint. A tree lacking in vigour is more susceptible to infection, so give correct cultural treatment as above.
SILVER LEAF see p.97.

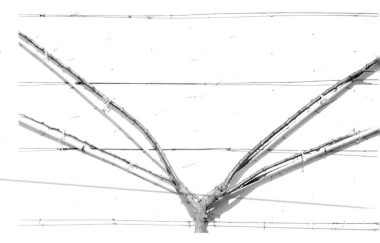

Apricot fan: (above) 2-year old showing formation of 4 ribs; (below) 4-year old in blossom demonstrating filling in of space on wall.

(Opposite) 'Alfred' is a mid-season apricot.

Figs

Figs like the sun and need plenty of warmth to crop successfully outdoors. The best way of growing them is as a fan against a south-facing wall. They do quite well in the south and west, but less so the further north they are planted. A fig can be grown in the open as a bush or standard, but only in milder areas. In a small garden it may be possible to place a fig in a sunny corner provided by two walls. It should also do well in a pot.

The choice of cultivar is important, because not all will ripen outdoors. Figs are susceptible to cold, and in areas where hard winters may be expected, the branch framework needs protection throughout the winter.

Figs grow on a wide range of soils, preferring chalk, but all must be well drained. Very fertile soils can induce too much growth, and it is better to have a light soil or a shallow soil over chalk.

Planting and root restriction

Figs are grown on their own roots; no rootstocks are available. The rooting area must be restricted to prevent the tree becoming too vigorous, large and unfruitful. Root restriction for a wall-trained tree can be provided by, for example, planting it in a narrow border 1½ to 2 feet (45–60cm) wide, bounded by a concrete path, or in a paved area, provided that there is not less than 6 cubic feet (0.17m³) of soil for rooting. The usual way is to construct an open-based trough with the top about 1 inch (2.5cm) above the surrounding soil level. The size of the container influences the eventual size of the tree. To cover a wall space of about 7 to 8 feet (2.1–2.4m) high by 10 to 12 feet (3–3.6m) wide, the trough should be about 2 feet long, 2 feet wide by 2 feet deep (60cm × 60cm × 60cm). Construct the sides with paving slabs 2 feet square (30cm²), or concrete, brick or some other solid material to stop the roots escaping outwards. The bottom should be left open to allow for drainage, but packed tightly to a depth of about a foot (30cm) with broken bricks or lumpy chalk to prevent strong tap roots forming. The bed may then be filled in with loam or good garden soil mixed with mortar rubble, and about 2 handfuls of bonemeal.

A young pot-grown plant is the best buy, to be planted in March to April when the danger of very severe frosts is over. Plant 9 inches (22cm) away from the wall. It should be turned out of the pot and the roots disentangled and spread out evenly in the hole prepared for it. The hole can then be filled in in the usual way.

If more than one fig is planted, allow 12 feet (3.6m) between them.

Pruning and training a fan

The fig is generally supplied by the nursery as a 2- or 3-year old plant. It may have a single stem or 2 or more ribs. Prune after planting in March. In the case of a single stem, cut it back to a bud at about 15 inches (38cm). If it has side shoots, lightly tip each shoot to a bud, removing no more than one-quarter to stimulate the production of more laterals. In the summer the new growths are trained fanwise to the wall as they extend, in the same way as for a peach (see p.109).

Pruning the cropping tree

It is important to understand how figs fruit in this country because this dictates the pruning. Here, figs bear 2 crops a year – but usually only one ripens. The successful crop starts as embryo fruits produced in the late summer at and near the tip of the young shoots. These fruitlets are about the size of sweet-pea seeds or smaller. Provided that the winter is mild, or that the young figs are protected against severe frost, they should develop and ripen the next summer, usually in August and early September. Fruits produced in the spring on the new growth do not usually ripen because our summers are too cool. These should be removed in the late autumn to concentrate the tree's resources into the embryo figs (see p.127).

In order to produce plenty of sturdy, short-jointed young shoots every year, on which the embryo figs are borne, the growing points of the shoots should be cut off when they have made 4 or 5 leaves, so inducing more shoots from the leaf axils. This should only be carried out when the buds have time to grow out and develop other shoots that can ripen

Trough made of paving slabs of 2 feet (60cm) square for containing root growth of a fan tree: the base is open but packed with brick rubble and chalk to a depth of 9 to 12 inches (22–30cm). Note the battening on the wall to hold the wires.

Fan planted 6 to 9 inches (15–22cm) away from the wall. The rim of the trough is an inch (2.5cm) above soil level to prevent any escape of roots, and for containing irrigation water.

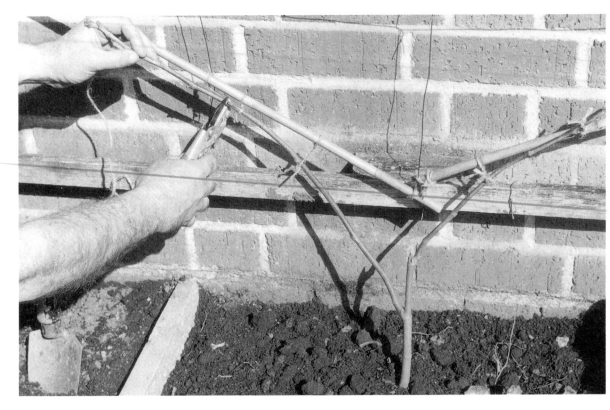

before leaf fall. In most areas this means up to the end of June. In July tie the shoots in to the wall, giving each room to develop and ripen.

Pruning while the tree is dormant is also necessary, but should be delayed until the end of April because in a severe winter some frost damage might occur. First, cut out all diseased or frost-damaged wood. Next, thin out the young shoots by cutting each alternate shoot back to 1 bud, to encourage new growth from the base. Train the others parallel to the wall. Aim for a 9- to 12-inch (22–30cm) spacing between shoots, and where there is a choice retain the best young growths with ripened and undamaged tips carrying the embryo figs. Cut out surplus shoots.

Renovation of a neglected fig

A neglected tree usually has a gaunt appearance with thick, bare wood at the base and the fruits borne only at the top. Hard pruning can stimulate dormant buds to produce new growth. If a lot of wood needs to be removed, spread the operation over three years.

Prune in late April when the danger of

(Above) *Two selected shoots are tied to canes at 20° horizontal and cut back to 18 to 24 inches (45–60cm).*

(Left) *Growing a fig 'St Johns' in a pot.*

(Above) 'White Marseilles', a good outdoor cultivar.

(Above right) 'Bourjasotte Grise', a cultivar that needs a very warm situation, and best grown under glass or in a pot.

Diagram of fig shoot in August:
A = next year's fruits;
B = fruits which will not mature before the frosts;
C = ripening fruits.

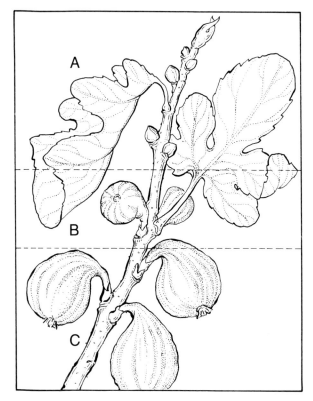

very hard frosts is over. In the pruning operations retain as far as possible the youngest and healthiest branches growing in the desired position. Cut out about one-quarter to one-third of the old, gaunt, unproductive branches, cutting back to young, healthy replacement branches wherever possible or, failing this, back to their point of origin. Make the cuts evenly over the whole tree so that a balanced head is maintained. A few limbs can be sawn back to ground level if need be, which may encourage the production of new shoots from the base. Figs are very susceptible to coral spot disease, so it is essential to protect all saw cuts with a wound paint. Remember that remaining old wood is to be removed in the late winter of the next 2 or 3 years.

This hard pruning should result in strong new shoots appearing in the early summer, and some selective thinning may be necessary. Train the remainder parallel with the wall to fill in available space as described in the training of a young fan-trained tree (see p.124).

Watering and feeding

Root restriction can lead to extreme dryness and starvation, resulting in fruitlet drop and poor fruit development. It is important, therefore, to keep the tree well watered whenever conditions are dry in the spring and summer, and to feed

it without encouraging excessive growth. Each spring apply a top dressing of Growmore, about 2 oz (55 g) over the rooting area, followed by a light mulch of well rotted stable manure. The mulch should help to keep the soil moist. During

(Above) Winter protection of a fan-trained fig. Immediately after leaf fall this wall trained plant was covered with dead bracken fronds.

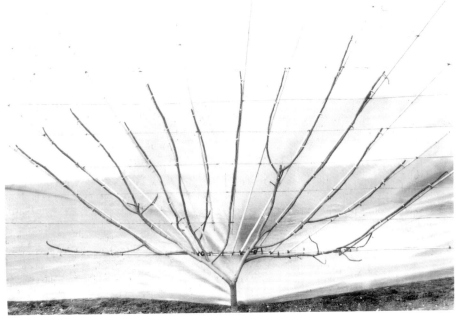

(Left) A young fan-trained fig showing the ribs radiating outwards.

the summer apply a liquid feed high in potassium (such as tomato fertilizer) about once a fortnight until the fruits are ripening.

Winter protection

In hard winters the branches bearing the embryo figs at their tips can be damaged by frost. They can be protected between November and the end of April, even to the end of May, provided that the buds are not breaking into growth, by tying over the branch framework a loose cover of straw, bracken, spruce boughs or material of a similar, open nature. A mulch round the base of the tree helps to protect the root system.

Root pruning

Unless the roots have been restricted, as mentioned earlier, root pruning is necessary occasionally (see pp.136-138).

Growing in a pot

Figs grow well in a pot that gives the necessary root restriction. In the summer, place the potted fig in the sunniest position possible – ideally, under glass, but a warm patio would do. In the winter it can be brought in to protect it against hard frost: a cool cellar or well-built garden shed are suitable. Cover it with a piece of sacking to give extra protection. If it is not possible to bring it under cover, protect the plant outside by burying the pot in a border and covering the top with a layer of straw or bracken. Bundle the branches together, tying straw or bracken round them.

The size of the pot influences the eventual size of the fig: the larger the container, the larger the plant. It can be grown quite well in a 10-inch (25-cm) pot, but because the root-run is so restricted watering is critical. Easier sizes to manage are 12- or 15-inch (30-38cm) pots, either clay or plastic. Ensure that the pot has plenty of drainage holes; a clay pot should be crocked.

A container-grown tree can be planted at any time, but March is the best month. Use John Innes potting compost No. 3. Firm well during potting and leave a 1-inch (2.5cm) gap at the rim for watering. Fill this with a bark mulch and stand

the container on bricks to ensure that water drains away.

Begin watering when the buds break, sparingly at first, but every day in hot weather when the leaves are fully developed. Feed with a high potassium liquid feed every 7 days until the harvest is finished.

It is desirable to develop and maintain a shrubby habit to the plant. This is done by pinching out the tips of the new shoots, as described for the fan-trained tree (see p.124).

Repotting is only necessary every 2 years. Do it in the late winter using John Innes potting compost No. 3, gently combing away some of the old soil from the root ball. Strong thong-like roots should be lightly trimmed. In the intervening years a little of the top soil can be carefully scraped away and replenished with fresh compost.

Harvesting

Figs are not ready for picking until they turn soft and hang downwards. Slight splits in the skin, or sometimes a drop of nectar exuded from the eye of the fruit, are indications that it is ready. Netting against blackbirds is usually necessary.

Recommended cultivars

White Marseilles, early.
St Johns, early; excellent for a pot.
Brown Turkey, mid-season; the most reliable cultivar.
Brunswick, mid-season.
White Ischia, mid-season, small fruits, good flavour; good for pots.
Rouge de Bourdeaux, mid-season, only suitable for a very warm situation; good in pots.
Bourjasotte Grise, late; only suitable for a very warm situation; very good flavour; excellent for growing in a pot.

Pests and diseases

RED SPIDER MITE and BROWN SCALE see p.119.
CORAL SPOT shows as numerous coral red spots on old and dead wood and can cause die-back of branches. Cut out and burn affected branches to a point well below the diseased tissues, and paint all the wounds with a protective paint.

Cobnuts and filberts

The cultivated cobnut is derived from *Corylus avellana*, the European hazel nut, and the filbert from *C. maxima*. They are easily distinguished by the length of the husk which encloses the fruit. The husk of the cobnut is short, and the nut protrudes. The filbert's husk is as long as or longer than the nut, which is hidden. Both are grown in the same way, and the term cobnut is used here to cover both.

The male and female flowers of cobnuts are separate, but borne on the same tree (monoecious). The handsome, long, male catkins are easily recognised, but the tiny red female flowers are not so obvious. It usually flowers in late January or February, according to season, and flowering may last from 4 to 6 weeks. The flowers are pollinated by the wind and are moderately hardy, but cannot withstand severe frosts or very wet and windy conditions. In its natural habitat the cobnut is a small woodland tree growing in light shade and protected by larger trees. In the garden it should be planted in a sunny or lightly-shaded position, but the site must be sheltered. (Avoid a frost pocket.) Trees growing in heavy shade do not crop well.

Cobnuts are self-fertile, but the blossoming of the two types of flowers does not always coincide and because the weather at flowering is frequently unfavourable, better pollination is obtained if 2 or more different cultivars are planted. Each tree may reach up to 15 feet (4.5m) across, so they are too big for a small garden. A good average yield from one tree is about 7 to 10 lb (3-4.5 kg), but individuals can give more in a favourable season with good weather during flowering. Cropping tends to be erratic.

Soils

Cobnuts are tolerant of a wide range of soils, and even thrive in poor, stony land, provided that it is well drained. Very fertile ground generally induces too much strong growth, and the best is a light, sandy loam with a slightly alkaline pH. Acid soils need liming to bring the pH to between 6.7 and 7.5

Tree form and spacing

Trees are grown on their own roots as an open-centred goblet shape on a short stem of about 12 to 18 inches (30-45cm) with a head consisting of 8 to 12 main branches. For ease of management the tree should be kept to a height of 6 to 7 feet (1.8–2.1m). They are planted at 15 feet (4.5m) apart.

(Below left) *Female flower with tiny red stigmas protruding from the bud, at the receptive stage. Male catkins beneath.*

(Below right) *The cobnut 'Nottingham' is a good pollinator and makes a small tree. Note the nut protruding from the husk.*

(Above) *The long male catkins of 'Cosford' in January: a good pollinator.*

(Right) *'White Filbert', the nut enclosed in the husk, of excellent flavour.*

(Left) *Vigorous laterals of the previous summer are cut back to 3 or 4 buds. Short twiggy shoots are not pruned.*

(Right) *Brutting: in August strong, young laterals are broken and left hanging.*

Occasionally trees are grown without a trunk, with several branches coming from the soil. Such bushes take up a lot of space and are difficult to prune, and so are not recommended.

Planting and formative pruning

Plant a 1-year-old rooted sucker or layer, or (preferably) a 2- or 3-year-old tree, already partly shaped by the nursery. Plant in the dormant season between November and March – although a container-grown cobnut can be planted at any time. Prune when the cobnut is dormant. If the tree consists of a single stem, cut it back to about 18 inches (45cm) from the ground. This promotes the growth of laterals in the following summer, some of which can be used to form main branches.

If the plant is weak at planting and carries only short laterals, it is best left alone for a year before formative pruning begins, except to cut out the centre back to 18 inches (45cm) and to remove any side shoots lower than 12 inches (30cm) from the ground.

A strong 2- or 3-year-old tree should have at least 4 to 6 branches. Cut off any below about 12 inches (30cm) back to the main stem to make the short trunk. Cut the others back hard to about 9 inches (22cm). This hard pruning stimulates the production of more shoots near to the ground which should form further framework branches that do not become too tall and out of reach. During the formative period for the next 2 or 3 years, thin new growth in the winter to allow no more than 10 leaders to grow upwards and outwards to form the goblet shape. Keep the centre open. When the required height of 6 to 7 feet (1.8–2.1m) is reached, top the branch by cutting to a bud or a weak lateral. This should be followed by the plentiful formation of side shoots that are eventually to bear the catkins and female flowers. Remove any growth in the centre as well as shoots on the trunk below the main branches. Pull up any suckers around the base; if they are too tough for this, remove them with a spade or a sharp knife below soil level. It is best not to cut them at ground level, for this results in more unwanted sucker growth.

It is not necessary to stake the tree, although a 1-year-old or weak tree would benefit from the support of a stout cane for the first year or two.

(Left) *The whole tree in flower in February before pruning.*

(Right) *The same tree after pruning: weak laterals bearing female flowers are left unpruned; strong laterals pruned to 3 or 4 buds at about 4 inches (10cm).*

Pruning the established cropping tree

An established tree should be pruned both in winter and in summer. Winter pruning should be carried out when the catkins are freely releasing their pollen and the female flowers are receptive, usually sometime in February. The movement of the branches during pruning helps to disperse the pollen, thus aiding pollination. The female flowers are easily seen at this time, so that none need be removed in error.

Winter pruning is fairly severe, but simple. Each branch should be treated like a cordon. Vigorous laterals produced in the previous summer (and which have been brutted – see *below*) should be cut back to 3 or 4 buds. These laterals for the most part carry the catkins, although there may be some female flowers near the base. Short, twiggy, weak growth may be left unpruned or pruned lightly, because this type of growth usually carries the female flowers.

Keep the tree to 6 or 7 feet (1.8–2.1m) high, if necessary cutting back to weaker branches at this height.

After a number of years the side growth may have become over-long and too thick. To prevent this, each year cut back about one-third of the heavier, older shoots to within 1 to 2 inches (2.5–5cm) of the branch, using long-handled pruners or a saw. New growth should appear from the stub in the next summer, and so the cycle is repeated. Thin and shorten any weak growth where necessary. Remove any growths crowding the centre, and any suckers around the base of the tree, with a small mattock, spade or knife.

Summer pruning is done in August, and is called brutting. This entails breaking by hand the strong laterals (about 12 inches/30cm long) of the current season's growth by about half of their length. The shoots are not completely broken off, but left hanging until the winter. Brutting reduces vigour, induces weaker growth more likely to carry female flowers, and helps the ripening of the nuts.

A neglected cobnut which has become overgrown and unproductive can be dealt with in a similar way. Thin the branch framework to restore the original goblet shape with the open centre. Cut out any heavy side branches larger than

 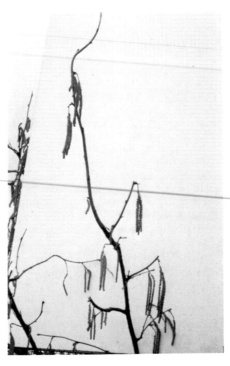

Close-up of a branch before pruning (left) and after (right).

2 inches (5cm) diameter back to their point of origin. Reduce the height by cutting each limb to a weaker branch at a more convenient level. Take out any branches crowding the centre. Spread the operation over 3 or 4 winters to lessen the shock to the tree. This hard pruning induces strong growth in the following summers which can be brutted or left in to form new framework branches where wanted.

Cultivation and manuring

Keep a weed- and grass-free area around the base of the tree over a radius of 2 feet (60cm). This is done by shallow hoeing, followed by an annual application of simazine to keep the ground clean if herbicides are preferred (see p.26).

In late January apply a top dressing of a balanced fertilizer (such as Growmore at 3 oz per sq. yd/100g/m²), over the rooting area, roughly equivalent to slightly beyond the spread of the tree. On light soils mulch the trees with well rotted manure or compost to a depth of 2 inches (5cm) over a radius of 18 inches (45cm).

Picking and storage

Cobnuts should be left on the tree until they are fully mature, a stage not usually reached until late September. Nuts picked too early do not keep but tend to shrivel. Start picking the nuts when the husks begin to turn yellow.

They may be stored in shallow layers in a dry, airy room or shed to dry. Alternatively, hang them up in nets.

Do not leave the harvesting until the nuts fall to the ground, as many are liable to be lost to mice and squirrels. Where these pests are troublesome, picking may have to be done early to get any nuts. Such slightly immature nuts do not develop their best flavour nor keep so long as ripe nuts. Turn the nuts occasionally to ensure that they dry thoroughly. If they become damp, they soon become mouldy and the kernels tainted. When dry, remove the husks and pack the nuts into earthenware jars, clean clay pots, or other suitable receptacles, and then store them in a cool, airy room or shed. If necessary, protect the nuts from mice.

Recommended cultivars

Cobnuts
Cosford, good pollinator.
Nottingham Cob (Pearson's Prolific), catkins numerous, good pollinator; a small tree.

(Above) *Removing a sucker, with a sharp knife, an annual winter job.*

(Right) *The purple-leaved filbert is ornamental as well as useful, with claret-red catkins followed by purple leaves in early summer.*

Filberts

Kentish Cob (Lambert's Filbert), the most widely planted; hardy and reliable; despite its name, it is a filbert; pollinated by 'Nottingham Cob'.

Red Filbert, excellent flavour; attractive, long claret-red catkins.

White Filbert, as above except for colour.

Purple-leaved Filbert, more ornamental, with purple leaves in spring; but yields a moderate crop; excellent flavour; long, dark red catkins.

Pests

APHIDS soil the leaves with honeydew and sooty mould, and WINTER MOTH caterpillars feeding during April and May cause holes in the foliage (*see* p.69). This can be unsightly, but neither pest has a serious effect on the tree.

SQUIRRELS may eat the whole crop, often starting before the nuts are fully ripe. Shooting or traps can be effective in reducing squirrel numbers, although this is not always possible in gardens.

NUT WEEVIL, a small brown beetle with a long curved snout, is indicated by holes in the shell. It lays eggs in immature nuts, and these hatch into small white maggots that feed on the kernel. In August, the maggots bore holes in the shell in order to come out and pupate in the soil. Light infestations are not serious, but if many nuts have been attacked, in subsequent seasons spray with permethrin or fenitrothion in late May, and again 3 weeks later.

NUT GALL MITES cause rounded, swollen buds, but are not a serious pest because infestations are generally light. No chemical controls are available to amateur gardeners. Any shoots which are heavily galled could be pruned out during the winter.

Diseases

BROWN ROT fungus (*see* p.70) causes the nuts to fall in July and August when they are fully grown but still unripe. The disease usually follows an attack by the nut weevil (*see* above). Collect and burn fallen nuts.

POWDERY MILDEW shows as white, powdery patches which may completely cover the undersides of young leaves. Spray with benomyl, bupirimate with triforine, carbendazim or thiophanate methyl according to the manufacturer's instructions.

GREY MOULD (*see* p.201) can cause die-back of branches.

HONEY FUNGUS *see* p.70.

Treatment of overvigorous unproductive trees

Before deciding the method to be used to check the growth of over-vigorous trees, some of the more usual reasons why the trees are vigorous or unproductive or both should be considered.

The trees may have been grafted on to very vigorous rootstocks. Provided that there is room and the cultural conditions are right, this is not a mistake because such trees usually bear heavier crops than the same cultivar on a dwarfing rootstock. However, they are much later coming into bearing than the more precocious, less vigorous rootstocks.

The trees may be over-vigorous and unproductive because they have been pruned too hard in the past. The effect of hard pruning is to cause most of the buds that remain to grow out as shoots instead of developing into fruit buds. Tree growth is strong but the crops are small. No pruning at all results in too many fruit buds and poor shoot growth. The aim in pruning should be to maintain a balance between fruitfulness and vigour.

Another common fault is the application of too much nitrogen. Trees so treated make lush growth but few fruit buds, and the fruits that are produced are usually large and of poor keeping quality.

It is possible to check growth in various ways. Lighter pruning in the winter and summer pruning (p.36) are examples. Another method is to grow the trees in grass (p.56), which competes for nutrients and water. Where the trees may be receiving too much nitrogen, nitrogenous manures should be reduced or cut out altogether.

Other more drastic ways of reducing vigour are root pruning and bark ringing. Both have their disadvantages, and bark ringing in particular should only be used when other methods have failed. Neither technique should be used on fruit trees which are growing poorly. Stone fruits should not be bark ringed because of the risk of silver leaf infection.

There are many other reasons for unfruitfulness, not always associated with excess vigour. Examples are poor pollination, starvation, bullfinch damage,

Root pruning a tree that is too big to lift:
(Left) First mark out the trench at a 2 to 4 foot (60cm–1.2m) radius.

(Opposite above left) Take out the trench to expose the roots.
(Opposite above right) Cut the thick anchorage roots with a saw.

(Opposite below) Leave intact, as far as possible, the thin fibrous feeding roots, before returning the soil to the trench.

frost damage, and lack of sunlight due to overcrowding or shading by taller plants or buildings.

Root pruning

Fruit trees that are producing poor crops because they are growing too vigorously can be induced to form fruit buds by root pruning. This is done in the winter (November/December) and means exposing and cutting back the thick anchorage roots. The thin fibrous feeding roots should be left undamaged as far as possible. A trench about 2 to 4 feet (60cm to 1.2m) radius, according to the size of the tree, should be dug round the tree and the thick roots exposed cut. Vigorous downward-growing roots should also be cut by undercutting.

Young trees can be lifted to make sure all the thick roots are cut, and replanted. Older trees too large to lift, should have the roots cut *in situ*. With these trees, it is often better to root prune in 2 stages,

Bark ringing:
(Far left) *make parallel incisions in the bark right round the trunk, cutting down to the heartwood. The width of the ring depends on the size of the tree.*

(Left) *Peel off bark.*

(Below) *Cover the 'ring' with adhesive tape wide enough to bridge the gap. Remove the tape in autumn when callusing is complete.*

tree with well rotted manure or compost, keeping the mulch away from the trunk.

Bark ringing

Bark ringing also can be used to bring over-vigorous trees into cropping, but it is only suitable for apples and pears. It is easier and quicker than root pruning, but can seriously damage, or even kill a tree if done incorrectly.

Ringing is done at blossom time. A complete ring of bark down to the hardwood is removed from the trunk or a branch, thus disrupting part of the vascular system. As a result, carbohydrates and other carbon assimilates accumulate above the wound so inducing better fruit set.

The width of the ring is determined by the age, size and vigour of the tree; the younger and smaller the tree, the narrower the ring. On larger trees it should never be more than $\frac{1}{2}$ inch (1cm) wide. With a sharp knife make two parallel cuts round the trunk, cutting through the bark and soft tissue below. Peel off the bark and soft tissue and cover the ring immediately with several turns of adhesive tape. The tape must be wide enough to bridge the gap and not fall on the wound beneath. The tape can be removed when callusing is complete, in the autumn.

doing one half one winter and the other half the next.

When refilling the hole, firm the soil well. Root-pruned trees need to be staked after the operation, and in dry spells in the following summer should be watered copiously. It also helps to mulch a young

Renovation of tree fruits

Pruning apple and pear trees to re-invigorate them should be done in the winter at any time from November to March, but avoid pruning in severe frosty weather. Stone fruits, for example cherries and plums, should be pruned when the sap is rising, i.e. in the early spring or immediately after cropping, at which times there is the least risk of infection by silver leaf and bacterial canker, which enter through pruning cuts. Even at that time avoid making large wounds on stone fruits; any such cuts must be protected immediately with a tree paint.

Before embarking on the task, if the trees are very large and there will be obviously a lot of work to get them back into shape and down to a more accessible height for picking and pruning, the gardener should consider whether the labour is worthwhile and the space the trees take up economically justified. Today, with certain fruits, especially apples, there are available trees grafted onto dwarfing rootstocks which will remain small and within 2 or 3 years from planting start to bear fruit. Within 7 or 8 years they are into full cropping.

Having taken these points into consideration, it is usually possible to rejuvenate a fruit tree. The most promising is one with a sound, healthy trunk and main branches which shows some sign of having made good growth and yielded fruit in the past.

Turning now to the tree in detail, there are two extremes as far as the neglected tree is concerned. Either it is too large and over-crowded, or it is starved and stunted. Readers must decide in which category their trees are.

The over-large and over-crowded tree

The first requirement is to get the trees adequately spaced. If necessary pull out any which are too close to their neighbours, but remember in the thinning process the need for cross pollination with certain kinds of fruits (see pp.216–221).

The next essential is to make sure that the main branches are well spaced. Remove any low branches which are an obstruction, are badly placed and crossing over the tree, and any tall branches, including vigorous centrally placed ones difficult to spray and pick. When removing a branch, cut back to the point of origin or to a limb large enough to take up the vigour. The latter should be not less than one third of the diameter of the branch removed. Do not cut back to an insignificant branch or leave a stub, otherwise the cut end is likely to die. Remove dead and broken branches. Saw cuts should be protected with an approved tree paint or grafting wax. Before painting, pare the edges of the wound with a sharp knife so that there is a smooth surface for painting.

Always undercut first and complete the cut from above. Where branches are too close together or one overshades another, one should be removed or shortened, so that they are at least 2 feet (60cm) apart when side by side and not less than 3 feet (90cm) apart when one is directly above another. This applies to the very large tree with many branches. With the smaller tree where the branches are not so numerous or so large, the pruning should be moderated accordingly.

The reduction in height and the cutting out of main limbs is called de-horning and if this involves the removal of a lot of wood, it is advisable to spread the renovation over a period of several years by treating a few branches each year to lessen the shock to the tree. The object is to achieve improved spacing of the limbs so that light and air can reach all parts of the tree as well as to make it easier to spray, cultivate and pick the fruit.

After such drastic pruning, the tree may react by producing a multitude of shoots in the summer. Where these are badly placed, for example in the centre of the tree, or where they are particularly overcrowded, for example at the end of a cut limb, then they can be removed or thinned before the growth has had a chance to harden.

It must be stressed that *very hard* winter pruning causes most of the buds that remain to grow out as shoots instead of developing into fruit buds. Tree growth is strong, but the crops small. No pruning at all results in too many fruit buds and poor shoot growth. The aim in pruning should be to maintain the correct balance between fruitfulness and vigour.

(Right) *An apple growing in grass and making poor growth.*

(Below right) *The same tree with grass and weeds cleared away and then mulched.*

Opposite:
(Top) *A large old apple tree before being reduced in height and after winter pruning.*

(Centre) *Height is reduced by cutting back to a lower branch large enough to take up the vigour.*

(Bottom) *Large wounds should have their edges pared smooth and the cut area is painted liberally with wound paint.*

If the tree is growing vigorously or has been subjected to very hard pruning in the past, then pruning should be relatively light to discourage shoot growth. Thin out where necessary, as described above, cut out crossing over laterals, thin any leaders in excess of those required for reasonable spacing and clusters of strong unproductive laterals which are overshading other spurs. (See also summer pruning, tying down, root pruning and bark ringing.)

The stunted and starved tree
With a weak tree bearing a mass of dense complex spur systems but making no new growth, the first task is to remove worn out and overshading spurs and to thin the others. This process allows more light to the remaining spurs and results in better quality fruits. It also increases fruit size as well as tree vigour which should be directed to encourage the formation of new shoots to be employed as leaders and laterals for the gradual replacement of worn out framework branches and spurs.

Finally do not expect an improvement overnight. The effect will not be noticed for at least 2 or 3 years and remember pruning is only one factor in the process of rejuvenation. There is also the need to feed the trees annually and to control pests and diseases. Thin growth, weak fruit buds, small leaves and early defoliation are symptoms of starvation and sometimes lack of water. The trees should therefore be fed, irrigated and, if need be, sprayed.

SOFT FRUITS

Soft fruits are most delicious when picked and eaten straight off the plant, having developed their full flavour. Shop fruit cannot have that extra flavour, as the fruit must be picked slightly earlier in order to reach the market when ripe. If the space available for fruit growing in the garden is limited, concentrate on growing the soft fruits, which have a more fragile flavour, but start to fruit relatively early in their life.

Strawberries, planted in late summer, will crop in just under a year. The next group, the cane fruits, i.e. raspberries, blackberries and hybrid berries start to fruit in the second year after planting.

The third group, the bush fruits, includes blackcurrants, redcurrants and whitecurrants, gooseberries, and blueberries.

There are two important problems related to soft fruits that need to be watched. These are attack by birds and infection by virus diseases.

The only certain method of protecting the plants from birds, which will attack both fruit buds in winter and fruits in summer, is to enclose them in a bird-proof cage. The framework of such a cage must be strong enough to withstand the weather, and the mesh of the netting must be small enough to prevent the entry of small bud-eating birds (such as bullfinches and sparrows). A walk-in cage about 6 or 7 feet (1.8–2.1m) high is most convenient for the bush and cane fruits. (Strawberries are only attacked at fruiting and can be protected then by a temporary net cage, see pp.147–149.)

The other problem is infection by virus disease. Soft fruits may succumb to one or other of a series of these diseases, resulting in poor growth, and little or no crop. Infected plants are incurable, and must be dug up and burnt.

It is especially important to start with healthy, vigorous plants, bought from a reputable nursery. For some fruits there are certification schemes; plants have been inspected and passed as being true to type, substantially free from pests and diseases and otherwise healthy. With such plants there is every prospect of high yields.

If you are sure your plants are healthy, it is convenient to propagate from them. But there is some risk, as virus infection does not always show obvious symptoms. (Plants raised from diseased cuttings or runners will never grow or crop satisfactorily, so it is always best to start with plants known to be healthy.)

All soft fruits, except blueberries, are self-pollinating, and one cultivar will set an adequate crop when grown by itself. A selection of cultivars is grown to extend the season of fruiting rather than to ensure crop setting.

It is usual to plant soft fruits apart from tree fruits because they are smaller, and most ripen earlier. There may also be occasions when it is necessary to spray tree fruits at a time when the soft fruits are ripening.

Renovation of soft fruits

Those taking over a neglected garden may find it better in the long run to uproot and burn all soft fruits, because in many cases they are unproductive through being infected with incurable virus diseases. It is unwise to replant fruit in the same position as before. Better to select a fresh area not previously used for fruit. After thoroughly preparing the ground, plant as suggested earlier with healthy young plants and canes. These should be acquired from a reliable source, preferably carrying the Ministry of Agriculture's certificate of virus-tested stock.

With bush fruits that have not been neglected for too long, it may be possible to rejuvenate them by cutting out old and useless wood and applying mulches, manures and fertilizers.

Ground which has been allowed to become overgrown with weeds needs to be thoroughly dug over and cleaned. This is an opportunity to incorporate organic manures, compost, or artificials suitable for the respective fruits. As far as possible avoid damage to the roots while digging.

(Above left) *Making good use of space: train blackberries and hybrid berries over an arch, but choose thornless cultivars.*

(Above right) *A temporary net cover for wall trained redcurrants and gooseberries, with alpine strawberries below. Canes are carefully placed to keep the net away from the foliage.*

(Right) *When making a simple fruit cage for temporary protection, a plant pot or jam jar on the top of each post will enable the net to be drawn over without being torn.*

Strawberries

Strawberries are the quickest crop to fruit after planting. Runners planted in July or up to the middle of September fruit in the following June or July. But the plants are liable to attack from certain soil-borne pests and diseases, and so are best grown in rotation (for example with vegetables). A strawberry bed is generally kept for 3 or 4 years and then cleared away before planting on new ground where strawberries have not been grown for at least 3 years. So in the garden the strawberries might include 1-year-old, 2-year-old and 3-year-old plants, and after the crop has been picked the oldest plants would then be dug out and new runners planted in fresh ground.

It is essential to buy plants from a reputable source, to be sure that they are healthy. In England and Wales a nursery that supplies plants which have been inspected and certified under the Ministry of Agriculture is the sensible choice. In Scotland it is illegal for a nursery to sell uncertified plants.

Preparation of the site

Soils rich in humus and which are well drained are best for strawberries. Few soils are like this, although in a good vegetable garden the humus content is likely to be adequate. It is difficult to get rid of perennial weeds, especially couch grass in an established bed, so great care has to be taken to remove all perennial weed roots when preparing for planting (see p.27).

A month before planting, dig in well rotted compost or farmyard manure at the rate of one barrowload to about 30 sq. ft (9m²). Rake off any organic material left on the surface which might harbour slugs, snails and millipedes. Just before planting, fork into the top soil a balanced fertilizer, such as Growmore at 3 oz per sq. yd (100g/m²). Water the land if it is dry, firm it, rake it, and finally mark it out for planting.

Planting

The earlier that strawberries are planted, the better the crop the following year. Planting as soon as runners are available in late June to mid-September allows the plants to become established and the flower buds to develop before the soil cools down in the autumn. Planting may be done later, up to May, provided that the soil and weather conditions are suitable. In areas where hard winters may be expected, delay planting until spring. The plants can be overwintered in a sheltered spot or open cold frame. Runners planted in the late autumn, winter or spring, should (preferably) not be allowed to fruit in their first season, but have the flowers removed to allow good strong plants to develop for cropping from the second year onwards.

Space the rows 30 to 36 inches (75–90cm) apart, and plant the runners 15 to 18 inches (38–45cm) in the rows. The wider spacings are for fertile soils. Make a hole with a trowel large enough to take the roots well spread out, and plant firmly. After planting, the crown must be at soil level (see illustration).

Black polythene as a mulch

Some growers may prefer to plant the runners through a black or blue polythene sheet laid over the soil, which keeps the weeds down and the fruit clean. Blue polythene creates cooler soil conditions than black and the fruits are slightly later but of better quality. Watering has to be carefully monitored and it is beneficial to put down a line of seep hose or drip irrigation underneath. A black polythene sheet, also available, has tiny slits in it which allow rainwater to percolate through but still stop weed growth.

First construct a slight ridge of about 3 inches (7.5cm) high down the centre of the row to be planted. This ridge allows the water to drain off the polythene to between the rows. It is extremely important that the soil is thoroughly moistened before laying the polythene. Use 150 gauge black polythene, 3 feet (90cm) wide; black dustbin bags cut into strips are useful. Lay the sheet down over the ridge and, using a *blunt* spade, force about 4 to 6 inches (10–15cm) of the polythene vertically into the soil on each side. It is important that the polythene is stretched tightly so that there are no hollows in which water can gather. When completed, there should be about a 6- to 12-inch (15–30cm) gap between one row

(Right) *Planting at 15 to 18 inches (38–45cm) apart, with rows 30 to 36 inches (75–90cm) apart.*

(Far right) *Close-up of planting; the roots well spread out in the hole.*

(Below) *After planting; the crown is level with the soil surface. If too deep, the plant may rot, and if not deep enough, the roots may dry out.*

(Below right) *Planting through slits in black polythene film.*

and the next to allow rain to permeate. On light soils where irrigation lines have not been laid, it may be necessary to water through the slits in very dry weather.

Plant the runners through small crosswise slits, and tuck the flaps back around the crown.

Cultivation

After planting keep the plants well watered until they have started producing new leaves. Watering may also be needed in periods of dry weather, especially on dry soils.

For strawberries, watering is best given in the morning so that the foliage is dry by nightfall. Water that settles on flowers is likely to increase the incidence of grey mould (botrytis) on the fruits, so that irrigation applied along the rows at soil level – such as drip nozzle and seep hose systems – are the most useful. Yields are increased by watering when the fruit is ripening. Watering in September increases flower bud development for the next year. Runner production is improved by watering in July and August.

Keep down weeds and surplus runners by careful hoeing and/or herbicide application (see p.27).

As the growing fruits begin to weigh down the truss, some kind of soil covering is necessary to keep the fruits clean. Straw is the most useful, but before strawing scatter slug pellets about 6 inches (15cm) apart along the rows and between the plants. Tuck the straw under the berries and cover the soil between the rows; this helps to keep the weeds down and to prevent soil compaction during picking. Alternatives to straw are dry bracken, specially-made strawberry mats, or a layer of black polythene down each side of the row.

It is important not to put down the straw too early in the season because it may prevent the free flow of heat upwards from the soil, so increasing the possibility of frost damage on cold nights. Frost protection during flowering can be given by spreading straw lightly over the plants on frosty nights, but it must be removed during the day. Strawing is not needed for plants planted through black plastic. Cut off any runners as soon as they are produced, unless they are wanted to fill gaps in the row or to establish a new bed. Some gardeners may

(Above) A strawberry plot, showing the use of plastic both as a mulch, and as a cover to obtain early fruits.

(Opposite above) Strawing down; first put down slug pellets, then tuck the straw under the berries and right across the row.

(Opposite below) Specially made mats are an alternative to straw. Be sure they are wide enough to keep the berries off the soil.

prefer a continuous or matted row in the second and third year rather than spaced plants. The yield is higher, although the quality of the fruits is not so good. In this case tuck the runners in so that they root in the row, but keep the ground clear between the rows.

Protection from birds and squirrels

It is necessary to net the whole plot of strawberries during the fruiting season. Use plastic or nylon netting draped over the posts, and wire or strong string at about 4 feet (1.2m) high. Picking is easier with the nets at this height, although with a small bed the nets could be draped over string stretched not less than 18 inches (45cm) above the rows. Manufactured fruit cages are also available, as well as cloches fitted with netting, as an alternative to glass or plastic. If squirrels are a problem use 1-inch (2.5cm) mesh galvanised wire netting.

Picking

Pick the fruits when fully ripe and dry. Put any diseased (rotting) fruits in a separate container and burn. Avoid bruising of the juicy berries by picking by the stalk rather than the fruit, although strawberries for jam can be picked without stalk and calyx.

After fruiting

As soon as picking is finished, cut off the old leaves using hand shears or a sickle, to leave about 4 inches (10cm) of leaf stem so that the crowns and young leaves are not damaged. Cut off unwanted runners, remove the old straw, leaves and weeds, and burn the lot to get rid of any pests and diseases present. Then fork in sulphate of potash between the rows at $\frac{1}{2}$ oz per sq. yd (15g/m²). If the soil is shallow or the plants weak, fork in Growmore at 2 oz per sq. yd (65g/m²) instead of the potash. If the ground is dry, water the plot thoroughly. The same programme should be repeated in the third year.

Propagation

It is not easy to buy certified strawberry runners in time for early planting (July/August), although it is possible to

obtain cold-stored runners from a few specialist strawberry growers. But it may be more convenient to keep a few healthy de-blossomed plants, ideally certified stock from the previous year, in a nursery bed to produce a supply of runners for the next planting. Usually these are grown on a 4-foot square (1.2 × 1.2m) planting with the runners trained towards the centre so there is no chance of mixing up the cultivars. Each block would consist of one cultivar. Do not allow the mother plants to flower because this delays the production of runners and reduces their vigour. Keep a good control over pests and diseases, particularly aphids which carry virus diseases.

If there is no room for a special runner bed, runners can be taken from healthy fruiting plants. Allow no more than 5 runners per plant, stopping the runner just beyond the plantlet.

The runners root more quickly if they are pegged down on to the soil's surface or, better still, rooted into small pots (3½-inch/9cm plastic or peat pots), plunged level, and containing John Innes compost No. 1. Pot-grown runners transplant better than open ground plants. Peg down the runners in late June or early July; U-shaped thin pieces of wire about 4 inches (10cm) long (straightened-out paper-clips) are ideal. Keep the runner beds well watered in dry weather. In about early August, when they are well rooted, cut the runners from the parent and plant out into their permanent positions.

The runner bed should be cleared away each year as soon as sufficient runners have been taken, and a new runner bed established on a fresh site. Replace the stock with new certified plants every 4 or 5 years, or even earlier if there is any suspicion of virus infection.

Extending the season

Early strawberries can be obtained by covering the plants in late winter with glass or plastic cloches, or with polythene tunnels. Strawberries under cloches may be 3 to 4 weeks earlier, and those under polythene 1 to 2 weeks earlier than un-protected plants. At the other end of the season late strawberries can be obtained by planting perpetuals (remontants) which crop from July until stopped by the

A low cage of netting protects strawberries from birds, but is high enough for easy picking.

Netted cloches over strawberries keep the birds off while giving plenty of ventilation.

autumn frosts (see p.153). Certain cultivars of the ordinary summer-fruiting strawberry, like 'Redgauntlet', in a warm summer or if protected in the spring, produce a second crop in the autumn. It is possible to extend the season even further by covering both types from mid-September onwards. Remove the cloches or polythene tunnels at the end of December.

Cultivation under protection
In general the cultivation of strawberries under protection is the same as for those in the open, except that watering and ventilation need particular attention. Usually 1-year-old plants are grown in this way rather than older strawberries, because they are liable to grow too large under cover, so impeding air circulation as well as making them prone to leaf scorch. The spacing is as recommended for outdoor culture, although a more economical use of the protection would be to double up on the spacing in the row, planting at 8 to 9 inches (20–22cm) apart and then, after harvesting, removing every other plant to leave them at 16 to 18 inches (40–45cm) apart.

Types of cloches. There are many types of cloches available, made of plastic or glass. The most important point is that they should allow sufficient room for development. The minimum width should be about 18 inches (45cm), preferably more, and the height about 12 inches (30cm).

Polythene tunnels. This method of protection consists of continuous tunnels made of polythene film (150 gauge/38mμ) supported on galvanised wire hoops to which it is held down tightly by string ties.

The usual width of polythene when purchased as a strip is 48 inches (1.2m). The film must be stretched out tightly over the hoops and each end secured either by tying to a stout wooden peg driven into the ground, or by burying in sufficient depth of soil to provide good anchorage.

The first 2 hoops at each end of the row should be spaced at only 6 inches (15cm) for extra support, the remainder spaced at 30 inches (75cm) apart. The hoops can be made from gauge 6 or 8 galvanised wire. The rings, one on each side of the

Propagation:
(Above) pegging down the young runners into 3-inch (8cm) pots plunged into the soil.

(Left) The roots have filled the pot, and the young plant is ready for planting out.

(Opposite above) Plenty of ventilation must be given on warm sunny days to strawberries under polythene film tunnels, by pulling up the sides, to help pollination and prevent the build up of high temperatures.

(Opposite below) The old leaves of 'ordinary' strawberries are cut off immediately after harvest and burnt. Cut about 4 inches (10cm) above the crown so that it is not damaged. Defoliation must not be delayed, otherwise next year's crop will be reduced.

(Above) *Grey mould infection of fruits: a very troublesome disease in wet weather (see p.157).*

(Left) *Barn cloches of glass being placed over maiden strawberries in late January/early February.*

hoop, facing outwards, are formed by holding the correct length for the leg ends (6in./15cm) of the wire in a vice and pulling the wire round a small piece of tubing of $\frac{1}{2}$ inch (1cm) outside diameter. The wire can then be bent over an arrangement of nails in a board to produce a half-circle.

Use of cloches and polythene tunnels. Plants are generally covered in February, although it can be done at any time from January to mid-March. Ventilation during the cold early days of spring should not be necessary, but as the plants start flowering some ventilation must be given, particularly on warm sunny days, to help pollination and to prevent the build-up of high temperatures which can result in weak drawn growth and fruit malformation. The cloches should be moved wider apart to allow more air movement, and the sides of the polythene tunnels be pushed up on one side. Ventilation should be continued whenever the weather is hot. Occasionally some rain should be allowed to reach the soil.

Immediately after the protected crop has been cleared remove the cover and cut off the old foliage and any runners. Apply sulphate of ammonia at $\frac{1}{2}$ oz per sq. yd (15g/m²), keeping the fertilizer clear of the crowns.

Choice of cultivars. Any of the ordinary summer-fruiting cultivars can be used. The heavy-cropping, reliable cultivars, although not the best-flavoured, are 'Cambridge Favourite' and 'Redgauntlet'. 'Redgauntlet' has the additional advantage in that if protected in the spring it will yield a second crop in the autumn after a warm summer. 'Honeoye' gives the earliest crop and has a good flavour, and so has the second early 'Cambridge Vigour'. 'Royal Sovereign', although poor in yield, is considered to be the best in quality.

Perpetual (remontant) strawberries
Perpetual strawberries carry on the succession of fruit after summer-fruiting cultivars are over. The amount picked from them at any one time is not great, but plants fruit more or less continuously from July to the end of November, when poor light and frosts finally stop development.

With many cultivars, fruit size is poor in the second and later years; most are therefore best grown as an annual crop, replanting each year with new plants. 'Gento' is an exception, as it yields good-sized berries in its second year.

Very few cultivars come within the certification scheme. If it is known that yours are not certified, it is as well to assume that they are carrying virus and to plant them as far as possible from summer-fruiting plants.

Because perpetuals fruit in summer when the weather is often hot and dry, it is important that the soil is fertile and moisture-retentive, although well drained. Plant from August to October or in the spring; watering may be needed to help the plants to become established. Late autumn or winter planting is not recommended because the young plants may not become sufficiently well established to withstand the winter.

The cultural requirements, including soil preparation and spacing, are the same as for ordinary strawberries.

Remove the first flush of flowers, usually in late May or early June, to ensure good pickings from August.

During dry weather in the growing season, water the plants thoroughly but try to keep the water off the berries to reduce the risk of grey mould.

If the plants are to be grown on for a second year, at the end of the season tidy up the rows by removing unwanted runners, weeds and any dead leaves. Then lightly fork between the rows. In January apply sulphate of potash as a top dressing at 1 oz per sq. yd (33g/m²).

Alpine strawberries
Alpine strawberries are selected strains of the wild strawberry *Fragaria vesca* subspecies *alpina*. The fruits are very small and rather dry, but have an excellent flavour and perfume. They make an ornamental edging to a border, producing masses of white flowers.

They are best grown from seed, the plants kept for only two years before re-sowing; they can be propagated by division. A few cultivars produce runners. But maintaining virus-free stocks is difficult because they soon become infected. Sow in the autumn or in the spring. Following autumn sowing, the seedlings should be over-wintered in a cold frame and planted out in May. With a spring sowing, sow in March and plant out in May.

(Above) 'Tamella' in a polythene tunnel grown through black polythene.

(Right) 'Royal Sovereign' is the best flavoured strawberry but only gives a moderate crop.

(Opposite above) Tunnel erection: the film being brought over the hoops.

(Opposite left) Securing the film with string.

(Opposite right) Alpine strawberries make a decorative edging.

Sow on the surface of John Innes seed compost in seed-trays, and cover lightly with sharp sand. Cover the boxes with glass and paper for shade, and keep at 65° to 75°F (18–24°C). Remove the covering when the seedlings appear. Germination can be slow and erratic.

As soon as the seedlings have 2 true leaves and are big enough to handle, prick them out into boxes at 1 inch (2.5cm) apart. Gradually harden them off, then once the danger of hard frosts is over, transplant at 12 inches (30cm) apart and 2½ feet (75cm) between the rows. They need watering in dry periods, and a foliar feed is also beneficial.

Picking. To bring out their full flavour and perfume, it is best to pick the fully ripe fruits in the evening, crush them slightly, sprinkle with sugar and leave the berries to soak overnight.

Recommended cultivars

Summer-fruiting cultivars (in season order)
Honeoye. Very early. Suitable for cloches and tunnels. Crops well, large fruits. Some susceptibility to red core and verticillium, some resistance to botrytis. Flavour excellent.
Tamella. Early first year, mid-season thereafter. Suitable for forcing. Crops heavily, very large firm fruits. Flavour fair.
Elvira. Early. Crops heavily, large soft fruits. Susceptible to mildew. Flavour good.
Idil. Early. Crops well, medium to large dark red fruits. Flavour good.
Cambridge Vigour. Early. Yield and fruit size good in first year, but both decline thereafter. Flavour good.
Royal Sovereign. Susceptible to diseases and cropping only moderate, but the flavour is very good.
Redgauntlet. Heavy cropper. Some resistance to red core, verticillium and botrytis. Produces a second crop in the autumn if protected in the spring or if the summer is hot. Flavour only fair.
Cambridge Favourite. Widely grown. Unfortunately becoming affected with a physiological problem called June yellows but there are clean clones available. Otherwise reliable and crops well. Flavour moderate.
Elsanta. Widely grown, vigorous, suits most soils. Crops well, yielding large firm

fruits. Some susceptibility to verticillium and red core. Resistant to mildew. Flavour very good.
Korona. Heavy cropper, large to medium, dark-fleshed fruits. Flavour good.
Hapil. Vigorous plant. Crops well on light soils and dry conditions. Fruits large, attractive orange-red. Flavour good.
Bounty. A heavy cropper of small to medium fruits. Size deteriorates in the second year. Flavour very good.
Cambridge Late Pine. A moderate cropper. Fruits dark crimson. The flavour is very good and very sweet, but certified stock is difficult to obtain.
Tenira. Crops well, good disease-resistance. In warm summers bears an autumn crop. Flavour very good.
Domanil. Late. Fruits large, dull dark colour. Flavour good. A heavy cropper.
Bogota. Very late flowering and fruiting. Medium to large orange-red fruits which freeze well. Moderately susceptible to verticillium and June yellows. Moderate cropper. Flavour good.
Pandora. A most promising cultivar because of its very late season and heavy cropping. It is male sterile, however, and a pollinator must be planted either as an adjoining row or interplanted as one plant in six. Suitable pollinators include 'Tenira' and 'Hapil'. Flavour very good.

Perpetuals (Remontant)
Rapella. Fruits ripen late summer. High-yielding medium to large fruits of good flavour. Freezes well. Shy runner producer and best propagated by division.
Aromel. Fruits medium to large, soft orange-red. Crops reasonably well. Flavour excellent.
Gento. Small to medium berries. Crops well. Flavour very good. Yields a fair crop in the second year.
Ostara. Heavy cropping, medium-sized, red, conical soft berries of good flavour. Susceptible to verticillium and red core.

Alpines
Baron Solemacher.
Alexandria.
Alpine Yellow. Yellow-fruited.

Promising new cultivars
Kouril. Late mid-summer cultivar. Good yields of large, well flavoured berries.
Mara de Bois. A perpetual, reputed to have a wild strawberry flavour.

Signs of virus; plants stunted and dying out. Dig up and burn such plants.

Rhapsody. Late. Attractive glossy fruits. Crops well. Resistant to red core. Does well in the North and in Scotland.

Pests

APHIDS (greenflies) breed rapidly on new growths from May onwards and, in addition to weakening and fouling infested plants, may spread virus diseases. Spray with pirimicarb, dimethoate or heptenophos in late April, and at other times if colonies are seen on the plants.

SLUGS eat ripening strawberries, and damage is best prevented by baiting with slug pellets well before putting down the straw. High humidity and the use of organic fertilizers and mulches tend to encourage slugs.

GLASSHOUSE RED SPIDER MITE infests strawberry leaves which become severely discoloured, bronzed and may die. Mites are more likely on plants grown in cloches or polythene tunnels. Spraying with malathion, pirimiphos-methyl or dimethoate may give some control but too frequent use will result in resistance being developed by the pest. Biological control with the predatory mite *Phytoseiulus* is possible, but does not work if non-selective insecticides are used against aphids because these also kill the predators.

EELWORMS, TARSONEMID MITES and VIRUS DISEASES all produce symptoms of stunting, distortion and discoloration in the plants that are superficially similar. Expert diagnosis and advice on treatment should be sought if such symptoms appear in a crop. Dig up and burn immediately any severely affected plants.

BIRDS such as blackbirds eat the ripening fruits unless plants are protected by netting (see p.147).

STRAWBERRY BEETLE takes seeds from the outside of strawberry fruits, which spoils their appearance and encourages rotting. The beetles are shiny, black, and about $\frac{1}{2}$ inch (1cm) long. They also feed on weed seeds, so keep the beds free of weeds to discourage the beetles. They can be killed with methiocarb slug pellets.

Diseases

VIRUS DISEASES are very troublesome on strawberries, causing stunting and a poor or non-existent crop. Affected plants show leaf symptoms including yellow edges, yellow or purplish mottling or blotching, or crinkling. Dig up and burn such plants. New plants certified free of virus disease should be planted on a fresh site, or in new soil, because some viruses are transmitted by soil eelworms.

The most common virus diseases of strawberries are spread by aphids (see above).

GREY MOULD caused by the fungus *Botrytis cinerea* can result in serious fruit losses in a wet summer. Affected berries rot and become covered with a brownish grey fluffy growth. As soon as the first flowers open, spray with benomyl, carbendazim or thiophanate methyl, repeating twice at 10- to 14-day intervals. Pick off affected fruits and remove them from the strawberry plot.

STRAWBERRY MILDEW causes the fruit lose its shine and the leaves to turn purple and curl upwards showing greyish lower surfaces. Spray with benomyl or carbendazim or thiophanate methyl according to the manufacturer's instructions, or dust with sulphur dust. Sulphur dust should not be used on ripening fruit to be canned or frozen, to avoid possible taint.

After harvesting, remove the old leaves by cutting or burning them off, or spray again with one of the above fungicides.

LEAF SPOTS may be produced by several different fungi, and show as circular purple, red or white spots, particularly on old leaves. In severe cases the leaves wither and disintegrate.

LEAF BLOTCH produces larger brown blotches with a purple border; blackening and rotting of the leaf and flower stalks occurs, followed by withering of fruits and death of leaves.

Remove and burn affected leaves. Mancozeb may also be effective used according to the manufacturer's instructions.

(Above) 'Cambridge Late Pine' has excellent flavour.

(Left) 'Rabunda', a heavy cropping perpetual cultivar.

(Opposite above) 'Cambridge Vigour'; 1-year-old plants crop earlier in the season than 2-year-old and older plants.

(Opposite left) Frost damage to flowers – a black "eye".

(Opposite right) 'Tamella' has very large fruits.

Raspberries

The raspberry is another fruit for quick cropping and comparatively heavy yields. From an established row of summer fruiting raspberries, a crop of about 1½ to 2 lb per foot (2–3kg/m) is a reasonable expectation. A row of autumn fruiting raspberries can produce about ¼ lb per foot run of row (0.6kg/m).

Raspberries have a perennial root system of suckering habit, and in summer-fruiting cultivars this produces canes each year which bear fruit the following year and then die. The canes of autumn-fruiting raspberries grow and fruit in one season. It is most important to begin with healthy plants, preferably canes certified as healthy and true to type under the Ministry of Agriculture's voluntary inspection scheme. Starting with healthy canes, a row of raspberries should give good crops for up to 12 years, after which they may start to degenerate from virus infection.

Site and soil

Raspberries flower in late spring and so usually escape frost damage to the flowers. But they need shelter from strong winds, which can break fruiting laterals, especially in cultivars with long ones, such as 'Malling Admiral'. A sunny position is preferable, although plants do grow satisfactorily in partial shade provided that the soil does not become dry.

Raspberries like a slightly acid soil (pH 6.5–6.7), well drained, but not drying out too quickly during the summer. They are intolerant of badly drained land, typically heavy clays, and on such soils the drainage must be improved (see below).

In soils where chalk comes near the surface, canes may grow poorly, and the leaves become yellow between the veins, a sure sign of iron deficiency (see p.24).

Preparing the site

For this long-term crop it is worth while preparing the site thoroughly, and such preparation should include the removal of all perennial weeds. Raspberries make deep roots as well as masses of fibrous surface roots, and so the organic material needs to be well mixed into the top 18 inches (45cm) of the soil.

Early autumn is the best time to start. Dig a trench 1 spade deep and 3 spades wide. Fork into the bottom a layer 3 to 4 inches (7.5–10cm) thick of well rotted manure or compost. Fill in the trench, and fork into the top soil a compound fertilizer such as Growmore at 3 oz per sq. yd (100g/m²).

Drainage can be improved on a small scale by incorporating builder's rubble and similar materials along the row well below the root area, i.e. not less than 1 spade depth. If there is still doubt about the drainage of the ground it would be best to plant the canes on a slight ridge about 3 or 4 inches high (7.5–10cm).

Planting

Planting is best done in November, but it can be done any time in the winter up to March, provided that the soil is neither frozen nor very wet. Space the rows 6 feet (1.8m) apart and the plants in the rows at 15 inches (38cm) apart. 'Malling Jewel' is slow to produce new canes, so plant 2 canes at positions 15 inches (38cm) apart.

Plant the canes shallowly about 2 to 3 inches deep (5–7.5cm), and spread the roots out horizontally to encourage suckers which represent the new canes. Planting too deep inhibits this suckering habit, especially on heavy soils. Keep the roots covered at all times during the planting operation.

Cut each cane to a bud at 9 to 12 inches (22–30cm) above the soil surface. Finally, mulch the row with a 2-inch (5-cm) layer of well rotted manure, compost or peat, to 6 inches (15cm) on either side of the row.

Support and training

Canes need to be tied to a post and wire system to prevent wind damage to the canes and fruits. There are several methods of providing this support. In all cases the posts are set 10 to 12 feet (3–3.6m) apart and 14-gauge galvanised fencing wire is used.

Single fence
The advantage of this is that individual canes are securely tied in and are well spaced for light and air; it occupies less space than other systems.

(Above left) Preparation
for planting: putting a
layer of manure in the
bottom of the trench,
before forking it in.

(Above right)
Raspberry supports for
rows longer than 12 feet
(3.6m) need to be strutted to
bear the weight of leaves
and crop in summer.

(Right) Pruning a newly
planted cane: cutting down
to 9 to 12 inches (22–30cm).

The 'fence' has three wires strained horizontally at 2½, 3½ and 5½ feet (0.75, 1, 1.6m) above the ground, and fixed to posts 7½ feet (2.3m) long, driven 18 inches (45cm) into the ground.

Parallel wires

Two sets of wires are stretched horizontally at 2½ feet and 5 feet (75cm and 1.5m) from the ground, and 2 feet (60cm) apart. The wires are fixed to posts along each side of the rows, or to crossbars 2½ feet (75cm) long, nailed to posts down the centre of the row.

The canes are kept upright by tying wires or strong fillis string across the wires at 2 feet (60cm) apart. With this system the support is not as firm as with the single fence, and it is not suitable for windy positions or for vigorous cultivars.

Scandinavian system

One set of parallel wires 3 feet (90cm) apart is strained horizontally at 3 feet (90cm) above the ground, and fixed to posts 5 feet (1.5m) long driven 1½ feet (45cm) into the ground and spaced at 10 to 12 feet (3–3.6m) apart. The canes are not tied but are woven around the wires. The system is very suitable for private gardens although it does take up more room than other systems. Young canes are less likely to be trampled on during picking, but there is a risk of breaking off fruiting laterals when picking.

Single post

The single post system is useful for a very small garden in which space is limited. A single post is driven in leaving about 6 feet (1.8m) out of the ground, and 2 or 3 canes planted around the base. The canes are secured by looping them to the post with strong fillis string.

Cultivation

In the first season while the summer-fruiting cultivars are producing next year's canes, the main job is to control the weeds. Remove any flowers produced on the original canes, so that the plant concentrates on producing new canes.

In established rows weed control throughout the season is just as important, but hoeing around the plants is likely to damage surface roots and suckers, and it is best to control weeds by mulching, adding to the previous year's mulch along the row in March. Keep

(Left) 'Malling Delight', an early to mid-season cultivar, with very large pale fruits.

(Left) Support by parallel wires: the double wires and cross ties prevent the canes falling in the row.

(Opposite above) 'Glen Moy', an early cultivar which crops well and is resistant to aphids, making it less prone to virus infection.

(Opposite left) Hoe out suckers between the rows, at an early stage while still soft.

(Opposite right) Removing the unwanted suckers later on, also any weaker shoots and those growing too far out from the row.

down weeds and unwanted suckers between the rows by hoeing or with herbicides (see p.27).

Suckering too far away from the row can be prevented by using some kind of physical barrier about 1½ feet (45cm) away from the row. For example, a sheet of thick plastic (500g) can be inserted vertically into the soil to a depth of 2 feet (60cm).

Some cultivars, such as 'Malling Promise', produce too many canes, and the row may become too crowded unless some of the new ones are removed in May and June. Aim to leave 8 to 10 canes per plant, removing the weak canes and those growing too far away from the rows.

Feeding and watering

Raspberries need potash for fruiting as well as nitrogen for cane production. In late January apply sulphate of potash at ¾ oz per sq. yd (25g/m²); every third year add superphosphates at 2 oz per sq. yd (65g/m²). In early March apply sulphate of ammonia at ½ oz per sq. yd (15g/m²) – if growth has been poor give 1 oz per sq. yd (33g/m²). Sprinkle the fertilizer along the row over a band 18 inches (45cm) wide.

In dry summers and particularly on light soils, watering is necessary to increase yields and obtain strong new growth of canes. If water is scarce, the most effective time to irrigate is just as the berries begin to swell in June. A minimum of 1 inch (4½ gal. per sq. yd/25 litres/m²), but preferably 2 inches, given at this time will increase berry size and new shoot growth. Another application of 2 inches after picking encourages vigorous growth of canes to carry next season's crop. Apply the water at the base of the plants rather than from overhead in order to lessen the risk of fungal infection of fruits and canes.

Picking

Pick the fruits when they are dry and well coloured, but firm. Over-ripe fruits do not make good jam or freeze well. Pull them off carefully, leaving the core (plug) and stalk on the plant. Fruits for showing are picked with core and stalk.

Pruning and training

As soon as fruiting is finished, cut the old canes down to ground level to allow room

for the new young canes which are to bear next year's crop. Do not leave any stubs. Select not more than 8 per plant of the strongest and healthiest of these, leaving sufficient to ensure a spacing of 3 to 4 inches apart (8–10cm), and remove the rest.

Raspberries grown on the single fence should be tied into the wires using 3- or 4-ply fillis string, spacing the canes at 3 to 4 inches (8–10cm) apart along the top wire. Secure them by continuous lacing with a knot at occasional intervals in case the string breaks later on. There may be some tall canes with many inches left unsupported; these may be bent over and tied again to the top wire to prevent them breaking in the winter. In early February cut the canes to a bud at about 6 inches (15cm) above the top wire.

No tying or tipping is done with the Scandinavian system. The new canes are carefully bent over the wire and twisted round each other and the wire. Divide the canes equally between the two wires aiming to get about 4 canes on the wire at any one point. If there are more than this, thin out the canes. The best time for this training is in late August or September while the canes are still pliable.

Propagation

Raspberries are easily propagated by forking up suckers which may have grown between the rows, and transplanting them. Such canes must be healthy, showing no signs of virus infection. This method is thus only to be used within the first few years of planting. Virus-infected canes are useless for propagation and should be burnt. Not only do they produce a poor crop but they are a source of infection for other canes.

Autumn-fruiting raspberries

These bear fruit at the top foot (30cm) or so of the current year's canes, ripening from September until the autumn frosts. A warm, sunny position is essential so that as many fruits as possible ripen before the start of the cold weather. The directions given on p.160 for soil preparation, planting and initial pruning, spacing and feeding are the same as for the summer-fruiting cultivars.

Most cultivars are fairly compact and can be supported by the parallel wire system, the wires at 2½ feet and 5 feet

Cut out the old canes of summer fruiting raspberries down to soil level as soon as fruiting is over.

Lace the remaining young canes to the wires at 3 to 4 inches (8–10cm) apart, using a continuous length of 3-ply fillis string. Twist ties could be used.

Opposite:
(Above left) *Tops of the
canes looped back on to the
top wire to keep them
secure for the winter.*
(Right) *In early February
prune the canes to about 6
inches (15cm) above the top
wire.*
(Below left) *In the
Scandinavian system the
new canes are woven
round 2 parallel wires in
late summer. The old canes
which have fruited have
been cut out.*
(Right) *The Scandinavian
system in summer; the
young canes grow up in the
centre of the 2 rows of
fruiting canes.*

'Autumn Bliss', an
autumn-fruiting raspberry
with large well-flavoured
fruits.

(75cm and 1.5m). All canes should be cut down to ground level in late winter. If the canes were left to grow for a second year, they would bear fruits on the part of the cane which did not crop in the first year. But for a heavy autumn crop all canes must be cut down in late winter. During the summer remove any suckers growing away from the rows. Thin the canes in the row to about 2 inches (5cm) apart, removing the weakest first. The canes can be allowed to grow into a bed about 15 to 18 inches (38–45cm) wide.

Recommended cultivars

Summer-fruiting

Glen Moy. Early. Canes erect, vigorous, numerous, spine-free. Fruits firm, well flavoured, of good size. Crops well. Some resistance to spur blight and certain strains of aphid, but susceptible to phytophphora. Not suitable for heavy wet soils. Not advisable to plant with 'Malling Promise' or 'Malling Jewel' because of possible virus infection.

Glen Clova. Early. Heavy cropper, fruits medium-sized, flavour good, canes vigorous and abundant. Tends to spread. Susceptible to virus infection. Should not be planted with 'Malling Promise' or 'Malling Jewel'.

Delight. Early mid-season. Large pale orange-red dessert fruits. Fruits crumbly, not suitable for freezing. Canes prolific and vigorous. Fruiting laterals long. Susceptible to spur blight and grey mould (botrytis). Resistant to some strains of aphid. Good cropper.

Malling Jewel. Mid-season. Good quality, heavy cropper, sparse in the production of canes, so plan 2 per station at 15 inches (38cm) apart. Tolerant of virus infection.

Glen Prosen. Mid-season. Canes of moderate vigour, sufficient in number, spine-free. Fruits firm, medium size, good flavour. Crops well. Susceptible to spur blight and cane botrytis.

Malling Admiral. Late mid-season. A very heavy cropper of good quality fruits. Canes prolific and vigorous. Fruiting laterals long. Some resistance to spur blight, mildew and cane botrytis.

Malling Joy. Late. Canes very vigorous, tall, stout, moderate in number. Fruiting laterals very long but strong. Fruits large, conical, firm, good flavour. Crops well. Resistant to aphids.

Leo. Very late. Fruits large, bright orange-red, firm, good, slightly acid flavour. Canes very vigorous, but slow to build up in the early years. Fairly resistant to spur blight, cane botrytis, and some strains of aphid. Susceptible to cane spot. Good cropper.

Autumn-fruiting

Autumn Bliss. Ripens mid-August onwards. Canes prolific, fairly erect and of moderate height. Needs minimal support. Fruits large, of good flavour. Crops very well. Good resistance to aphids.

Zeva. Flavour fair. Fruits crumbly, medium to large. Cropping moderate to good. Canes prolific, moderate vigour. Ripens early September onwards.

Heritage. Flavour fair. Berries firm, small to medium. Cropping good. Canes numerous and vigorous. Ripens mid-September onwards. Requires a warm situation.

Promising new cultivars

Glen Lyon. Early. Canes vigorous, spine-free. Large fruits, firm, pale, of good flavour. Crops well.

Augusta. Very late, following 'Leo'. A potentially useful cultivar to fill the gap between 'Leo' and 'Autumn Bliss'.

Pests

RASPBERRY BEETLES lay eggs in the blossom and the grubs feed at the stalk end of the ripening fruit. They are often first noticed when the fruit is picked. Spray the young fruitlets with malathion, fenitrothion or derris when the first pink fruit is seen. A second application of derris can be given 2 weeks later. Spray at dusk to reduce the danger to bees.

APHIDS are potentially serious pests because they spread virus diseases but the prevention of virus transmission is not easy. Tar oil sprayed on the dormant canes in December or January kills off overwintering eggs, and spraying pirimicarb, dimethoate, or heptenophos in late April kills any aphids that have escaped the winter treatment.

LEAFHOPPERS cause a whitish mottling of the upper leaf surface. They are pale yellow, sap-feeding insects and are controlled by spraying with dimethoate.

LEAF AND BUD MITES cause pale yellow blotches on the upper leaf surface, frequently mistaken for virus infection. The microscopic mites feed on the underside of the leaves. Heavy infestations can

Autumn-fruiting raspberries: all canes are cut to the ground in late winter.

cause uneven fruit ripening and distorted leaves. None of the insecticides available to amateurs gives good control, but benomyl, used against spur blight and cane spot, can check infestations. Apply it in late March, with 2 further applications at 14-day intervals. 'Malling Jewel' can be heavily infested, but 'Malling Promise' is less susceptible.

Diseases

VIRUS DISEASES, which may be aphid- or eelworm-borne, frequently cause yellow mottling or blotching of the leaves, which may be distorted. Canes eventually lose vigour and cropping capacity, although virus-tolerant cultivars can be infected with virus and still crop reasonably well. Canes and stools showing symptoms should be removed and burnt; they cannot be cured. The soil should be changed or another site chosen for new disease-free canes.

SPUR BLIGHT shows around the nodes on the canes as blotches which are first purple and then silver. Buds at affected nodes die and any shoots produced die back in spring. Burn badly diseased canes. When the buds are $\frac{1}{2}$ inch (1cm)

long, spray with Bordeaux Mixture or liquid copper, or with benomyl, carbendazim, thiophanate methyl or thiram, following the manufacturer's instructions in every case.

CANE SPOT affects canes, leaves and fruit, showing first as small purple spots and then as elliptical greyish blotches with a purple margin. Remove and burn badly diseased canes. Spray as for spur blight following manufacturer's instructions.

CANE BLIGHT causes withering of leaves and die-back of fruiting canes through infection at ground level where a dark area develops on the canes. Affected canes become brittle and snap off easily. Cut diseased canes hard back to below soil level and burn them, and disinfect the pruning tool. As the new canes grow, spray with bordeaux mixture or other copper fungicide.

HONEY FUNGUS *see* p.70.

GREY MOULD (*see* p.157) is sometimes troublesome. For control, spray with benomyl, carbendazim or thiophanate methyl.

IRON DEFICIENCY (*see* p.24) shows as irregular yellowing between the veins. It is frequent on raspberries and should not be confused with symptoms of virus.

Blackberries and hybrid berries

Blackberries grow wild in the hedgerows of Britain, but the cultivated kinds are more productive, and include thornless forms which make training and picking much easier.

Hybrid berries are the results of crosses between various *Rubus* species, principally the blackberry, dewberry and raspberry. Some ('Loganberry', for example) are not as vigorous or as aggressively thorned as many blackberries, and are therefore more suited to the small garden. There are also thornless forms. Hybrid berries are grown in the same way as blackberries, except where specially mentioned in the text.

A reasonable annual yield from a well-grown blackberry or hybrid berry can range from 10 to 30 lb (4.5–13.5kg), depending upon the size of the plant and the cultivar.

There is a limited certification scheme for blackberries and hybrid berries, which at present covers the blackberry 'Ashton Cross' and the hybrid berries 'Tayberry' ('Medana') and 'Sunberry'. Virus-free stock of other hybrid berries, including the loganberry, are released from time to time by fruit research stations, so it is as well to check whether any are available before buying.

Site and soil

The canes can be damaged or killed by very cold drying winds and by hard frosts in the winter; cold, exposed sites should therefore be avoided. The blossoms of blackberries and most hybrid berries are seldom damaged because they flower late in the spring. Some support is needed, and they can be grown in rows on wires or trained against walls or over arches.

Blackberries tolerate partial shade, provided that the soil is not dry; nevertheless, they grow best in full sun. Hybrid berries always require plenty of light.

Blackberries can grow in soils with slightly impeded drainage, but the ideal soil for them is a deep, well-drained medium to heavy loam holding an adequate moisture supply in summer. Light soils are suitable, provided plenty of bulky organic material is incorporated before planting. Shallow soils over chalk are unsuitable because of the likelihood of iron and manganese deficiencies, and dryness.

Soil preparation and planting

Blackberries are a long-term crop, and all perennial weeds in the plot need to be cleared before planting. Herbicides can be used (*see* p.27). Deep digging before planting is essential for good root growth. On light soils, dig in a 2-inch (5-cm) layer of well rotted manure or compost at each planting site over an area of about 2 feet square (60cm²). In the final preparations, fork in 3 oz (85 g) of Growmore or equivalent compound fertilizer over the same area.

Plant between October and March, whenever soil conditions are suitable. Plant shallowly to encourage the production of suckers, which will grow into the new canes. Spread the roots out horizontally, covering with about 3 inches (7.5cm) of soil, and firm. Space hybrid berries and the moderately vigorous blackberries 8 to 10 feet (2.4–3m) apart, but up to 12 feet (3.6m) on good soils, and up to 15 feet (4.5m) for a vigorous cultivar like 'Himalaya Giant'. If more than one row is to be planted, allow 6 to 7 feet (1.8–2.1m) between the rows.

Immediately after planting, cut the cane(s) to a bud at about 9 inches (22cm) above the ground to encourage the production of strong new canes for fruiting two seasons ahead. Then mulch the young plant with well rotted manure or compost to a depth of about 2 inches (5cm).

Supports, training and pruning

Whether grown in the open or on a wall, blackberries need support for the canes, erected at planting time. Four wires (galvanised, 10-gauge/3.15mm, is recommended) should be stretched at 12 inches (30cm) apart, with the lowest at 3 feet (90cm) from the ground and the top one at 6 feet (1.8m).

(Opposite) *Growing hybrid berries (both thornless types) over an archway in one of the model fruit gardens at Wisley.*

(Opposite left) *Four methods of training blackberries.*

A. Fan: *for limited spaces, and cultivars which produce strong rather rigid canes, e.g. 'King's Acre Berry' and 'Smoothstem'.*

B. Alternate bay: *young canes from two neighbouring plants are trained towards each other, while the older, fruiting canes are in the alternate bay.*

C. Rope: *for cultivars with thin, flexible canes, e.g. 'Tayberry', 'Loganberry'. About 20 to 25 canes are needed per plant, to allow for loss and damage; remove any in excess in early summer.*

D. Weaving: *for vigorous cultivars, e.g. 'Bedford Giant', 'Himalayan Giant'. This system needs a lot of handling.*

Young growth is shown as dotted lines; older, fruiting canes are shown as a solid line. The wires are spaced at 3 feet (90cm), 4 feet (1.2m), 5 feet (1.5m) and 6 feet (1.8) above ground.

(Opposite right) *After planting, the cane is cut back to a bud about 9 inches (22cm) above soil level.*

In the open the wires are fixed to posts of $7\frac{1}{2}$ to 8 feet (2.2–2.4m) driven $1\frac{1}{2}$ to 2 feet (45–60cm) into the ground, and spaced at 12 to 15 feet (3.6–4.5m). To strain the wires tight, use straining bolts at one end of the row, and wire staples to secure the wire to the intermediates and the other endposts. On a wall or fence the wires are threaded through vine eyes driven or screwed into the brickwork or woodwork.

In the first summer tie in the new canes as they grow to the lower wires. In the next and following years, the current year's growths are tied in and kept separate from the older canes bearing fruit. This helps to avoid any spread of disease from the old to new canes, and makes picking, winter pruning and tying easier. There are various training methods, as shown in the photographs and diagrams.

The fan or rope is best where space is limited. The rope trained one way saves double handling of the canes, but requires more room. The weaving system is recommended only for very vigorous varieties.

As soon as picking is finished, cut out the old canes and re-tie the new ones to the wires in their place. With the rope system, for example, tie 3 or 4 canes to each wire, except the top wire which is left clear for the new canes next summer. The maximum recommended length of cane is 8 to 9 feet (2.4–2.7m). If there are few new canes, the best of the old canes can be kept, but they produce lower quality fruits in their second year. In areas where extreme frosts are usual,

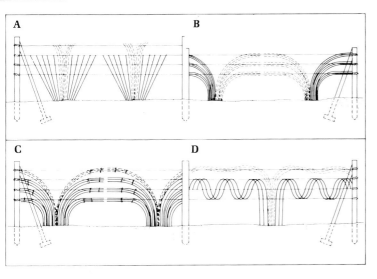

loosely bundle the new canes together for winter protection. They are untied and spaced out, in spring, just before the buds break.

Cultivation, feeding and watering

Keep the weeds under control by shallow hoeing or herbicides. Unwanted canes growing too far away from the row should be pulled out as they appear.

In late January each year apply $\frac{1}{2}$ oz sulphate of potash per square yard ($15g/m^2$) as a top dressing, and then a mulch of well rotted manure or compost. If no organic manure is available, apply a nitrogen fertilizer, such as sulphate of ammonia at 2 oz per sq. yd ($65g/m^2$) in the spring. Every third year apply superphosphates at 2 oz per sq. yd ($65g/m^2$).

The optimum time to apply water in dry weather is when the first berries begin to colour. This increases berry size and promotes strong new cane growth for the next year. Apply at least 1 inch ($4\frac{1}{2}$ gal. per sq. yd/25 litres/m²), and preferably 2 inches, of water at a time, Irrigate at ground level to reduce the risk of fungal infection on the fruit and young canes.

Picking

Blackberries and hybrid berries are picked with the plug. For showing, they must be picked with the calyx and stalk. Avoid handling the berry. Preferably pick when dry and not when wet with rain because the fruits soon rot in damp conditions.

Propagation

Most cultivars are easily propagated from rooted tips. At the end of July, bend over the tip of the shoot and bury it in a hole in the soil about 6 inches (15cm) deep. Tread the soil gently so that the tip is held firmly. It will root during the summer and winter and be ready to be cut from its parent and be transplanted in the following spring. Cut it off with about 12 inches (30cm) of the old cane.

Leaf bud cuttings taken in July, August or September can also be used to produce new plants. They may be rooted under mist, in a propagating frame or cold frame, using a 50:50 peat and coarse sand rooting medium. Rooting takes place in 6 to 8 weeks, after which the young plantlets may be hardened off and then lined out for a year in nursery rows 1 foot (30cm) apart. Late-taken cuttings are best put into 5½-inch (14cm) pot of John Innes compost No. 1 and kept in a cold frame until spring (see photos pp.176–177).

Recommended cultivars

Blackberries
Bedford Giant. Early (July). Vigorous and thorny. Fruit large to very large, very sweet but no pronounced blackberry flavour. Not suitable for a small garden. Plant 15 feet (4.5m) apart.
Ashton Cross. Moderate vigour, thin wiry canes. Crops well. Fruits small to

(Above) *Cutting out to the ground the old canes after fruiting.*

(Below) *The best of the new canes are tied in, here using the fan system.*

(Left) *Tying the canes together loosely for winter protection.*

(Right) *In July or August tips of young canes are inserted in holes about 6 inches (15cm) deep, with one side sloping towards the parent cane.*

(Below) *The rooted tip is dug up and severed from the parent plant in late winter.*

(Above) 'Kings Acre Berry' trained on the rope system. Note that the top wire has been left clear for the new young canes in the summer.

(Left) 'Loganberry': there are both thorned and thornless selections available.

(Opposite above) Japanese wineberry is very ornamental, with red stems in winter. Fruits are rather insipid, but make nice jam.

(Opposite left) Blackberry 'Oregon Thornless' has ornamental foliage.

(Opposite right) 'Tayberry', a bland, sweet fruit, which makes excellent jam.

medium, of sweet wild blackberry flavour. Plant at 10 feet (3m) apart.

Fantasia. Mid-season to late with a long cropping season. Very vigorous, long canes with powerful but widely spaced thorns. Crops exceedingly heavily. Fruits very large, shiny black, good flavour. Plant at 15 feet (4.5m).

Loch Ness. Mid-season to late. Canes thornless, of moderate vigour, stout and semi-erect. Berries shiny black, long, attractive, good flavour. Crops well. Plant at 8 feet (2.4m).

Himalaya Giant. Early to mid-season. Very vigorous, and thorny. Crops heavily. Moderate flavour. Not suitable for a small garden. Plant at 15 feet (4.5m).

Marion. Very vigorous and thorny. Crops well, good flavour. Plant at 12 feet (3.6m).

Oregon Thornless. Mid-season to late. A thornless form of the parsley-leaved blackberry, more suitable for the garden. Mild blackberry flavour. Ornamental foliage. Plant at 10 feet (3m).

Hybrid berries

Tayberry. Early. Thorned, moderate vigour, crops heavily. Fruits medium to large, mild sweet flavour. Makes

flavour. An ornamental species rather than a fruit crop. Plant at 8 feet (2.4m).

Kings Acre Berry. Dark shiny red fruits, medium size. Vigorous. Plant at 12 feet (3.6m).

Smoothstem. Very late. Vigorous, thornless, rigid canes. Fruits acid. Needs a sunny position to ripen. 'Thornfree' and 'Black Satin' are similar. Plant at 8 feet (2.4m).

Promising new cultivar

Silvan. An early, dark red hybrid berry of medium to large size and good flavour. Crops well. Canes vigorous and thorny.

Pests

RASPBERRY BEETLE grubs attack the fruits of hybrid berries and blackberries. They can be controlled on a hybrid berries by spraying with malathion, fenitrothion or derris, applied as soon as most of the blossom falls, with a repeat application when the first fruit is colouring. Spray blackberries with one of these materials at dusk as the first flowers open.

APHIDS and LEAFHOPPERS see p.168.

Diseases

CANE SPOT (see p.169) can be troublesome on loganberry and other hybrid berries. Remove and burn diseased canes. Spray with Bordeaux Mixture or liquid copper or benomyl or carbendazim or thiophanate methyl as recommended by the manufacturer.

SPUR BLIGHT (see p.169) and GREY MOULD (see p.157) can affect loganberries and other hybrid berries.

VIRUS DISEASE can cause stunting of canes and a reduction in crop. Diseased plants should be burnt and healthy plants obtained.

(Above) *At the end of the summer, the plantlets should be ready to plant out.*

(Opposite above) *A bud, with leaf and stalk, is cut from the stem.*

(Opposite below) *It is then inserted in a rooting medium in a cold frame: rooting should take place in 6 to 8 weeks.*

excellent jam. Plant at 8 feet (2.4m). 'Tayberry Medana' is from virus-tested plants.

Tummelberry. Mid-season. Canes moderately vigorous, wiry and more winter-hardy than 'Tayberry'. Fruits roundish, good size, red, of sharp aromatic flavour. Crops well. Plant at 8 feet (2.4m).

Sunberry. Mid-season. Very vigorous, rather spiny canes. Medium-sized, dark red berries of excellent flavour. Crops well. Plant at 12 feet (3.6m).

Loganberry LY59. Thorned. Crops well, moderate vigour, long berries, excellent acid flavour. Plant at 8 feet (2.4m).

Thornless Loganberry. A thornless sport of the loganberry. A healthy stock is now available (L654).

Boysenberry. Large purplish fruits. Moderate vigour. Tolerates dry soils. There is a thornless form. Plant at 8 feet (2.4m).

Japanese wineberry, (*Rubus phoenicolasius*). Moderate vigour. Canes covered with soft, red bristles. Fruits very small, wine-red, sweet, without much

Blackcurrants

The main season for the blackcurrant crop is July, but by choosing the right cultivars for succession, fresh fruit can be provided from the end of June until September. The fruits are high in vitamin C, freeze well and are excellent for jam.

A well-grown, mature bush reaches about 5 to 6 feet (1.5–1.8m) in height and spread, and such a bush should easily yield 10 lb (4.5kg) or more of fruit annually. Blackcurrant bushes are potentially long-lived, yielding satisfactorily for 15 years or more.

The best fruits are produced on 1-year-old wood, on shoots made in the previous summer. To encourage the production of vigorous young growths the plants need plenty of organic manure and hard pruning. The plants are grown as stooled bushes – a bush with a number of shoots growing from ground level. There is a certification scheme (see p.29) for blackcurrants.

Site and soil

The best position in the garden for blackcurrants is an open and sunny one, although they tolerate some shade for part of the day. They flower early and the flowers are very susceptible to cold, and so should not be planted in a frost pocket. If there is no alternative site, be prepared to protect the bushes at this time. Shelter from north and east winds is essential. Blackcurrants will grow on a wide range of soils, provided that they are of good depth, 15 inches (38cm) or more, and have a reserve of moisture yet are well drained. They are better able than other soft fruits to grow in soils less than well drained. The optimum soil pH is 6.7, just below neutral, so very acid soils will need liming.

Soil preparation and planting

It is best to obtain 2-year-old certified bushes. Younger plants are not certified, but are acceptable provided they have been propagated from disease-free plants.

Before planting, remove all perennial weeds (for herbicides see p.26) and dig in well rotted manure at a rate of at least a barrowload per 30 square feet (9m²) or a 2- to 3-inch (5–8cm) layer over the whole area. Remember that blackcurrants need as much organic manure as can be made available. Just before planting, fork in a compound fertilizer such as Growmore at 3 oz per sq. yd (100g/m²).

Planting can be carried out from October to March, preferably in the autumn while the soil is still warm enough to encourage some root growth. Plant at between 5 and 6 feet (1.5–1.8m) apart each way; allow the wider spacing for vigorous cultivars such as 'Boskoop Giant' and 'Blacksmith'. The compact-growing cultivar, 'Ben Sarek', can be grown at 4 feet (1.2m) apart. Plant about an inch (2.5cm) deeper than each plant was in the nursery, as indicated by the soil marks on the shoots, and then cut them all down to 1 bud above soil level. This stimulates shoot production from the base, and lays the foundation for a strong-stooled bush.

Cultivation

After planting apply a mulch 2 to 3 inches (5–8cm) deep of well rotted bulky organic matter to the soil, taking care not to cover the pruned shoots. For blackcurrants it is important to replenish this mulch annually, and for an established bush this means covering an area of 18 inch (45cm) radius round the bush, to 2 to 3 inches deep (5–8cm) with well rotted organic material, such as manure, garden compost, mushroom compost or old straw.

Weeds can be controlled by shallow hoeing, so that the surface roots are not disturbed. A thick mulch helps to suppress the weeds.

Feeding and watering

In January each year apply a potash fertilizer, for example sulphate of potash at ¾ oz per sq. yd (25g/m²), as a top dressing over the rooting area, and in March apply nitrogen as Nitro-chalk on an acid soil, or sulphate of ammonia on an alkaline one, both at 1 oz per sq. yd (33g/m²).

In most years watering in dry spells

'Ben Sarek' makes a small compact bush, is quite hardy and resistant to mildew.

(Left) Planting a 2-year-old blackcurrant; it is planted 1 or 2 inches (2.5–5cm) deeper than it was in the nursery to encourage the stool system of growing.

(Right) All shoots are cut back to within an inch (2.5cm) of the soil immediately after planting.

between May and early August increases fruit size and encourages shoot growth. Apply at least 1 inch (4½ gal. per sq. yd/25 litres/m²), preferably 2 inches, to the base of the plant, extended to at least 2 feet (60cm) either side of the plant. Overhead irrigation is liable to increase the risk of fungal infections, so one of the low-level systems of watering, such as lay-flat tubing, is best.

Pruning

After the first growing season 7 or 8 strong shoots should have been produced by a 2-year-old bush. These should be left to bear fruit the following summer. Any weak growth can be pruned to an inch (2.5cm) of soil level. Bushes from 1-year-old rooted cuttings should be cut down again to within an inch (2.5cm) of the soil surface.

Established bushes should be pruned by cutting out one-quarter to one-third of the wood each year. A little selective pruning can be done immediately after picking, if necessary, to remove low-lying and broken branches. This improves air

(Above) *Established bushes of 'Amos Black' before pruning.*

(Right) *Pruning of the bushes completed.*

(Opposite above) *After planting mulch with rotted manure or compost, taking care to leave the shoot stubs uncovered.*

(Opposite below) *Cutting out old, low-lying branches.*

circulation, giving better ripening of the wood. The main pruning is done after leaf fall in autumn, or in the winter – but preferably in the early part of the winter.

Cut out the oldest branches bearing few young growths, together with badly placed and low-lying branches. Keep strong, young, upright shoots. Old wood is almost black; young wood is light brown to golden. Cut as low down as possible to stimulate vigorous growth of shoots at or near the base of the bush.

Weak shoots and those with withered tips (those affected by die-back or mildew) should be removed at their base.

Old, neglected bushes, provided that they are not infected by gall mite or reversion, can be rejuvenated by cutting all the branches to within an inch (2.5cm) of the ground during the winter. This stimulates production of new shoots in the following spring. If these are crowded, thin them out in the subsequent autumn, leaving the strongest and best placed to bear fruit in the second year.

Picking

If the fruits are to be used soon after picking, they may be stripped from the stalk, but be careful not to break the skin. But the currants keep better if picked by strig (the whole bunch). Fruit for showing must be picked by the strig with a full complement of berries.

Propagation

Blackcurrants are easily propagated from hardwood cuttings taken in the autumn, but the latter must be taken only from healthy plants. Select strong, healthy shoots from the current season's growth, of about pencil thickness 8 to 10 inches (20–25cm) long. Cut to just below a bud at the base, and at the top cut off the un-ripened tip, to just above a bud. Remove any remaining leaves, but leave all the buds on the shoot; each will grow out into a shoot, making a stooled bush. Make a slit in the soil about 10 inches (25cm) deep, and if the soil is a heavy clay, sprinkle some sharp sand along the bottom to help drainage. Push the cuttings into the slit so that 2 buds are left above soil level. Space them at 6 inches (15cm) apart; if there is more than one row allow 3 feet (90cm) between them. Firm the soil around the cuttings and again following frosts in winter.

(Above) A 4-year-old blackcurrant bush needing little pruning, but showing the difference between the younger light coloured shoots and the older darker brown wood.

(Opposite above) 'Boskoop Giant' is an early cultivar with large, sweet berries. It is too vigorous for a small garden.
(Opposite left) 'Ben Lomond', a heavy-cropping and fairly hardy cultivar with some resistance to mildew.
(Opposite right) Blackcurrant buds at the late grape stage with the first flowers open: the time to spray against big bud mite.

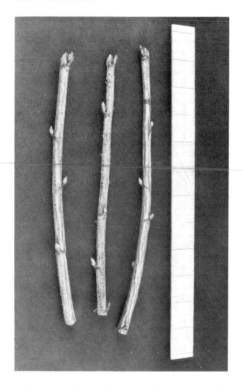

As an alternative, cuttings can be inserted through small slits in a 12-inch (30cm) wide black polythene film laid along the row with its edges buried to prevent it blowing away. The polythene prevents weed growth and reduces loss of soil water and heat, so benefiting the rooting of the cuttings.

After a year the cuttings should have rooted and be ready for planting out.

Recommended cultivars

Boskoop Giant. Early. Large sweet berries. Very vigorous. Flowers early, prone to spring frost. Plant 6 feet (1.8m) apart.

Blackdown. Second early. Berries sweet. Cropping good. Vigour moderate, spreading. Resistant to mildew. Plant at 5 feet (1.5m) apart.

Wellington. Mid-season. Berries sweet, medium to large. Heavy cropper. Vigorous, spreading. Plant 5 × 6 feet (1.5 × 1.8m) apart.

Blacksmith. Mid-season. Berries large, tender, flavour good. heavy cropper. Very vigorous. Plant at 6 feet (1.8m) apart.

Ben Nevis. Mid-season. Berries medium-large, skin thick, flavour fair. Cropping heavy. Some resistance to mildew. Fairly hardy. Plant 5 feet (1.5m) apart.

Ben Lomond. Mid-season. Berries large, trusses short, flavour good, but acid. Bush upright, spreads a little with crop. Flowers late, some resistance to frost and mildew. Cropping good. Plant at 5 feet (1.5m) apart.

Ben Sarek. Mid to late. Large berries on short strigs. Small, compact bush of medium vigour, suited to the small garden. Crops heavily and branches may need support. Resistant to gooseberry mildew, some resistance to leaf midge and has considerable tolerance to frost and cold at flowering time. Plant at 4 feet (1.2m) apart.

Baldwin (Hilltop Strain). Mid-late. Berries medium, hang well without splitting. Acid flavour, rich in vitamin C. Cropping good. Vigour moderate, fairly compact. Plant at 5 feet (1.5m) apart.

Black Reward. Late. Medium-sized berries. Crops well. Some frost-hardiness. Vigorous. Plant at 6 feet (1.8m) apart.

Jet. Very late. Very long strigs of small to medium berries, distinctive acid flavour. Flowers very late, usually escapes spring frosts. Extremely vigorous, not for a small garden. Plant at 6 feet (1.8m) apart.

Promising new cultivar
Ben Alder. Late. Good for juice, crops well. Flowers late – useful in frosty areas.

(Above left) Cuttings 8 to 10 inches (20–25cm) long of current season's wood: note that all buds are left on.

(Above) Straight-back trench with (left to right) 3 blackcurrant, 3 gooseberry and 3 redcurrant cuttings, all spaced at 6 inches (15cm).

Big bud mite: (left and centre) Infested shoots showing the rounded buds; (right) healthy shoots with pointed buds.

Pests

BLACK CURRANT GALL MITE is the most significant pest and it destroys buds and also transmits reversion disease. The minute mites feed and breed within the buds, which become swollen and round, throughout the year and in spring migrate to young buds. Hand-picking and burning the 'big buds' in the winter may limit infestations; spraying with carbendazim when the first flowers open and on two further occasions at 14-day intervals may also give some control. Destroy badly infested bushes that crop badly.

APHIDS infest leaves and stems. Control by spraying with tar-oil winter wash during the dormant period, or with pirimicarb, dimethoate, or heptenophos applied just before flowering.

LEAF MIDGE LARVAE are tiny orange-white maggots that feed between the folds of leaves at the shoot tips, from May onwards. The leaves are prevented from expanding and become stunted and twisted. There are 3 or 4 generations: the first is the most harmful because it can reduce shoot growth. Thorough spraying of the shoot tips with dimethoate or fenitrothion may control the larvae.

CAPSID BUGS (see p.201) make leaves at the shoot tips distorted and tattered with small holes.

Diseases

REVERSION is a serious disease which causes a severe reduction in crop. Although certain typical symptoms are produced on flower buds and leaves, these are difficult for an amateur to identify, and specialist advice is best sought in June or July if bushes fail to give a satisfactory crop. Once confirmed, diseased bushes should be dug up and burnt.

LEAF SPOT produces small, dark brown spots which coalesce until the whole leaf surface becomes brown. Affected leaves fall prematurely and there may be a reduction in crop the following season. Spray immediately after flowering with a copper fungicide.

Thiophanate methyl or benomyl also controls this disease if applied according to the manufacturer's instructions. Rake up and burn diseased leaves.

AMERICAN GOOSEBERRY MILDEW (see p.201) is sometimes troublesome late in the season.

HONEY FUNGUS see p.70.

Redcurrants and whitecurrants

Redcurrants and whitecurrants are fairly easy to grow; they are not troubled by reversion disease, and they are long-lived. They fruit on short spurs produced on the old wood, and in clusters at the base of the young laterals made in the previous year. The whitecurrant is a sport (mutant) of the red and needs the same cultural treatment.

Both are usually grown as open-centred bushes on a short stem of about 4 to 6 inches (10–15cm) or as cordons in single, double, or triple form. Cordons trained against walls or fences are particularly suitable for small gardens. Occasionally, redcurrants are grown as fans, espaliers or standards. However, birds may be a problem, attacking the fruit buds in the winter and eating the ripening fruits in the summer. Netting is the only sure method of control.

A reasonable annual yield from an established bush is 10 to 15 lb (4–5kg), and from a single cordon 1 to 2 lb (0.5–1kg).

There is no certification scheme for red- or whitecurrants, so it is important to obtain healthy plants from a reliable source. Bushes 2- and 3-years-old are usually available in nurseries. Choose a plant with a clean stem of 4 to 6 inches (10–15cm) and a well-balanced head of vigorous shoots. Younger rooted cuttings are suitable for training as bushes or cordons; older partly-trained single, double, or triple cordons can also be obtained, but are more expensive.

Site and soil

The ideal site is sunny, sheltered from strong winds, and not in a frost pocket. But redcurrants tolerate partial shade and fruit successfully when grown against a north-facing wall or fence, although the fruits ripen later, and do not have as much colour or flavour as those in full sun. Redcurrants flower when frosts are still likely, and the bushes will need shelter from low temperatures at flowering time or the fruit set may be reduced.

Strong winds may be another problem and in early summer can break vigorous young shoots. With young bushes which are still forming their framework it is worth while staking and tying important shoots.

The plants need a well drained fertile soil, slightly acid to netural. Shallow soil over chalk and badly drained plots are unsuitable.

Potash is an important nutrient for red- and whitecurrants, so it is worth while checking that potash levels are always adequate.

Soil preparation and planting

In early autumn, before planting, fork in a compound fertilizer such as Growmore at 2 oz per sq. yd (65g/m²), plus sulphate of potash at ½ oz per sq. yd (15g/m²). On poor or light soils first dig in a 1½- to 2-inch (3–5cm) layer of well rotted manure and then rake in the fertilizers.

Plant the currants between mid-October and March, whenever soil conditions are suitable, but preferably in autumn when the soil is still warm. Space the bushes at 5 feet (1.5m) apart in the row, with 6 feet (1.8m) between the rows. Space single cordons at 15 inches (38cm) apart and double cordons at 30 inches (75cm) apart. Cordons need support, and each should be planted to a bamboo cane which in turn should be tied to horizontal wires at 2 feet (60cm) and 4 feet (1.2m) from the ground. Multiple cordons need a cane for each stem.

After planting, mulch with a 1- to 2-inch (2.5–5cm) layer of well rotted manure, peat or garden compost over a radius of about 10 inches (25cm) around each plant.

Bush form

Pruning

At planting. The aim is to produce an open, goblet-shaped bush of 8 to 10 main branches, on a short stem. After planting, prune the leader of each branch to an out-ward-facing bud about half-way down its length. If the branch is too drooping, cut to an inward-facing bud or to a suitable upright side shoot, which is also cut back to half.

Remove any shoots on the main stem less than 4 inches (10cm) from the ground to produce a clean stem. Prune any shoots crowding the centre to 1 bud.

'Jonkheer van Tets', a very early, heavy cropping redcurrant.

A fan-trained redcurrant ('Red Lake') against a fence. The panel is 6 feet (1.8m) wide and 7 feet (2.1m) high.

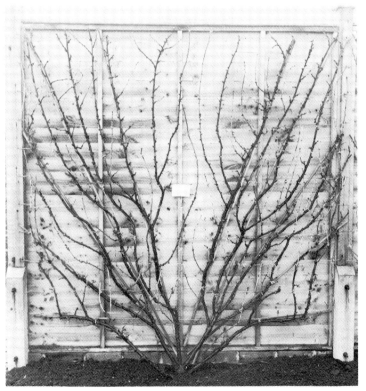

Established bushes. For the first few winters after planting, the framework should be shaped. Prune each branch leader by half to a bud facing in the required direction of growth, usually to an outward facing bud. Cut the lateral shoots to 1 bud, unless they are needed to fill in a gap in the framework, when they can be treated as leaders and cut to half their length. Shoots crowding the centre are also cut to 1 bud. Remove any suckers and also shoots less than 4 inches (10cm) from the ground. Any shoots which may have died back in the previous summer through disease must be pruned back to healthy wood.

In subsequent winters, after the framework is established, cut the main leaders to leave about 3 inches (8cm) of the previous summer's growth. Continue to cut the laterals to one bud because this encourages the production of fruit spurs – clusters of fruit buds close to the framework branches. Cut out old, unfruitful branches, leaving vigorous young laterals to replace them.

Summer pruning is desirable although not essential, because it allows more light and air into the centre of the bush to help

(Left) *A well grown 2-year-old redcurrant bush at planting. Roots are well spread out and the bush planted to the same depth as in the nursery.*
(Below) *After planting, the leaders are pruned by about half to an outward facing bud.*
(Opposite left) *The stem should be 4 to 6 inches (10–15cm) long. Remove any laterals below this.*
(Opposite right) *Summer pruning: in the third week of June cut the current season's laterals back to 5 leaves. The leader is not pruned.*
(Opposite below left) *A branch of a redcurrant bush before pruning.*
(Opposite below right) *The same branch after pruning: laterals have been cut to about an inch (2.5cm) except where needed to fill in gaps. Branch leaders have been pruned by about half to outward facing buds.*

to ripen the fruit and the new wood. At the end of June cut back all the current season's new shoots to about 5 leaves. Do not prune the leaders.

Cordons

Pruning

At planting. Cordons are also grown with a clean stem of 4 to 6 inches (10–15cm), so remove any laterals below 4 inches (10cm) from the ground. After planting, cut back the leader by half, and side shoots on the main stem to 1 bud. Tie the cordon to the cane.

Established cordons. For the first few winters after planting, the emphasis is on training a straight stem up to 5 or 6 feet (1.5–1.8m). Remove about one-quarter of the previous summer's growth from the leader to stimulate the production of side shoots.

Cut laterals to 1 or 2 buds and remove any suckers at the base of the stem, as well as any shoots coming off it below 4 inches (10cm) from the ground. This hard pruning of the laterals encourages the development of fruiting spurs close to

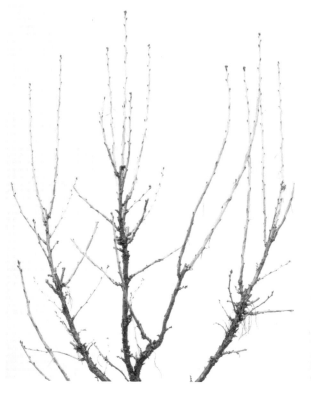

'Red Lake' is a mid-season cultivar of good flavour.

the main stem. After some years these spurs may become too long and branched; they should then be shortened and simplified by cutting back into older wood. When the cordon has reached 5 or 6 feet (1.5–1.8m), prune the leader to 1 bud each winter.

Some pruning should be carried out at the end of June by pruning all current season side shoots to 5 leaves. Do not prune the leader of a young cordon, but tie it to the cane during the summer. Once it has reached the desired height, prune it to 5 leaves and to 1 bud in winter.

Each stem of a multiple cordon is treated in the same way.

Feeding, watering and weeding

In February apply sulphate of potash at $\frac{3}{4}$ oz per sq. yd (25g/m²) or liberal dressings of bonfire ash. On poor soils also apply a compound fertilizer such as Growmore at 2 oz per sq. yd (65g/m²). A mulch of manure is also beneficial, especially when the soil is light and/or the plants are young. This mulch helps to conserve soil moisture which may be reflected in larger fruits.

Watering in dry spells from May to early August increases growth and yield. The plants need at least $4\frac{1}{2}$ gal. per sq. yd (25 litres/m²), but preferably twice that in a watering. The area watered should extend at least 2 feet (60cm) on either side of the plant or row.

Weeds also need to be controlled throughout the growing season, by shallow hoeing or preferably by mulching or herbicides (see p.26).

Picking

Redcurrants are picked on the strig with the full complement of fruits on the truss. The fruits are thinner-skinned than blackcurrants, so are more easily squashed if picked one by one.

Propagation

New plants are easily grown from hardwood cuttings taken in the autumn or early winter. Strong, healthy shoots of the summer's growth about 12 to 15 inches (30–38cm) long are suitable for cuttings. Trim off unripe wood at the top of the cutting, pruning to just above a bud, and to just below a bud at the base. Remove all buds except 3 or 4 at the top so that a clean stem is formed.

'White Grape' ripens in mid-season.

Make a slit in the soil with a spade, or dig a straight-backed trench, and insert the cuttings to about half their length, with the remaining buds 6 to 7 inches (15–18cm) above ground level (see photo, p.198). Space the cuttings 6 inches (15cm) apart in the row. Firm the cuttings after insertion and again after frosts during winter. They should have rooted a year later and have produced a good shoot from each of the buds left on the cuttings. The rooted 1-year-old plants are then ready for planting out.

A bush is formed by cutting back all shoots to about 4 buds. Remove shoots growing from the main stem at less than 4 inches (10cm) from the ground to create a short stem. For cordons select the strongest shoot (for a single cordon) or the 2 strongest shoots (for a double cordon), remove the tips and tie them to vertical canes. Cut the remaining laterals to one bud.

Recommended cultivars

Redcurrants
Jonkheer van Tets. Very early; good flavour. Heavy cropping.
Earliest of Fourlands. Early.

Laxton's No. 1. Early. Good flavour.
Red Lake. Mid-season. Good flavour. Heavy cropper.
Stanza. Mid- to late season. Good flavour. Heavy cropper.
Rondom. Late.
Wilson's Long Bunch. Late.
Redstart. Late.

Whitecurrants
White Grape. Mid-season. Good flavour.
White Dutch. Mid-season.
White Pearl. Mid-season. Large berries.

Pests

BIRDS, especially pigeons and blackbirds, attack ripe fruits, and in many areas damage can be avoided only by erecting netting to exclude them.
APHIDS infest leaves and shoots, causing reddish blistered foliage, but can be controlled by a tar oil spray applied to dormant bushes during the winter, or by spraying with pirimicarb, heptenophos, or dimethoate just before blossoming.
GOOSEBERRY SAWFLY and CAPSID BUGS see p.201.

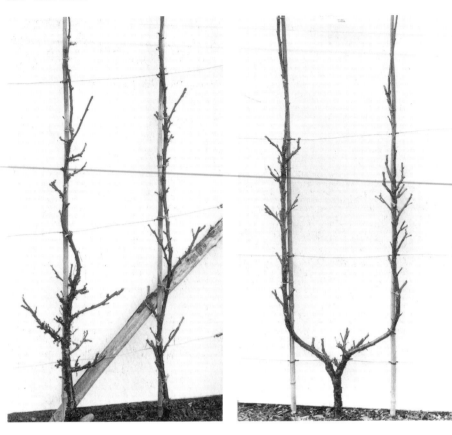

(Far left) *Two single cordons of whitecurrant 'White Grape' (left) and redcurrant 'Red Dutch' (right).*

(Left) *A whitecurrant trained as a double or U cordon.*

(Below) *Blistering on redcurrant leaves caused by aphids.*

(Opposite left) *Winter pruning a cordon: cut the previous summer's growth to 1 or 2 buds. Note that redcurrants form clusters of fruit buds on the older wood and the base of young laterals.*

(Opposite) *Cuttings of 12 inches (30cm) or more, taken from well ripened 1-year-old shoots: all but the top 3 or 4 buds have been removed.*

(Opposite below) *Cuttings inserted 6 inches (15cm) apart through black polythene, which controls weeds and helps to keep the soil moist.*

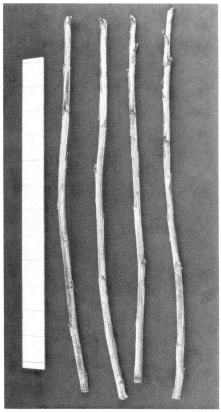

Diseases

CORAL SPOT shows as numerous coral pink spots on old and dead wood and can cause die-back of branches or even the death of a plant. Cut out and burn affected branches to a point well below diseased tissues, and paint all wounds with a good protective paint.

LEAF SPOT causes small brown spots on the leaves which eventually wither and fall prematurely. Spray as for blackcurrants (see p.185).

Gooseberries

Gooseberries grow well in Britain's cool summer climate and are fairly long-lived, lasting possibly 20 years or more.

They are usually grown as open-centred bushes on a short stem, 4 to 6 inches (10–15cm) long, although they are also grown in trained forms, such as single, double, or even triple cordons, and occasionally as fans or espaliers against walls and fences. More rarely they are grown as standards on a 3½- to 4-foot (1–1.2m) stem.

A well-grown mature bush should yield an average of at least 8 to 10lbs (3.6–4.5kg) each year, and a single cordon about 1 to 2lb (0.5–1kg) of fruit.

There is a limited certification scheme for gooseberries which at present covers the cultivar 'Invicta' and the 'Jubilee' clone of 'Careless'. Possibly more will be added in the future. However, virus infection is relatively unimportant in gooseberries, and provided that the plants are obtained from a reputable source, there should be no problems in this respect.

Site and soil

Shelter is essential because gooseberries flower very early in the spring, and also the young shoots are easily broken by strong summer winds. A sunny position is best, but they do tolerate partial shade. Plants can be grown on a north-facing fence or wall. Avoid a frost pocket.

A well drained, slightly acid medium loam soil suits gooseberries best, although they tolerate a wide range, provided that they are not waterlogged. Shallow or light sandy soils may be too dry for vigorous growth and good fruit size, unless heavily manured with bulky organic materials to improve their moisture-holding capacity.

Soil preparation and planting

It is important that the ground is free of perennial weeds before planting. If necessary use a herbicide to clear the land (see p.26). On a light soil, dig in a 1½- to 2-inch (4–5cm) layer of well rotted farmyard manure or compost over the whole area. Gooseberries have a relatively high requirement of potash, so

in the final preparation before planting fork in some sulphate of potash at $\frac{3}{4}$ oz per sq. yd (25g/m²). A soil of low fertility also needs an application of a compound fertilizer such as Growmore at 2oz per sq. yd (65g/m²).

Plant at any time during autumn and winter when soil conditions are suitable. Two- and 3-year-old plants are usually available from nurseries. Choose a plant with a well-balanced head of strong young shoots on a clean stem of 4 to 6 inches (10–15cm).

Space bushes 5 to 6 feet (1.5–1.8m) apart or 4 to 5 feet (1.2–1.5m) on light soils. Plant single cordons 1 foot (30cm) apart in the row and 5 feet (1.5m) between the rows. Allow the same spacing for each vertical stem of a multiple cordon. Plant each cordon to a bamboo cane which in turn should be tied to horizontal wires at 2 feet (60cm) and 4 feet (1.2m) above ground level, fixed to the wall or fence. A mulch after planting helps to conserve soil moisture in the growing season and to prevent weed growth.

Bushes

Pruning at planting
The aim is to obtain an open-centred goblet-shaped bush consisting of 6 to 8 main branches. Prune the leader – last summer's growth – of each branch by half to an appropriate bud according to whether the cultivar is of drooping or upright growth. If the branch is weeping, cut to an upward-pointing bud; if upright, cut to an outward-facing bud. Remove any shoots on the main stem lower than 4 inches (10cm) from the ground to create the clean stem. Cut back to 1 bud any growth crossing over the centre.

Established bushes

Formative winter pruning should continue for a number of years. Cut back the new leading shoots by about half to a bud facing in the required direction of growth, usually to an inward-facing bud, or upright lateral in that most gooseberries are of a weeping habit. This should produce strong branches for the support of heavy crops of fruit. The formation of fruiting spurs is encouraged

'Careless', a reliable cultivar which crops well.

A fan-trained gooseberry against a north-facing fence.

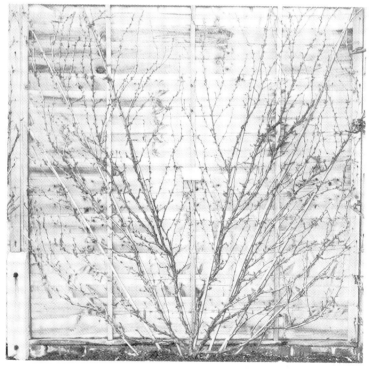

by cutting back laterals (previously summer-pruned – *see* photo) to about 3 inches (8cm), pruning to a bud. Remove all weak shoots.

After some years, the leading shoots of an established bush may be pruned harder. Cut out weak shoots and old branches, and thin out any main branches if the centre is too thick. Suitably placed vigorous young shoots should be left to replace old unproductive branches that are removed. Cut any laterals not required as replacement branches to 3 inches (8cm), but where they are crowded or if large fruits for eating are wanted rather than smaller ones for cooking, prune them harder. Keep the centre open to allow sunlight and air in, to ripen the wood and fruits, as well as to reduce the risk of mildew infection.

Summer pruning is not essential, but it has several advantages. It removes any mildew or aphids on the tips of the shoots, lets in sunlight, and improves air circulation and spray penetration so reducing the risk of fungal troubles. It also helps to prevent young laterals breaking during heavy rains in the early summer.

From the third week of June shorten all laterals of the current season's growth to 5 leaves.

Cordons

Pruning at planting

Shorten the leader by half to an outward-facing bud, and the laterals to 3 buds. Cut away side shoots below 4 inches (10cm) from the ground back to the main stem, to give a clean stem of about 4 to 6 inches (10–15cm). Tie the cordon to the cane with a figure-of-eight tie using soft fillis string.

Established cordons

Formative pruning continues for the next few winters until the cordon has reached the required height, which is usually about 5 to 6 feet (1.5–1.8m). Lightly prune the leader, removing about one-quarter of the previous summer's growth, so stimulating the production of side shoots. Cut laterals, previously summer-pruned, to a bud at about 3 inches (8cm), and remove any suckers around the base as well as any shoots coming off the main stem lower than 4 inches (10cm). This pruning of laterals promotes the development of fruiting spurs close to the main stem. After some years they may become over-long, and should be shortened by cutting back into older wood. When the cordon has reached its required height, cut the leader to 3 buds, or fewer if it is becoming too tall.

Start summer pruning at the end of June, pruning all laterals of the current season's growth to 5 leaves; this pruning should be finished by mid-July. Do not prune the leader, but tie it to the cane as it grows throughout the summer.

Birds

Protection of the fruit buds from birds, especially bullfinches, may be necessary throughout the winter. Netting is the only sure method of protection. Delay winter pruning of plants that have been attacked until the buds are beginning to break so that cuts can be made to a living bud.

Cultivation, feeding and watering

It is best not to dig the ground between the bushes or damage may be caused to

(Above) A newly-planted 3-year-old bush on a 6-inch (15cm) stem, before pruning.

(Left) The same bush after pruning.

(Below) Pruning a drooping leading shoot to an upward pointing bud.

(Opposite above) An established bush of 'Keepsake' before pruning (left) and after pruning (right).
(Opposite below) A close look at one branch before pruning (left) and after pruning (right) laterals pruned to 1 bud and crowded spurs thinned out.

Thinning and harvesting

For large berries, and when a heavy crop has been set, thinning is necessary. Start from about the third week in May, when the thinnings are a useful size for cooking. Remove every alternate fruit, going over the bushes a number of times, leaving some berries to ripen to their full size, colour and flavour for dessert use.

Propagation

Young bushes can be grown from cuttings in the same way as described for redcurrants (p.190) but they do not root so readily. Cuttings are taken in mid- to late September. Dip them in a hormone rooting-powder for hardwood cuttings. Insert the cuttings to half their length, spacing them 6 inches (15cm) apart in the row.

It is usual to remove the lower buds leaving about 4 at the top on well-ripened wood from which the young branches can develop. But it has been found that gooseberries root better if all the buds are left on the cutting; and this is recommended when cuttings are rooted in poor

(Far left) Summer pruning of a gooseberry bush, starting from about the third week in June. (Left) Cuttings usually have the lower buds removed before insertion (see below)

the roots. Keep weeds under control by mulching or by herbicide application. Should any gooseberry shoots appear from the ground, pull them out, or the advantages of growing the bush on a stem will be lost.

Potash is necessary for gooseberries, which are very susceptible to deficiency; it shows as marginal scorching on the leaves. An annual application in the late winter of sulphate of potash at $\frac{1}{2}$ oz per sq. yd (15g/m²) plus Growmore at 2 oz per sq. yd (65g/m²) should supply adequate nutrients. On a light soil mulch plants with well rotted manure or compost, keeping the material away from the stem. If growth has been poor in the previous summer, give more nitrogen by applying sulphate of ammonia at 1 oz per sq. yd (33g/m²) in March.

Water in dry weather to obtain good fruit size and strong growth. Apply at least 4½ gal. per sq. yd (25 litres/m²) and preferably 9 gal. (50 litres) of water at a time. Do not let the soil become too dry before a heavy watering when the berries are ripe or nearly ripe because they may split.

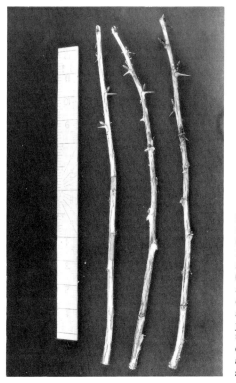

(Opposite above) 'Leveller', a mid-season cultivar. (Opposite left) 'Howard's Lancer', a mid- to late-season green gooseberry. (Opposite right) A standard gooseberry is an attractive form but is rarely seen. It has a stem 3½ to 4 feet (1–1.2m) long and is usually grafted onto R. divaricatum or Ribes aureum. Note the strong staking.

conditions. It is also beneficial to leave one or two leaves on at the top. The use of black polythene mulch, as described for blackcurrants (see p.184) also encourages successful rooting of the cuttings.

One year later, the rooted cuttings should be dug up when dormant, and the lower side shoots removed, thus creating the necessary clean stem, before planting out.

Recommended cultivars

Green
Keepsake. (Berry's Early Kent). Mid-season, but the earliest for picking green for tarts. Bush vigorous, spreading. Susceptible to frost damage. Flavour good.
Careless. Mid-season. Moderately vigorous, spreading. Crops well. 'Jubilee' is a virus-tested selection of 'Careless' which crops more heavily. Flavour fair.
Invicta. Mid-season. Vigorous, spreading and thorny. Crops heavily. Resistant to mildew. Flavour good.
Greenfinch. Mid-season. Vigorous, upright. Crops well. Resistant to mildew. Flavour fair, only suitable for cooking.
Lancer. Late. Very vigorous, strong, spreading. Berry large, pale, greyish green. Cropping heavy. Flavour good.

Red
May Duke. Early. Picked green for earliness. Moderately vigorous, upright. Crops well. Flavour fair.
Whinham's Industry. Mid-season. Very vigorous. Berry medium to large. Tolerant of poor soils. Susceptible to mildew. Crops heavily. Flavour very good.
Lancashire Lad. Mid- to late. Moderately vigorous. Stunted on poor soils, but crops well on good land. Some resistance to mildew. Flavour fair.
Lord Derby. Late. Bush small, pendulous habit. Berry very large, dark red almost black. Cropping moderate. Flavour good.
Captivator. Late. Moderately vigorous, spreading habit. Almost thornless. Berries small, dark red, sweet. Cropping moderate.

White
Whitesmith. Mid-season. Vigorous, upright, then spreading. Berry large. Cropping heavy. Flavour very good.
Langley Gage. Mid-season. Vigorous, upright. Berry medium, silvery white, transparent. Cropping good. Flavour excellent.

On an old cordon the spurs will need shortening and thinning out.

Yellow
Golden Drop. Early, mid-season. Neat, upright, compact habit. Berry greenish yellow, small. Flavour very good.
Leveller. Mid-season. Moderately vigorous, spreading, but rather weak on poor soils and needs good drainage. Berry very large, yellow-green. Flavour good.

The Worcesterberry
The Worcesterberry, *Ribes divaricatum*, is a North American plant, at one time thought to be a cross between the gooseberry and the blackcurrant. The bush is extremely vigorous and very thorny with long arching laterals. It is similar to the gooseberry in growth habit, leaf, flower and fruit, but the berries are small, dull, reddish purple and of pleasant flavour suitable for culinary uses and making jam. It crops well and is immune to American gooseberry mildew.

Culturally, it is treated in exactly the same way as the gooseberry.

The Josta
The 'Jostaberry', of complex parentage, is a cross between blackcurrant and goose-

Summer pruning of a young cordon, starting in the third week of June, cutting the laterals to 5 leaves. The leader is not pruned.

berry. The dull black berries, like very large blackcurrants, are borne in small clusters and have a sharp pleasant flavour, excellent for jam and other culinary uses. The plant is extremely vigorous, upright, spineless, self-fertile and crops well. It is resistant to American gooseberry mildew, blackcurrant leaf spot and gall mite, though the flowers can be damaged by spring frosts.

It crops on both old and young wood. It can be grown as a stooled bush like a blackcurrant, or as a half-standard on a clean stem of about 2½ feet (75cm) when it requires staking. Prune in winter, spurring back some of the young laterals to about 5 inches (13cm), leaving others full length. Also cut out some of the older wood regularly.

Pests

BULLFINCHES eat the buds in winter and there may be hardly any left after severe attacks. 'Leveller' is particularly susceptible to bullfinch damage. Erecting netting over the plants from about November to April is the only certain preventive measure.

GOOSEBERRY SAWFLY and MAGPIE MOTH CATERPILLARS feed on the leaves, reducing them to a skeleton of veins. Look out for the first signs of attack from April onwards. Hand-pick and destroy caterpillars if there are a few bushes. Otherwise, spray with malathion, permethrin, fenitrothion or derris when larvae are seen. Gooseberry sawfly can have three generations during the summer.

CAPSID BUGS suck sap from the shoot tips, causing the foliage to develop many small holes. Growth can be checked. Spray at the end of flowering with fenitrothion or dimethoate. These sprays also control aphids.

Diseases

AMERICAN GOOSEBERRY MILDEW affects leaves, shoots and fruits, producing a white powdery coating. Diseased shoots become distorted at the tips and should be cut out. Apply benomyl or bupirimate with triforine or carbendazim or thiophanate methyl as instructed by the manufacturer.

LEAF SPOT commonly causes spotting and early leaf fall. If a systemic fungicide is not being used, spray immediately after flowering with mancozeb according to the manufacturer's instructions, or spray with a copper fungicide.

GREY MOULD. Die-back of a bush branch by branch until the whole plant is killed may be caused by grey mould. Cut out all dead wood back into living tissues, paint the larger wounds, prune to provide plenty of light and air within a bush and see that soil conditions are good.

HONEY FUNGUS *see* p.70.

Highbush blueberries

The American highbush blueberry is derived from *Vaccinium corymbosum* and *V. australe*. It is related to our indigenous bilberry or whortleberry *V. myrtillus*, but is much more productive and is also a larger plant. The berries are up to ¾ inches (2cm) across, blue-black when fully ripe, and covered in a waxy white bloom which makes them seem light blue. Their taste is sometimes bland when raw, but they are excellent cooked and they freeze or bottle very well. The plant is slow to start cropping, yielding lightly at first, but by the fifth year should give at least 5 lb (2.25 kg) per bush each year, increasing to at least 10 lb (4.5 kg) when fully grown.

Blueberries need a very acid soil with plenty of summer moisture. They do not grow satisfactorily in alkaline or neutral soils. Although there are ways of reducing the pH of the soil, naturally alkaline soils tend to revert to their original high pH within a very short time unless special steps are taken to prevent it. These are described later, but each grower must make a personal decision whether the trouble and expense is worthwhile before planting this crop.

Highbush blueberries are hardy and deciduous, and when fully mature reach a height between 5 and 6 feet (1.5–1.8m). They are decorative as well as productive, and with some cultivars the leaves turn red and gold in autumn.

Site and soil

The most suitable sites are in full sun or light shade, sheltered from strong winds. The right soil is vital for blueberries: it must be definitely acid, with a pH between 4 and 5.5, ideally about 4.5, and well drained. In soils with a pH above this the plants become increasingly likely to suffer from a deficiency of iron or manganese, which induces yellowing of the leaves (chlorosis). The best soils are well drained, light sandy loams, very high in acid organic matter content.

Heavy soils, those of low organic content, or with a pH above 5.5 up to

(Opposite right) A blueberry in flower in mid-May makes a decorative shrub.

(Opposite below) Fruiting blueberry, 'Berkeley'.

Mulching a pruned bush with peat.

about 6, need a very generous application of an acid peat such as sphagnum moss peat. Fork a 3- to 4-inch (8–10cm) thick layer into the top 6 inches (15cm) of soil. A heavy clay needs more than this plus sharp (acid) sand to improve the texture and drainage. Soils with a pH 6.5 or more also need an acidifying agent such as flowers of sulphur or iron sequestrene (see p.8). Near-neutral, neutral and alkaline soils are very difficult to acidify and maintain at an adequate pH because of the seepage of alkaline water into the rooting area. On such soils it is necessary to grow blueberries in containers or to make special planting sites. The containers, at least 15 inches deep and 15 inches wide (38 × 38cm), should be filled with an acid compost. Plastic pots of 18 inches (45cm) in diameter are ideal. Crock the base of the pot with broken clay pots, bricks, clinker or gravel to ensure that the drainage is efficient.

Water generously throughout the growing season with rain-water whenever conditions are dry. Give the plants a high-potash liquid feed every 10 days from the start of flowering until the berries begin to ripen.

Another alternative is to make special planting sites each about $2\frac{1}{2}$ feet by $2\frac{1}{2}$ feet, and $1\frac{1}{2}$ feet deep (75 × 75 × 45cm). Line the sides and the base of the hole with heavy-grade black polythene, so that alkaline water from the surrounding soil does not permeate the rooting area. Prick the polythene at the bottom of the hole with a garden fork so that the water can drain away. Then fill the hole with an acid compost such as is prepared for ericaceous plants.

Raised beds
Badly-drained clays are not suitable for special sites because they would act as a sump. On such soils blueberries must be grown in raised beds or in the containers previously mentioned.

The sides of a raised bed may be constructed of a solid material such as bricks or old railway sleepers, or of peat blocks, minimum size 12 × 6 × 6 inches (30 × 15 × 15cm). The bed must be at least $1\frac{1}{2}$ feet (45cm) deep by 4 feet (1.2m) wide; the length depends on the number of blueberries to be planted. For only 2 plants at 4 feet (1.2m) apart, it would need to be 8 feet (2.4m) long.

A raised bed tends to dry out more quickly than level ground, and unless there is a plentiful supply of soft water it should be sited in light shade rather than full sun.

To prevent alkaline water from the clay permeating into the bed, lay a sheet of heavy-grade black polythene over the site, on a 6-inch (15cm) camber for drainage to the sides. Turn the edges of the polythene slightly upwards to prevent water flowing into the bed. If the side walls are solid, drainage holes have to be made in them, although this is not necessary with peat walls.

Before building a peat wall, the blocks must be thoroughly soaked. They are then laid so that the natural strata are horizontal. Build the wall in steps with a pronounced batter so that the walls recede. Spike each block to the one beneath with spliced bamboo. These precautions prevent the bed from bursting outwards.

Fill the bed with an acid peat or bark compost. Always keep the bed well watered in the summer because it is very important that it does not dry out.

Planting

Plant between November and March with 2- or 3-year-old plants spaced 5 feet (1.5m) apart each way. Mulch after planting with a 3-inch (8cm) layer of acid peat or bark over the whole area.

Cultivation, feeding and watering

Blueberries have surface-feeding roots as well as deeper roots for taking up moisture, and do not tolerate root disturbance. Any weeding is best done by hand, but provided that a thick mulch is maintained around the plants, weeds should not be a problem.

Annual feeding is necessary to encourage strong new growth. In early March apply John Innes base fertilizer, without chalk (acid-based) at 2 oz per sq. yd (65g/m²). In early April apply sulphate of ammonia at 1 oz per sq. yd (33g/m²). Fork fertilizers gently into the mulch without disturbing the roots.

Top up the mulch annually in spring to maintain a depth of 3 to 5 inches (8–13cm). Old sawdust from conifers can be used instead of peat, but the amount of sulphate of ammonia then needs to be doubled because decomposing sawdust competes with the plant for nitrogen. Other good acidic mulches are old pine-needles and granulated conifer bark. Do

(Above) *Temporary netting erected over the bushes at fruit ripening, supported by bamboo canes, held by rubber joints. The wire netting at the base is to keep out rabbits.*

(Opposite above) *Starting to prune a fruiting bush in early March; some of the older, less productive wood is cut out at or near the base.*

(Opposite left) *Pruning completed. About a quarter of the bush has been removed.*

not use manure, mushroom compost or lime of any kind.

Blueberries require plenty of moisture in the growing season, and in the drier parts of the country watering is needed in dry weather. With natural soft water, an application of 1 inch (2.5cm) every 10 days – 4½ gal. per sq. yd (25 litres/m²) – maintains the water supply, but in hard water areas the application has to be moderated. Hard water is better than no water, but collected rain-water is an even better alternative.

Pruning

Blueberries are grown as stooled bushes like blackcurrants. Pruning is not necessary until the third or fourth year after planting. The best fruit is produced on 2- or 3-year-old wood, so pruning must stimulate strong new growth from or near the base each year.

Prune in early March, by which time it should be apparent which wood is carrying fruit buds. Cut out the oldest, unproductive wood, removing about one-quarter of the bush. Cut some branches back to the base and others back to strong upright shoots. Remove low branches too near the ground and any weak, spindly growth.

Certain cultivars, in particular 'Berkeley', are reluctant to produce strong new replacement growth and they crop quite well on older branches. Provided that they have a good, strong framework, these cultivars need only the removal of weak or old wood. But if the whole framework is weak, hard pruning is needed, supplemented by nitrogen applications to stimulate new growth. If there is no growth, check on other factors such as the soil pH, drainage and nutrition other than nitrogen.

Harvesting

The fruits are borne in clusters and they do not all ripen at once, so selective picking is necessary. Ripe berries are blue-black with a white waxy bloom and are soft. They should leave the cluster easily and are picked by rolling the berries between the forefinger and thumb.

It is important not to pick the fruits too early because immature fruit has an inferior flavour. Even when the berries turn blue, they should be left on the bush for a few days to ensure that they develop their characteristic taste.

Propagation

The usual method in Britain is to take softwood cuttings in late June or early July when the shoots are 4 to 6 inches (10–15cm) long. Remove the lower leaves, leaving 3 or 4 at the top. Dip the base of each cutting into a hormone rooting powder, and then insert them into a rooting medium consisting of 1 part peat to 3 parts coarse sand, in a pot or box. Place this in a partly shaded propagating-case with a bottom heat of 68°F (20°C). They should root and after about 4 weeks be ready to pot up into pots containing equal parts of peat and sand. They should then be placed in a cold frame for gradual hardening off. Shade the frame in hot weather and give the plants high potash liquid feed every 10 days until growth stops in the autumn.

The young plants can then be planted out in nursery rows and grown on for a year before transplanting into their permanent positions.

Pollination

Trials in the USA have shown that cross-pollinated blueberries are more productive than those self-pollinated. So plant at least two different cultivars. A

ratio of a row of one cultivar to two rows of a different cultivar is adequate for good cross-pollination.

Recommended cultivars

A good deal of breeding work is being carried out in the USA, and cultivars superior to those presently available will probably be introduced in due course. In the meantime, the following have proved to be quite successful in this country, given the right conditions.

Earliblue. Early. Strong, upright growth, large berries, good quality. Attractive autumn colour.

Bluetta. Early. Compact, moderate vigour. Berries medium-sized. Yield very good.

Bluecrop. Early. Upright and vigorous. Berries large, light blue, firm, good quality. A good cropper. Orange and red autumn colour. Strongly recommended.

Spartan. Mid-season. Vigorous, upright. Large firm berries, dark blue. Yield good.

Herbert. Mid-season. Much-branched, fairly spreading bush of moderate vigour, producing very heavy compact clusters of large berries. The best-flavoured cultivar. Moderate autumn colour.

Ivanhoe. Mid-season. Strong, upright growth with tight clusters of highly flavoured dark berries. Attractive autumn colour.

Berkeley. Mid-season. Bush vigorous, open, spreading and very productive. Berries very large, light blue, firm with a mild, sweet flavour and of good quality. Strongly recommended.

Coville. Very late. Bush vigorous, upright and productive. Fruits large, in long open sprays. The berries can be left on the long bush to ripen fully without dropping. Of good quality.

Pests and diseases

BIRDS are the main problem. It is essential to net the plants well before the berries are ripe.

APHIDS and CATERPILLARS (see p.68) are rarely troublesome.

GREY MOULD (see p.201) causes die-back of a bush branch by branch.

(Above left) 'Earliblue' is an early blueberry, which also has good autumn colour.

(Below left) 'Bluetta', an early-ripening berry of good size.

(Above) Cutting out the thick, old dark brown wood with long-arm pruners.

Four Plans for Fruit Gardens

A is a plot with fruit and vegetables (30 ft × 38 ft). B is a larger fruit garden, 30 × 60 ft, as at RHS Garden, Wisley. C and D are the same size, but show different layouts.

Key

Ab	Apple (bush form)
Ac	Apples (cordon)
Ad	Apples (dwarf pyramid)
B	Boysenberry and Blackberry trained over an arch
Bc	Blackcurrants
G	Gooseberries
H	Hybrid berries
Mc	Morello cherry (bush)
Mcf	Morello cherry (fan)
P	Pears (espalier)
Pc	Pears (cordon)
Pe	Peaches (fans)
Pl	Plums (bush)
Plf	Plums (fan)
Rs	Raspberries (summer fruiting)
Ra	Raspberries (autumn fruiting)
Rc	Redcurrants (bush)
Rcc	Redcurrants (cordons)
Rcf	Redcurrant (fan)
Rc/G	Redcurrant or gooseberry

Work in the Fruit Garden

A brief outline of the various tasks which should be done is given on these pages. For full details of each operation turn to the chapter dealing with the fruit in question.

The timing of spray applications for control of pests and diseases is based on the stages of bud development. Dates for these stages can only be approximate because the rate of growth varies according to locality and season. For full details of each control see the paragraphs headed Pests and Diseases in the chapter on the fruit concerned.

For full details of herbicides mentioned see pages 26–27.

JANUARY

Inspect fruits in store and remove any that are rotten.

Continue planting fruit trees and bushes when soil conditions are right.

Select and heel-in scionwood in a cold, sheltered, shaded position for grafting later.

Apply potash to strawberries, gooseberries, red- and whitecurrants and a balanced fertilizer to cobnuts and filberts.

Check all tree-stakes and ties, and make sure they are firm and sound.

Continue pruning of apples and pears except in hard frost. Collect and burn the prunings. Prune newly planted cane fruits. Continue pruning established and newly planted bush fruits.

Pests and diseases
Spray dormant fruit trees, canes and bushes with tar oil to control overwintering aphid and sucker eggs – unless this was done in December.

Inspect apples and pears for canker and treat where necessary.

Spray peaches and nectarines against peach leaf curl. Repeat in 10 to 14 days. Fan-trained trees can be protected by covering them with a polythene cover.

FEBRUARY

Inspect fruits in store and remove any that are rotten.

Continue planting fruit trees and bushes when soil conditions are right.

Apply simazine to the soil around established fruit trees and bushes (except stone fruits).

Apply potash to apples, pears and plums. Apply nitrogen in early February to trees in grass, and in late February to those in cultivated land.

Mulch young trees, bushes and cane fruits with manure or compost.

Prune newly planted and established stone fruits (except pyramid plums – see April) as growth begins in late February.

Complete the formative pruning of newly planted apples and pears, and continue pruning the older trees except in hard frost.

Prune cobnuts and filberts provided the catkins are fully open and releasing pollen; otherwise delay until March.

Prune established autumn-fruiting raspberries. Tip summer-fruiting raspberries. If not already done, cut down newly planted canes to 9 to 12 inches (22–30cm).

Cover strawberries for an early crop with polythene tunnels or glass cloches early in the month.

Protect the blossom on wall-trained trees by draping with hessian, double thickness netting or equivalent whenever frost is expected. Hand pollinate if flowering is early and insects scarce.

Pests and diseases
Complete tar oil spraying early in the month.

Spray peaches and nectarines against peach leaf curl. Repeat in 10 to 14 days, but finish before the middle of the month.

Inspect apple and pear trees for canker and treat if necessary. Spray severely infected trees. Protect all large pruning cuts.

MARCH

Finish all planting of trees and bushes, early in the month.

Prune cobnuts and filberts if not done in February.

Apply potash to cane fruits.

Complete mulching of young trees, bushes and cane fruits.

Apply nitrogen to blackcurrants.

Apply simazine or dichlobenil around established fruit trees and bushes (except stone fruits). Paraquat/diquat can also be used to kill annual weeds and shallow-rooted perennials.

Give a second application of nitrogen to pears in grass.

Cleft graft apples, pears and plums.

Protect the blossom on wall-trained trees when frost is forecast (see February). Hand pollinate if flowering is early and insects are scarce.

On established acid cherries prune out a proportion of older wood, if not done after cropping.

Untie and retrain canes of blackberries and related fruits which have been bundled together against winter damage. Train on to wires before the buds burst.

Prune blueberries.

Plant strawberry runners. Sow seeds of alpine strawberries.

Pests and diseases
If a winter wash has been applied, control of aphids, suckers and scale insects may not be necessary; but if aphids are present spray with a systemic insecticide.

Spray apples against scab according to the manufacturer's instructions.

Spray pears against scab according to the manufacturer's instructions.

Spray blackcurrants against leaf spot, mildew and grey mould according to the manufacturer's instructions. Spray against aphids if present.

Spray gooseberries against gooseberry mildew according to the manufacturer's instructions.

APRIL

Early-flowering fruits may need some protection from frost by covering with hessian, double thickness nylon or fish netting, or similar materials whenever frost is imminent. Uncover immediately afterwards so that pollination is not impeded.

Ventilate protected strawberries on sunny days. If growth is poor apply a light dressing of nitrogen. Finish planting runners by mid-April. De-blossom spring-planted summer-fruiting strawberries in their first year.

Prune gooseberries and red- and white-currants left unpruned during the winter because of the likelihood of bird damage.

Prune pyramid plums in their early years.

Hand pollinate wall-trained peach and nectarine flowers and then spray at midday with a fine mist to help setting in dry conditions.

Untie and retrain branches of wall-trained figs that have been bundled together for protection, at the end of the month. Prune as necessary. Leave until May in cold districts.

210

Finish planting raspberries and cut back the newly planted canes. Check on netting for bird protection and prepare supports.

Graft top fruits, using whip-and-tongue grafts. Top-working top fruits to change the cultivar can also be done this month.

Pests and diseases
Do not use insecticides during flowering of any crop as bees and other pollinating insects may be killed.

Continue scab control on apples and if not already done, control aphids, apple suckers, and caterpillars before open blossom. Start spraying against mildew according to manufacturer's instructions if using thiophanate methyl or benomyl.

Continue with scab control on pears; also control aphids, suckers and caterpillars and, if necessary, pear midge before open blossom.

Spray peaches and nectarines at petal fall against aphids.

Spray plums at white bud against aphids and caterpillars.

Control aphids and caterpillars on cherries before open blossom.

Spray blackcurrants with carbendazim as the first flowers open against big bud mites. Spray for aphids if present. Continue spraying against leaf spot, mildew and grey mould.

Continue control of gooseberry mildew on gooseberries. Start spraying against leaf spot; control aphids, sawflies and capsids, if necessary.

Inspect strawberries for aphids and spray if necessary. Spray to control leaf spot and blotch early in the month. Spray at first open flower against grey mould on plants under glass or polythene.

Spray raspberries against spur blight if necessary.

Spray new canes of blackberries against spur blight.

The stages in apple fruit bud development: (Top to bottom) *Bud-burst, mouse-ear, green cluster.* (Opposite top to bottom) *Pink bud, full bloom, fruitlet.*

MAY

Pick protected strawberries and gooseberry thinnings.

Open one side of fruit cage to allow easier access for pollinating insects.

Protect blossoms from frost when necessary. Keep the grass short.

Ensure no plants suffer from lack of water after flowering, particularly wall-trained stone fruits.

Ring-bark over-vigorous apple and pear trees.

De-blossom newly planted fruit trees.

Start de-shooting wall-trained peaches and nectarines, with some light thinning. The polythene cover can now be removed, although it can be left on for extra warmth if necessary.

On wall-trained plums and damsons remove shoots growing directly towards or out from the wall.

Shorten leaders of all mature trees grown in a restricted form.

De-blossom spring planted runners of summer fruiting strawberries. Clean up weeds and put down slug pellets before strawing. Continue to ventilate protected plants on sunny days. Net against birds. Remove flowers formed on perpetuals. Plant out seedlings of alpine strawberries. Control weeds in soft fruits by hoeing or herbicides. Start netting all soft fruits at the first sign of ripening.

Pull out unwanted shoots of raspberries causing overcrowding or growing between the rows.

Thin gooseberries in late May if large dessert fruits are required.

Pests and diseases
Never apply insecticides during flowering: they may kill bees and other pollinating insects.

Control apple sawfly, aphids and capsid bugs at petal fall. Continue scab and mildew control.

Continue control against pear scab.

Control aphids and sawfly on plums at cot split (about 8 days after petal fall), if necessary.

Continue control on currants of big bud mite, aphids, leaf spot and gooseberry mildew as necessary.

Continue control on gooseberries of mildew and leaf spot. Control sawfly caterpillars and aphids if present.

Spray raspberries against grey mould.

Spray loganberries and blackberries against cane spot and spur blight in mid-May. Spray against grey mould.

Spray strawberries against mildew according to the manufacturer's instructions. When first flowers open, spray against grey mould. Control slugs if present.

JUNE

Pick strawberries, raspberries, red- and whitecurrants, gooseberries and cherries.

Irrigate tree, bush and cane fruits as necessary.

Keep the grass short and weeds under control.

Continue disbudding on wall-trained peaches and nectarines and tie in selected shoots. Thin fruits.

Thin plum fruits in two stages, first in early June and finally in late June.

Continue removing any shoots from fan-trained cherries and plums, that are growing directly towards the wall. Pinch back other laterals and tie in.

If set of apples is heavy, thin lightly. Wait until after the June drop for the final thinning.

Thin pears if fruit set is heavy.

Pinch out tip buds on young shoots of mature figs at 5 leaves.

Continue to net soft fruits against birds, where necessary.

Straw down strawberries (or use black polythene or mats). Ventilate protected strawberries. Remove cloches and tunnels when fruiting has finished. Peg down runners for new plants, otherwise remove them.

Continue to select raspberry shoots and loosely tie in. On newly planted canes prune down old canes once new shoots are produced.

Train in new shoots of blackberries and hybrid berries.

Thin gooseberries and use thinnings for cooking. Summer prune at end of June.

Summer prune bush and cordon red- and whitecurrants at the end of June.

Pests and diseases
Continue to spray apples regularly against scab and mildew. Inspect for red spider mite and spray if present. Spray against codling moth about mid-June and again 3 weeks later. Spray against bitter pit in mid-June if necessary.

Inspect stone fruits for red spider mite and aphids and spray if present.

Continue leaf spot and gooseberry mildew control on currants.

Inspect gooseberries for caterpillars of gooseberry sawfly and magpie moth and control if present. Spray against leaf spot after harvest if necessary.

Control grey mould and mildew on strawberries. Control slugs if present.

Spray raspberries and loganberries at dusk against raspberry beetle; at first pink fruit on raspberries or 80% petal fall on loganberries, and again after 14 days. Spray cane fruits against spur blight and cane spot. Spray against grey mould as the first flowers open.

JULY

Pick strawberries, gooseberries, currants, blueberries, blackberries, raspberries, cherries and peaches.

Check trees for tie constriction.

Complete thinning of apples. Support heavily laden branches. Irrigate if necessary.

Begin summer pruning of all trained forms at the end of month but delay if conditions are wet.

Prop up heavily laden branches of plums and damsons.

Continue training of fan-trained plums and cherries. Complete pruning of cherry trees.

Continue training of wall-trained peaches and nectarines. Protect fruits against birds.

Immediately after raspberries have fruited, cut out old canes and tie in new ones. Remove unwanted suckers and control weeds.

Immediately after summer-fruiting strawberries have fruited, cut off the old leaves and remove straw; remove surplus runners and all weeds, burn all the debris and apply simazine for long-term weed control. Continue propagation of new plants.

Training new canes of blackberries etc. Tip layering for new plants can be done at the end of the month.

Pests and diseases
Apply a second spray to apples against codling moth caterpillars (3 weeks after the first). Continue regular sprays against mildew until mid-July. Continue spraying against bitter pit if necessary. Check whether scab is present and if necessary continue spraying until mid-July. Inspect for woolly aphid and treat if found.

Spray blackberries at dusk against raspberry beetle at first open flower.

On currants and gooseberries continue to control sawfly caterpillars, leaf spot and gooseberry mildew after harvesting.

Control slugs on strawberries if present. After harvest, spray for powdery mildew if troublesome.

AUGUST

Pick strawberries, blackberries, hybrid berries, blueberries, raspberries, gooseberries, blackcurrants and redcurrants, figs, plums, damsons, cherries, peaches, apples and pears.

Continue pruning of restricted forms of apples and pears. Begin pruning of over-vigorous trees. Support heavily laden branches. Tie down laterals of spindle-bush trees where necessary. Protect fruits against birds.

Immediately after wall-trained peaches and nectarines have fruited, cut out the shoots which have borne fruit and dead wood and tie in replacement shoots.

Prune plums and damsons after fruiting, and cut out any broken branches. Remove dead wood on fan-trained plums, shorten pinched-back shoots and tie in.

Break (brut) laterals on cobnuts and filberts.

Prepare new strawberry beds and plant out rooted runners. Apply simazine for weed control in established strawberries only.

Continue pruning and tying-in of raspberries.

Continue training new canes of blackberries etc.

Pests and diseases
On apples continue spraying against bitter pit.

If necessary, spray stone fruits after harvest (but not before mid-August) against bacterial canker.

Continue with leaf spot control on gooseberries and currants after harvesting, and with control of gooseberry mildew if necessary.

On strawberries continue to spray against powdery mildew, if troublesome.

SEPTEMBER

Pick perpetual strawberries, autumn-fruiting raspberries, blackberries, blueberries, plums, damsons, peaches, figs, and early and mid-season apples and pears, cobnuts and filberts.

Order new trees and bushes.

Complete summer pruning of apples and pears.

Prepare for fruit storage by cleaning wooden trays and boxes.

Prune plums and damsons immediately after picking.

Complete pruning of wall-trained peaches and nectarines.

Remove dead wood on wall-trained cherries, shorten pinched-back shoots and complete tying-in. Cut out or tie down strong vertical shoots.

Continue planting strawberries.

Complete the pruning and tying-in of summer-fruiting gooseberries.

Prune blackcurrants. Take cuttings from healthy bushes.

Cut off mildewed tips of gooseberry shoots and burn. Take cuttings.

Cut off old canes of blackberries and hybrid berries after fruiting and tie in the new. In very cold districts bundle the canes together after leaf fall and tie to a lower wire sometime in October or November before hard frosts.

Pests and diseases
Give final sprays to apples against bitter pit.

OCTOBER

Pick strawberries, raspberries, blackberries, plums, apples and pears.

Store fruit of sound condition. Bring down the temperature by ventilating at night. Do not mix late apples in the store with earlier cultivars, and keep apples and pears separate.

Apply dalapon round established apples and pears for couch grass control.

Remove broken branches from stone fruits and protect the wounds.

Prune blackcurrants if not already done. Take cuttings from healthy bushes.

Prune gooseberries, red- and white-currants at leaf fall (if bird damage is likely, pruning can be left until spring). Take cuttings.

Finish pruning of blackberries and hybrid berries.

Cover perpetual strawberries to extend the season. Complete the planting of runners by mid-October. Tidy up beds and remove dead leaves from perpetuals.

Order new fruit trees and bushes and start planting immediately after leaf fall. Prepare the ground for planting before the trees arrive.

Pests and diseases
Greaseband apple, pear, plum and cherry trees to trap female winter moths.

Apply final spray at leaf fall to stone fruits against bacterial canker.

Spray peaches and nectarines against peach leaf curl; this will serve as the mid-October spray against bacterial canker.

NOVEMBER

Complete picking of all but the very late apples and pears.

Ventilate the fruit store at night to bring down the temperature.

Ensure the fruit cage is closed and the netting in good order.

Plant new trees and bushes as soon as possible, and prune after planting.

Root prune over-vigorous trees after leaf fall.

On summer pruned apples and pears, where secondary shoots have been produced, prune back to mature wood.

Prune established apples and pears immediately after leaf fall. Carry out the formative pruning of dwarf pyramid, espalier and fan forms of apples and pears (thereafter prune in summer). Young tip-bearing cordons or those lacking in vigour can be tipped (thereafter prune in summer).

Apply dalapon for couch grass control round established apples, pears, black-currants, gooseberries and cane fruits.

Complete pruning of blackberries and hybrid berries.

Complete pruning of raspberries. Check supports and wires and ensure canes are securely tied.

Prune currants and gooseberries. Take cuttings from healthy bushes.

Weed strawberries, remove runners. Remove old and dead leaves from perpetuals.

In cold districts loosely bundle fig branches together and cover with mats or straw to provide winter protection. Mulch the rooting area with straw or bracken.

In cold districts loosely bundle the new canes of blackberries and hybrid berries together and tie to a wire for winter protection.

Pests and diseases
Net or cotton all fruits (but especially gooseberries and plums) against bullfinches where possible.

Inspect apples and pears for canker and treat: spray severely infected trees according to the manufacturer's instructions.

Spray peaches and nectarines against peach leaf curl just before leaf fall if not already done.

DECEMBER

Complete picking very late apples, before hard frosts come.

Inspect stored fruits, and remove rotten ones.

Plant all fruits when soil conditions are suitable. If the soil is too wet, loosen the bundles, remove the packing material and heel the plants in. If the soil is frozen keep the plants in a cool, frost-proof place. Ensure roots do not dry out and plant as soon as possible.

Prune apples, pears, bush and cane fruits. Continue pruning except in hard freezing conditions, dealing with the young trees first, and then the older trees. Collect the prunings and burn.

Apply simazine to clean soil around established strawberries for weed control.

Untie those laterals on spindlebush apple trees which have 'set' at the required angle.

Check the condition of all stakes, supports and ties for trees. Look for and remedy wind rocking or constriction.

Erect a polythene cover over fan trained peaches and nectarines against peach leaf curl.

Pests and diseases
Start spraying of dormant tree, bush and cane fruits with tar oil winter wash to control aphids, sucker and scale insects.

Complete the spraying of stone fruits by the end of the month.

Inspect apples and pears for canker and treat where necessary.

APPENDIX
Pollination of tree fruits

Pollination and subsequent fertilization are essential processes for the production of good crops of fruit. Pollination is simply the transfer of pollen grains to the stigma of a flower and in tree fruits is mainly the work of bees and other insects.

Many of the important tree fruits are self-incompatible, which means cross-pollination is necessary if they are to set good crops. Some are self-fertile, for example peaches, nectarines and certain plums and gages, but even with these, cropping is improved if cross-pollination is provided. Cross-pollination means the transfer of pollen from one flower of one cultivar to that of a different cultivar, but of the same kind of fruit.

Apples

All apples show some degree of self-incompatibility; some apples set no fruit at all when self-pollinated, others can set a fair crop in favourable conditions. Cropping is much more satisfactory and consistent with cross-pollination. Most apples are diploid (having 2 complete sets of chromosomes in each body cell) and are suitable as pollinators, although some are triploid. Triploids are poor pollinators and need two diploid cultivars to cross-pollinate the triploid and each other.

In the table opposite cultivars are grouped according to their flowering season. In selecting cultivars for cross-pollination, choose those from the same group, if possible, although the flowering period of those chosen from the preceding or following group should overlap sufficiently for cross-pollination to take place, except for Group 7. 'Crawley Beauty' usually flowers after all other cultivars and sets an adequate crop on its own. A few apples are cross-incompatible and these are listed in the notes to the table.

In most seasons and districts flowering follows a regular sequence, but variations occur from year to year and from district to district. Cultivars react differently to winter temperatures and this may cause some cultivars to flower earlier than others in some seasons and later, or at the same time, in others; in the same way variation may occur between cultivars growing in one part of Britain compared with those in another in the same year.

Pears (see table 9, p.218)

Cultivars of pears are more incompatible than apples and very few fruits are produced from self-pollination. 'Conference', though sometimes reported as self-fertile, is almost self-incompatible, although it may set parthenocarpic (seedless) fruits, some of which are normal in shape. Most pear cultivars are diploid; a few are triploid or even tetraploid. Triploid cultivars behave in the same way as triploid apples and should have two other cultivars to pollinate both the triploid cultivars and each other. Two cultivars are tetraploids: 'Improved Fertility' is self-fertile, but a sport of 'Williams' known as 'Double Williams' is self-incompatible.

Two incompatibility groups are known in pears. Cultivars in these groups are all self- and cross-incompatible, that is, they will neither set fruit with their own pollen nor with the pollen of any cultivar within the same group. These are:

INCOMPATIBILITY GROUP I
Fondante d'Automne, Laxton's Progress, Louise Bonne of Jersey, Précoce de Trévoux, Seckle, Williams' Bon Chrétien.

INCOMPATIBILITY GROUP II
Beurré d'Amanlis, Conference.

Three diploid cultivars, 'Bristol Cross', 'Beurré Bedford' and 'Marguerite Marillat', produce little good pollen and are, therefore, useless as pollinators.

In the table on p.218 the cultivars are divided into 4 groups according to flowering season. Where possible, select from the same flowering group when choosing cultivars for mutual cross-pollination, although in many cases the flowering period of cultivars in adjacent groups provides sufficient overlap.

Table 8   Flowering of apples

Flowering Group 1: very early
Gravenstein (T)
Lord Suffield
Mank's Codlin (B)
Red Astrachan
Stark Earliest (Scarlet
  Pimpernel)
Vista Bella (B)

Flowering Group 2
Acme
Alkmene
Adam's Pearmain (B)
Baker's Delicious
Beauty of Bath
Beauty of Blackmoor
Ben's Red (B)
Bismarck (B)
Bolero
Cheddar Cross
Christmas Pearmain (B)
Devonshire Quarrenden (B)
Egremont Russet
George Cave
George Neal
Golden Spire
Idared
Irish Peach
Kerry Pippin
Keswick Codlin (B)
Laxton's Early Crimson
Lord Lambourne
Maidstone Favourite
Margil
McIntosh Red
Melba (B)
Merton Charm
Michaelmas Red
Norfolk Beauty
Owen Thomas
Rev. W. Wilks (B)
Ribston Pippin (T)
Ross Nonpareil
St Edmund's Pippin
Striped Beefing
Warner's King (T)
Washington (T)
White Transparent

Flowering Group 3
Acme
Allington Pippin (B)
Arthur Turner
Barnack Orange
Baumann's Reinette (B)
Belle de Boskoop (T)
Belle de Pontoise (B)
Blenheim Orange (TB)
Bountiful
Bowden's Seedling
Bramley's Seedling (T)
Brownlee's Russett
Charles Ross
Cox's Orange Pippin
Crispin (T)
Discovery
Duchess Favourite
Elstar
Emperor Alexander
Emneth Early (Early
  Victoria) (B)
Epicure
Exeter Cross
Exquisite
Falstaff
Feltham Beauty
Fiesta
Fortune (B)
Gavin
Granny Smith
Greensleeves
Grenadier
Hambling's Seedling
Holstein (T)
Hormead Pearmain
James Grieve
Jerseymac
John Standish
Jonagold (T)
Jonathan
Jupiter (T)
Karmijn de Sonnaville (T)
Katy (Katja)
Kidd's Orange Red
King of Tompkins County (T)
King Russett
Lane's Prince Albert
Langley Pippin
Loddington (Stone's)
Lord Grosvenor
Lord Hindlip
Malling Kent
Mère de Ménage

Merton Knave
Merton Prolific
Merton Russet
Merton Worcester
Miller's Seedling (B)
New Hawthornden
Norfolk Royal Russet
Ontario
Peasgood's Nonsuch
Polka (B)
Queen
Red Victoria (B)
Redsleeves
Reinette du Canada (T)
Rival (B)
Rosemary Russet
Rubinette
St Cecilia
St Everard
Spartan
Stirling Castle
Sturmer Pippin
Sunset
Taunton Cross
Tom Putt
Tydeman's Early Worcester
Wagener (B)
Waltz
Wealthy
Worcester Pearmain
S.T. Wright
Wyken Pippin

Flowering Group 4
Annie Elizabeth
Ashmead's Kernel
Autumn Pearmain
Barnack Beauty
Cellini
Chivers' Delight
Claygate Pearmain
Cornish Gillyflower
Cox's Pomona
D'Arcy Spice
Delicious
Duke of Devonshire
Dumelow's Seedling
  (Wellington)
Ellison's Orange
Encore
Gala
George Carpenter
Gladstone (B)
Gloster 69

Golden Delicious
Golden Noble
Hawthornden
Herring's Pippin
Howgate Wonder
Ingrid Marie
Jester
Joybells
King's Acre Pippin
Lady Henniker
Lady Sudeley
Laxton's Pearmain
Lord Burghley
Lord Derby
Mannington's Pearmain
Merton Joy
Monarch (B)
Orleans Reinette
Pixie
Sir John Thornycroft
Superb (Laxton's) (B)
Tydeman's Late Orange
Winston
Woolbrook Russet
Yellow Newtown (B)

Flowering Group 5
Coronation (B)
Frogmore Prolific (B)
Gascoyne's Scarlet (T)
Heusgen's Golden Reinette
King of the Pippins (B)
Merton Beauty
Mother (American)
Newton Wonder
Northern Spy (B)
Reinette Rouge Etoilée
Royal Jubilee
Suntan (T)
William Crump
Woolbrook Pippin (B)

Flowering Group 6
Bess Pool
Court Pendu Plat
Edward VII
Laxton's Royalty

Flowering Group 7: very late
Crawley Beauty

(B) Known to be biennial or irregular in flowering. (T) Triploid.

Colour sports usually flower at the same time as the cultivar from which they originated.

The following combinations are incompatible: Cox's Orange Pippin pollinated by Kidd's Orange Red and the reverse. Cox's Orange Pippin is ineffective on Holstein and Suntan, and the reverse. Golden Delicious may be ineffective on Crispin (Mutsu).

Table 9   **Flowering of pears**

Flowering Group 1: very early	Louise Bonne of Jersey	Durondeau	**Flowering Group 4: late**
Brockworth Park	Marguerite Marillat (M.S.)	Fertility	Beth
Maréchal de la Cour (T)	Packham's Triumph	Fondante d'Automne	Beurré Bedford (M.S.)
Précoce de Trévoux	Passe Crasanne	Fondante Thirriott	Beurré Mortillet
	Princess	Hessle	Bristol Cross (M.S.)
Flowering Group 2	Seckle	Jargonelle (T)	Calebasse Bosc
Baronne de Mello	St Luke	Joséphine de Malines	Catillac (T)
Bellissime d'Hiver	Uvedale's St Germain (T)	Laxton's Early Market	Clapp's Favourite
Beurré Alexandre Lucas (T)	Vicar of Winkfield (T)	Laxton's Progress	Doyenné du Comice
Beurré d'Amanlis (T)		Laxton's Satisfaction	Glou Morceau
Beurré d'Anjou	**Flowering Group 3**	Le Lectier	Gorham
Beurré Clairgeau	Belle-Julie	Merton Pride (T)	Improved Fertility
Beurré Diel (T)	Beurré Dumont	Nouvelle Fulvie	Laxton' Foremost
Beurré Giffard	Beurré Hardy	Olivier de Serres	Laxton's Victor
Beurré Six	Beurré Superfin	President Heron	Marie Louise
Comtesse de Paris	Black Worcester	Roosevelt	Napoleon
Doyenné d'Été	Concorde	Souvenir du Congrés	Nouveau Poiteau
Duchesse d'Angoulême	Conference	Thompson's	Onward
Easter Beurré	Doyenné Boussoch (T)	Triomphe de Vienne	Pitmaston Duchess (T)
Emile d'Heyst	Doyennée George Boucher	Williams' Bon Chrétien	Santa Claus
	Dr Jules Guyot		Winter Nelis
	Duchesse de Bordeaux		Zépherin Grégoire

(T) Triploid. (M.S.) Male sterile (ineffective as a pollinator). Onward is ineffective on Doyenné du Comice, and *vice versa*.

Plums

Myrobalan or cherry plums are diploids and are self-compatible. Most other plums, damsons and bullaces grown in this country are hexaploids and may be completely self-compatible, partly self-compatible or completely self-incompatible. All except the completely self-compatible cultivars require pollinators to set fruits. Cross-incompatibility also occurs, three groups being known:

INCOMPATIBILITY GROUP I
Jefferson
Coe's Golden Drop
Allgrove's Superb
Coe's Violet Gage
Crimson Drop
All pollinations fail.

INCOMPATIBILITY GROUP II
President
Late Orange
Old Greengage*
Cambridge Gage
'Late Orange' × 'President' fails both ways.
'Late Orange' or 'President' pollinated by 'Cambridge Gage' or 'Old Greengage' sets a full crop.

'Cambridge Gage' or 'Old Greengage' pollinated by 'Late Orange' or 'President' sets only 2%.

INCOMPATIBILITY GROUP III
Early Rivers
Blue Rock
'Early Rivers' pollinated by 'Blue Rock' sets a full crop.
'Blue Rock' pollinated by 'Early Rivers' sets a very poor crop.

In a protracted flowering season the time of start of full bloom from the earliest cultivar to the latest is about 20 days. In the table opposite this has been divided into 4-day periods and the cultivars divided into 5 flowering groups. When selecting pollinators for cultivars which occur in either Compatibility group A or B, choose those whose flowering group is the same as or adjacent to that of the cultivar to be cross-pollinated. A pollinator may be selected from any of the three compatibility groups.

*Four cultivars, perhaps bud sports, are distributed as Old Greengage. They are all in Group II. The differences are mainly in flower and leaf characters.

Table 10   **Flowering of plums**

Compatibility Group A *Self-incompatible*	Compatibility Group B *Partly self-compatible*	Compatibility Group C *Self-compatible*	*Unclassified*
Flowering Group 1: early Black Prince Grand Duke Heron Jefferson Late Orleans Mallard	Angelina Burdett Blue Rock Utility	Monarch	Olympia
Flowering Group 2 Admiral Avalon Black Diamond Coe's Crimson Drop Coe's Golden Drop Coe's Violet Edwards President Valor	Ariel Curlew	Brahy's Greengage Brandy Gage Denniston's Superb Goliath Guthrie's Late Prosperity Reine-Claude de Bavay Warwickshire Drooper	
Flowering Group 3 Allgrove's Superb Bryanston Gage Late Orange Reeves Seedling Washington	Belgian Purple Cox's Emperor Early Laxton Early Rivers Goldfinch Laxton's Delight Merton Gem Reine-Claude Violette Sanctus Hubertus	Aylesbury Prune Bastard Victoria Bonne de Bry Bountiful Czar Golden Transparent Herman Laxton's Cropper Laxton's Gage Laxton's Supreme Manns No. 1 Merryweather Damson Opal Pershore Purple Pershore Severn Cross Thames Cross Victoria	Archduke Laxton's Abundance Swan Wye Cross
Flowering Group 4 Count Althann's Gage Kirke's Peach Wyedale	Cambridge Gage Farleigh Damson Stint	Blaisdon Red Bradley's King Damson Early Transparent Gage Giant Prune Ontario Oullins Gage	
Flowering Group 5 Delicious Excalibur Fogmore Damson Late Transparent Old Greengage Pond's Seedling Red Magnum Bonum White Magnum Bonum		Belle de Louvain Belle de Septembre Gisborne's Kentish Bush Laxton's Blue Tit Marjorie's Seedling Shropshire Damson (Prune)	Pacific Teme Cross

Table 11 **Flowering of acid and duke cherries**

Capable of pollinating sweet cherries in flowering periods below	Cultivar	Degree of compatibility †	Picking season
	Duke cherries		
Group 3	May Duke	p.s.c.	Early mid-season
	Royal Duke	p.s.c.	Late mid-season
Group 4	Archduke	p.s.c.	Late mid-season
Group 5	Belle de Chatenay	s.i.	Very late
Group 6	Ronald's Late Duke	s.c.	Very late
	Acid cherries		
Group 4	Kentish Red*	s.i. or s.c.	Mid-season
	Wye Morello	s.c.	Late
Group 5	Montmorency	s.c.	Late
	Morello	s.c.	Late
	Flemish Red	s.c.	Late

† p.s.c = partly self-compatible; s.i. = self-incompatible; s.c. = self-compatible
* Kentish Red exists in 2 forms, one is self-incompatible and the other self-compatible

Cherries

Most sweet cherries, except for universal donors (see below), are not only completely self-incompatible, but also cross-incompatible with certain other cultivars. This means that none of the older cultivars of sweet cherry sets fruit with its own pollen nor with the pollen of any variety within its own incompatibility group, but does set fruit when pollinated by any variety in another group provided that they flower at the same time. The only exception to self-incompatibility is found in the last group shown in the table after group 13, represented by the Canadian cultivars 'Stella' 'Lapins' and 'Sunburst' and also the American 'Starkrimson', all of which are self-fertile and universal donars. The groups are indicated in tables 11 and 12.

The acid and duke cherries are tetraploids. Some are self-fertile, others are self-incompatible and require cross-pollination, but there are no known cases of cross-incompatibility in the acid and duke cherries. They are, however, capable of pollinating sweet cherries although most of them flower rather too late to be very useful.

The cultivars are arranged in flowering periods so that any cultivar in one of the periods flowers sufficiently close to any other in the same period, or in the period either directly preceding, or immediately following it; for example, the ideal pollinators for 'Roundel' are to be found within the same flowering period (3), but it could also be pollinated by any cultivar in flowering periods 2 or 4, provided that the cultivar chosen is not the same incompatibility group. Thus 'Merton Heart' in flowering period 2, 'Elton Heart' in flowering period 3, or 'Emperor Francis' in flowering period 4 will be found satisfactory.

There are two types of universal donors, the self-fertile and the self-infertile. The self-fertile cherry cultivars will set a crop with their own pollen and cross-pollinate any other cultivar, provided it is within the same flowering period or in the period directly preceding or following as there is usually an overlap. Similarly, the self-infertile universal donors will pollinate other cherry cultivars but not themselves.

Table 12   Flowering of sweet cherries

Incompatibility Groups	Flowering period 1 (Earliest)	Flowering period 2	Flowering period 3	Flowering period 4	Flowering period 5	Flowering period 6 (Latest)
Group 1	Early Rivers (E)	Bedford Prolific (EM) Black Circassian (EM) Knights Early Black (EM)	Roundel (M)			
Group 2		Bigarreau de Schrecken (EM) Mermat Merton Favourite (EM) Waterloo (M)	Frogmore Early (EM) Merton Bigarreau (M) Merton Bounty (EM) Van (LM)	Belle Agathe (VL) Merton Crane (M)	Black Elton (M)	
Group 3			Merton Marvel (LM)	Emperor Francis (LM) Napoleon (LM) Ohio Beauty (L)		
Group 4			Merton Premier (EM)	Kent Bigarreau (LM)		
Group 5					Late Black Bigarreau (LM)	
Group 6	Werder's Early Black (E)	Merton Heart (EM)	Early Amber (EM) Elton Heart (M) Governor Wood (EM)	Amber Heart (M)		
Group 7				Bigarreau Hâtif Burlat (E)	Hooker's Black (LM)	Bradbourne Black (LM) Géante d'Hedelfinger (LM)
Group 8			Peggy Rivers (EM)			
Group 9				Merton Reward (M)	Merton Late (VL)	
Group 10						Noble (L)
Group 11			Vic (LM)			
Unknown incompatibility			Hertford (LM) Inga (M)	Summit (LM) Colney (L)		
Universal donors self-infertile	Noir de Guben (LM) Nutbery Black (EM)	Merton Glory (EM)	Vega (M) Merchant (EM)	Smoky Dun (M)	Bigarreau Gaucher (L) Florence (L)	
self-fertile			Starkrimson (M)	Lapins (L) Sunburst (L) Stella (LM)		
Self Compatible						

Season of ripening: (E) = early; (EM) = early mid-season; (LM) = late mid-season; (L) = late; (VL) = very late

Index

Wisley Handbooks

THE COMPLETE SERIES